THE WAY WEST

THE WAY WEST

TRUE STORIES

AMERICAN FRONTIER

Edited by

JAMES A. CRUTCHFIELD

WITH AN INTRODUCTION BY PAUL ANDREW HUTTON

A TOM DOHERTY ASSOCIATES BOOK

NEW YORK

THE WAY WEST: TRUE STORIES OF THE AMERICAN FRONTIER

Copyright © 2005 by James A. Crutchfield

Introduction copyright © 2005 by Paul Andrew Hutton

A Forge Book
Published by Tom Doherty Associates, LLC
175 Fifth Avenue
New York, NY 10010

www.tor.com

Forge® is a registered trademark of Tom Doherty Associates,
LLC.

Library of Congress Cataloging-in-Publication Data

The way west : true stories of the American frontier / edited
by James A. Crutchfield.
    p. cm.
  ISBN-13: 978-0-765-30452-0
  ISBN-10: 0-765-30452-X
  1. West (U.S.)—History—anecdotes. 2. West (U.S.)—Social
life and customs—Anecdotes. 3. Frontier and pioneer life—
West (U.S.)—Anecdotes. 4. West (U.S.)—Biography—
Anecdotes. I. Crutchfield, James Andrew, 1938–

F591.W3 2005
978'.02—dc22   2005045066

First Hardcover Edition: May 2005
First Trade Paperback Edition: May 2006

Printed in the United States of America

0 9 8 7 6 5 4 3 2 1

To the men and women of
Western Writers of America,
who preserve the heritage and traditions
of the American West
through the written word

CONTENTS

INTRODUCTION

THE HISTORY OF AMERICA is, at its core, the story of the American West. In 1893, America's greatest historian, Frederick Jackson Turner, postulated that the origins of American exceptionalism were to be found in the movement of successive frontiers across the North American continent. Turner's "Frontier Thesis" has been celebrated, debated, condemned, and deconstructed, but never supplanted as the only coherent explanation of the first epoch of American development. It is the inspiration for the modern academic field of Western History and for the outstanding narratives of frontier America represented in this new volume from the Western Writers of America.

Strength of narrative has always been a hallmark of Western nonfiction. From John Smith's imaginative narrative of Virginia through a hundred memoirs patterned after it, to the early American histories of Filson, Flint, Irving, Bancroft, and—greatest of them all—Parkman, the power of the strong narrative has reigned preeminent in frontier stories. As often as not, these tales were grand adventure narratives—both a blessing and a curse to the evolution of frontier nonfiction. At their worst they dissolved into the colorful but melodramatic tripe of D. M. Kelsey and J. W. Buel, but at their best they evolved into the classic histories penned by Parkman and Theodore Roosevelt.

These frontier tales usually dealt with the cis–Mississippi West. With the exception of memoirs, many of the best written by women, there was little produced on the trans–Mississippi West until well into the twentieth century. At the same time that Professor Turner's numerous disciples came to dominate the academic world of American history, journalists, popular writers, and film-makers also discovered the western story. Lavish frontier melodramas based on history had helped to shape the silent screen—*The Covered Wagon, The Iron Horse, Pony Express, Wild Bill Hickok,* and *Flaming Frontier* to name but a few. In the thirties these epics had given way to fictional, action-oriented potboilers that mimicked the incredible commercial success of the western novels of Max Brand and Zane Grey. This changed in the late 1930s as the nation responded to the passing of the last pioneer generation. Suddenly aware that western sto-ries would soon be taken to the grave as these old-timers passed on, writers hurried to record their stories. Some of the best of these appeared as a result of oral histories compiled by government employees through the WPA and the Federal Writers Project. On the big screen, on the radio, in magazines, and in books the story of the American frontier found a new mass audience hungry for true tales of the Old West.

In Hollywood the epic historical Western again came to dominate the genre. *Billy the Kid, Robin Hood of Eldorado, The Plainsman, Frontier Marshal, Drums Along the Mohawk, Jesse James, Union Pacific, Northwest Passage,* and *They Died with Their Boots On* all presented a glossy, romanticized version of frontier history. Providing source material for these Hollywood epics, while also appearing regularly on bestseller lists and in *Saturday Evening Post* maga-zine serials, were a gaggle of colorful histories by writers such as Walter Noble Burns, Stuart Lake, Frederick Bechdolt, and William McLeod Raine.

This boom in Western nonfiction continued throughout the 1940s, al-though it was slowed a bit by the war, reaching its climax in the 1950s with the advent of television. In the 1940s and 1950s westerns made up some 30 percent of Hollywood's product. The new medium of television followed this trend, especially after the 1955 success of Walt Disney's *Davy Crockett* on ABC and *Gunsmoke* on CBS. By 1959, there were forty-eight prime-time westerns on the three national networks. Many of these shows dealt directly with historical characters—Wild Bill Hickok, Annie Oakley, Kit Carson, Wyatt Earp, Pat Garrett, Cochise, Bill Longly, Johnny Ringo, Ranald Mackenzie, Daniel Boone, Jesse James, Temple Houston, Roy Bean, Elfego Baca, Texas John Slaughter, and General George Custer all had their own series. Almost every television western—from *Cheyenne* to *Wagon Train*—was steeped in history. This encouraged a new boom in western nonfiction by talented popular histo-rians such as Dee Brown, Stanley Vestal, James Horan, Mari Sandoz, John My-ers Myers, Bernard DeVoto, David Lavender, Alvin Josephy, and Paul I.

Wellman to name but a few. This was a golden age for western history both in terms of popular writing as well as in academic circles, where Turner's disciple Ray Allen Billington strode across the field like a Goliath. He was instrumental in founding the Western History Association in 1962.

The Western Writers of America (WWA), founded in 1952, did not at first recognize nonfiction writing with a coveted Spur Award. That was rectified in 1954 with the first nonfiction Spur awarded to David Lavender for his classic fur-trade history, *Bent's Fort*. In 1981 a Spur Award was established for short nonfiction, in 1990 another was established for juvenile nonfiction, and in 1992 the first Spur was awarded for documentary scriptwriting as the WWA sought to expand its recognition of historical writing. In 1993 the nonfiction Spur category was divided into "historical" and "contemporary" categories in recognition of the impressive body of publication on the period after 1900 in the West, and in 1994 a nonfiction biography category was established. By this time nonfiction writers made up over a third of the total WWA membership.

The WWA also recognized nonfiction writers with its lifetime achievement award, called the Saddleman Award when established in 1961 and then renamed the Owen Wister Award in 1991. Nonfiction award winners for lifetime achievement have included Mari Sandoz (1964), Alvin M. Josephy, Jr. (1966), Nellie Snyder Yost (1975), C. L. Sonnichsen (1980), Eve Ball (1982), Bill Gulick (1983), Dee Brown (1984), Leon C. Metz (1985), Don Worcester (1988), Robert M. Utley (1994), David Lavender (1996), Dale Walker (2000), and David Dary (2002).

Even before its expansion of the Spur Awards, the WWA had long recognized the importance and vitality of nonfiction writing through a series of nonfiction anthologies. Harry Sinclair Drago initiated the WWA anthology concept and edited several volumes of fiction. By 1958 there had been six such volumes published. It was only natural for the WWA to expand into nonfiction and there soon followed such anthologies as *Trails of the Iron Horse, The Women Who Made the West*, and *Water Trails West*, all from Doubleday, and *Pioneer Trails West*, edited by Don Worcester, for Caxton. The WWA anthology tradition has been kept alive in recent years by publisher Tom Doherty through the Forge imprint. The success of *American West: Twenty New Stories from the Western Writers of America*, edited by Loren D. Estleman in 2001, and *Westward: A Fictional History of the American West*, edited by Dale Walker in 2003, has encouraged this current volume edited by longtime WWA Secretary-Treasurer and seasoned historian James A. Crutchfield.

Crutchfield has assembled a remarkable cadre of authors—including Saddleman and Wister winners Dary, Gulick, Metz, Utley, Walker, and Elmer

Kelton—covering such diverse and fascinating topics as cowboys both in the colorful past and the challenging present, the forgotten saga of women in the California gold rush, steamboating in the Pacific Northwest, journalists in the gold rush, and even the amazing story of a Hawaiian outlaw. Many of these tales deal with now-obscure individuals or forgotten stories, while others bring new insight to famous characters and events such as the battle of the Alamo, both Crazy Horse and Custer, the legendary Pancho Villa, young Buffalo Bill, and the storied Texas Rangers.

Join the Western Writers of America on a journey back in time and lose yourself in the colorful history of the American West. Here is history with the hide still on—steeped in lore and rich in detail—as only the talented members of the WWA can tell it.

—Paul Andrew Hutton

THE WAY WEST

SURVIVAL OF THE COWBOY

Darrell Arnold

MUCH OF THE LORE of the American West is based on the traditional cowboy, that man on horseback who tends cattle. To the surprise of many, that man is still out there on western ranges as we enter the twenty-first century. It is interesting to examine how the cowboy has survived and whether he will continue to do so.

At the end of the nineteenth century, people were proclaiming that the days of the cowboy were over. The time of the big trail drives had ended, and settlers were pouring into the West. Much of the once-open range was wrapped in barbed wire. America was the industrial powerhouse of the world. Railroads laced the mountains and plains, electricity was finding its way into rural America, and machines were taking over. It didn't look like there was going to be much of a future for cowboys.

But cowboying went right on. There was still a good and large market for beef, and there was still a lot of western land that, at that time, was best suited for grazing.

Though it was no longer possible to ride from Mexico to Canada without being stopped by a fence, it was still possible to find vast areas of the West not fenced up in small pieces. Big ranches of tens and hundreds of thousands of acres existed in large numbers in every western state. Ranchers claimed or bought up the necessary water rights and continued to turn range grasses into beef on all the land unsuitable for farming or settlement. And, early in the 1900s, that amounted to many millions of acres of land.

There were numerous large ranches owned by large companies, and there were thousands of smaller ranches owned by individual families. And on much of the range, the cow work had to be accomplished the same old way—by a highly skilled man on a horse. Despite early automobiles and motorcycles and airplanes, the very best way to get around on the land was to use a horse. And the most efficient way to work cattle was with a horse and a rope.

Men still had to scatter the cattle over the land, making sure they had access to water and that they thoroughly utilized available grazing. By riding out on the land, men could read the range—they could evaluate the condition and varieties of grasses; they could spot and eliminate invading plant species that weren't good for cattle ranching; they could find and eliminate predators; they could patrol for rustlers; they could find where water might be drying up and where windmills might come in handy.

And they still had to gather cattle for vaccinating, branding, sorting, and shipping. They still had to ride through the animals year-round to check on their condition and to doctor them when necessary. It was not uncommon for a man to ride a horse fifty miles in a day doing his routine ranch work. The man on horseback was the basic and fundamental tool of ranching.

On some of the larger ranches, it was possible for a cowboy to be just a cowboy. He was a hired man on horseback, highly skilled in the arts of riding, roping, shooting, shoeing, reading the range, and reading and working cattle. That's all he had to do—stay mounted and work cows. The ranch could hire crews of men to do the other jobs, the less glamorous jobs. They could hire men to build fences, to repair windmills, to farm hay fields, to work on machinery, to construct sheds, and to paint barns. All the cowboy had to do was to be a cowboy. He was the truest and purist of the breed, and he was very proud of it.

On the smaller outfits, of course, the rancher also was the cowboy. Not only did he know how to do and have to do the cowboy's job, but he also had to be the windmiller, the fencer, the plumber, the mechanic, the carpenter, the painter, and the business manager. But he was still a working cowboy. He earned a living, much of the time on horseback, tending to cattle.

As automobiles were improved, it became possible to haul a horse in the back of a pickup and reach remote ranch locations. By the '50s, trailering had become common. Cowboys embraced trucks and trailers as more efficient ways to get out to where the cattle were, but they still used their horses in the same time-honored way to accomplish the work. And trailering and trucking soon became the most common way to move cattle from summer to winter ranges and back again or to move them to market. The cowboy, the man on horseback, still was there, and he still was doing the job, but he had learned to use improving technology to make his cowboying job a little easier and a lot more efficient.

Another invention that changed the face of ranching was lightweight and durable plastic pipe. Prior to its widespread use, cattle could utilize only ranges close to waterholes. Ponds were dug but were often unreliable, and it was often prohibitively expensive to drill wells. Further, even drilled wells often produced little or no water in areas where it was most needed. And even if the wells were good, keeping the windmills that pumped water to the surface in good repair could be time consuming and expensive. But if a ranch had even one good well where electricity was available, water could be pumped through plastic pipes to storage tanks and watering troughs all over the ranch.

Up to the mid-1960s, cowboys and ranchers had battled rustlers, drought, predators, prairie dogs, locusts, flash floods, range fires, unpredictable cattle markets, and unsympathetic bankers. But, in the '60s, a new and far more dangerous obstacle appeared. This was the environmentalist, the environmentalist who hated the rancher.

Many of the early-day ranchers were the reason for this negative feeling toward the cowboy. When land was plentiful and use of public lands for grazing came almost free and very easy, many ranchers overgrazed the ranges. Some of those ranges never recovered from that misuse.

The environmental movement quite correctly pointed out that public ranges, in some cases, had been mismanaged and abused. But the problem was many environmentalists decided that the sins of the few were the common practices of the many. They blanketly condemned all ranchers as evil destroyers of the range. They demanded that all grazing on America's public land be stopped. They assailed grazing leases as a welfare system for cowboys. The cowboy and the rancher had become bad guys in the eyes of the public.

Such condemnation was bewildering to the ranching community. Their ancestors had indeed overgrazed the ranges, but after the time that ranches became smaller and fenced up, and after the time the government started carefully regulating the amount of time cattle could be held on public lands, ranchers had started to become careful husbanders of their land and their leases. They had to keep the ranges in good condition if their livelihoods were to continue to sustain them. They had to keep the land in productive condition if they were to have ranches to pass on to their children and grandchildren.

Ranchers had come to see themselves as the ultimate stewards of the land, be it public land or their own titled properties. They kept fences up, planted quality grasses, burned off brush, and improved springs and water sources. Not only did their efforts make the land better for their cattle, but wildlife benefited as well. Ranchers saw themselves as the greatest environmentalists of all.

The "greens," of course, saw things differently. Their ranks were swelled by hoards of recreationalists who demanded equal access to and use of the public lands. Public lands in pretty mountain country became the most contested areas. Hikers and mountain bikers did not want to share the national forests with cattle. Every time they had to step over a cow pie on a public trail, they raised a noisy objection. "Cattle Free in '83" became one of their rallying cries. They wanted cattle permanently removed from all federally managed lands.

Scientifically, such removal didn't hold up to scrutiny. Historically, land has always been grazed by something. Before cattle, it was bison, pronghorns, bighorn sheep, prairie dogs, deer, and elk. Land and grazing animals evolved together, and ecosystems developed a benefit-for-all strategy. Recent studies, including one on the expansive Gray Ranch in Arizona, indicate that land left ungrazed becomes stagnant and unproductive. The studies indicate that grazing is part of nature's system of overall ecological balance and harmony.

Still, in some areas of the West, the greens won. They wanted those dirty, destructive cows off of the public lands. They even wanted them off the pretty mountain meadows that were privately owned. Their constant ruckus caused the U.S. Forest Service to eliminate some grazing permits. And, without the grazing permits, some ranchers could no longer sustain their ranching operations.

Ranchers had only one choice left. That was to sell their land. And who was standing there ready to buy it? Subdividers. Thousands of them. The developers bought those pretty mountain meadows and started carving them up into building sites of forty acres or smaller.

The people who bought those mountain "ranchettes" were mostly well-to-do suburban or urban people who wanted to have their own little piece of the West where they could keep a horse and live in the wide-open spaces. The once-beautiful mountain meadows became crowded subdivisions with houses, pavement, powerlines, fences, noise, pollution, and congestion. Wherever there was a five-acre pasture with a horse on it, the land quickly became a big square patch of bare dirt, destroyed way beyond what a rancher's cattle ever did. And where once there were herds of deer and elk spending quiet winters in the river valleys, there were now houses and fences blocking their migration routes and domestic dogs chasing them through the woods.

Ironically, many of the new people wanted to experience the spirit of the

West by becoming "cowboys" themselves. They bought horses, pickups, and trailers, and they built stables alongside their homes. And they dressed in hats, jeans, and cowboy boots. They became part of what some have referred to as "the great western scare." They loved the cowboy, but they detested the cow.

It didn't take long for more enlightened environmentalists to see that they really hadn't won at all. What they had done was to run off the only people who were willing to pay, through grazing fees, for the privilege of living on and managing the land as wide-open space. In their place came thousands of homeowners, whose individual fenced parcels could no longer support the natural ecosystems they once had.

The environmentalists had created a monster far worse than the hated ranchers. What once had been open country that provided habitat for both man and wildlife had become housing sprawl. The open spaces were lost. There was no going back to the days of pristine country managed for cattle and wildlife. Environmentalists brought about the destruction of beautiful mountain lands they thought they were going to preserve.

Thankfully, the West is a very big stretch of country, and there are still many good-sized ranches that have managed to hold out as havens for ranching and the traditional cowboy. Even more thankfully, many environmentalists have begun to see that they might be wrong and have begun to seek accommodation with ranchers. They have discovered that one of the very best ways to preserve open space is to make sure that ranchers are helped and encouraged to stay on the land. Some came to realize that once the land is sold out of ranching, the open space is gone forever.

Where does all of this leave the cowboy/rancher as he enters this newest century? He is facing many battles. Some are long established and familiar struggles, while others are newer and potentially far more damaging.

Weather and the elements will always be a problem. If global warming is indeed occurring, as science seems to indicate that it is, then a cowboy/rancher in the future might find that his once well-watered grazing lands have become generally and consistently drought stricken. The rancher will have to find ways to adjust to a changing western environment.

Then there is the all-important problem of the cattle market. The first thing the rancher must do is raise a product that the public wants. Today, that product is lean beef. Tomorrow it may be fat beef. Whatever the public demands is what he's going to have to be able to produce.

Another market problem is that very little of what the consumer pays at the grocery store ever gets back into the rancher's pocket. The vast majority of that money goes to the middlemen—the store owner, the packager, the transporter, the meat packing company, and the feedlot operator. The rancher is left with very little. The commercial rancher is one of the few businessmen in the world who has nothing to say about the price he gets for his product.

A rancher also has to have a knowledgeable and understanding banker. Many ranchers make money only once a year, in the fall, when they take their calves to market. For the entire rest of the year, they have to operate at a deficit. They depend on a banker who knows how their business works and knows they can't make monthly payments on loans. A rancher makes yearly payments on loans. In today's world, it has become harder and harder for ranchers to find bankers who understand their business.

And the twenty-first-century cowboy has to accept and use more technology. He has already learned that just because grandpa raised Herefords is no reason to keep raising Herefords. Genetics, cross-breeding, and hormone technology all play a big part in a rancher producing the optimum beef animal given his ranch's weather, terrain, grasses, etc. And the world has come so far that just supplementing his horsebacking with a horse and trailer won't do. The modern cowboy is going to have to become computer literate. He may even have to carry a cell phone. Regardless, in order to survive, he will have to run his operation as tightly as any large corporation does, always being careful to optimize his product and minimize his expense.

Another problem is the nature of the cow business in general. There are fewer and fewer ranches that can afford to hire a crew of cowboys. If they can, then the hired cowboy can barely afford to keep himself alive, but at least he's doing a job he loves to do. On many of those ranches, the rancher and his wife and children are the only cowboys on the place.

Some larger ranches may be able to afford a ranch hand or two, but those hands have to be willing and able to do more than just cow work from horseback. They have to be all-around hands. There again, wages are barely enough to keep one man going. If the hired man happens to have a wife and child on the way, it can get real tough. Sometimes the ranch can pay a little extra if the cowboy's wife will cook for the crew. In many instances, the wife may get a job in town, which not only helps out but probably pays as much or more than the cowboy's job. What it boils down to is she gets a good job so her man can keep being a cowboy.

Many ranch cowboys today are "day-work" cowboys. They hire out as cowboys by the day and then go to work at other jobs when there isn't enough cow work to sustain them.

In the past thirty years, the ranks of governmental natural-resource managers have been infiltrated by people with a specific environmental agenda.

There was a time when the Bureau of Land Management was operated by people who had grown up in ranching or were sympathetic to ranchers and other land lessees. The same thing used to be the case with the U.S. Forest Service. In fact, the Taylor Grazing Act of 1934 was passed as much for the benefit of cattlemen and sheepmen as for the protection of the federal rangelands.

One of the things these new young, environmentally aware federal employees want to do is to reestablish wildlife habitats and ranges as they existed before white men took over the West. Many of them favor the reintroduction of grizzly bears and the gray wolf to their historic range. That historic range pretty well takes in every rural area of the West.

Of course, such reintroduction could wreak havoc on livestock and is, therefore, a serious threat to ranching. Further, the protection of other wildlife species, including box turtles, minnows, prairie dogs, and butterflies, could seriously limit the ability of ranchers to graze their animals on federal lands.

Today, to further complicate the issue, many governmental land managers are anti-cow. In fact, they are anti every use except for species preservation and recreation. They don't like cattle, they don't respect ranching, and they don't like to have to lease any federal land to the families who have traditionally depended on those leases for their cattle.

Much of what the cattle-free ranks claim is no longer true, their conclusions being based more on emotion than science. It doesn't matter to them if the rancher has a wildlife-rich ranch of deep waving grass and crystal-clear streams. It matters not that he is caring for the land in a manner that is absolutely the best management possible for the range and is better management, in fact, than the understaffed federal agencies can provide.

To these people, the rancher is a relic of the past. He's not like them. He's a rancher; he has cows; he has to go. The situation has gone beyond getting cattle off the range. It has become virtual racism against cowboys. It is very similar to the zealous public pressure that forced the Native Americans off of these same lands, lands that the white man wanted, during the nineteenth century. There is irony that the cowboy now knows what the Indian felt like. To the rancher, those who persecute him are just as bigoted and malevolent as Indian haters of a hundred years ago.

The rancher is going to have to find ways to help the "antis" understand that he is good, not bad, for the range, and he is actually their best line of defense from ultimate land destruction by developers.

It is every cowboy's dream to someday put together a group of cows and have a little ranch of his own. That was possible all the way up into the '60s and '70s. Not so, today. There is virtually no land available in the West, not even the most marginal land, that is cheap enough for a man to buy and start a cattle ranch on. If a rancher has to pay more than $50 per acre, he just won't be able to make it pay as ranch land. And finding land that cheap is next to impossible today. The land is just too valuable for its potential use as development property and residential sites.

A young cowboy might be able to make a go of it if he inherits the family ranch, and if the ranch's debt load isn't too steep. That is about the only way it can be done.

If that family rancher wants to make a go of it, then it helps a lot to have some government grazing leases that permit him to carry more cattle than his own ranch would carry without those leases. Or he has to have enough titled land to support his own operation. Even then, he will probably live a lean existence, barely surviving from one cattle market to the next.

There are always some ranch lands that get purchased by someone who wants to keep them in ranching. But more likely than not, the purchasers are large corporations or rich individuals who don't have to make the land pay as a ranch. Or, they may even need it to lose money for tax purposes.

The time is already here when one of the only ways to save what is left of western rangelands may be to have a wealthy owner—someone like Ted Turner—buy it up and determinedly keep it as rangeland, for the sake of our heritage and for the sake of the environment. They have to have enough money so they can put the land in conservation easements to keep them from being subdivided. They have to be committed to keeping some western lands free from development just because having such lands is good for our collective wide-open-space-loving American souls. And if those land owners are willing to run cattle on their ranches (Turner is not), then some traditional style of ranching may be saved.

Another problem facing the rancher/cowboy is his public image. After all, people who own so much land have to be rich, right? Wrong. What the general public has little understanding of is that ranchers cannot exist without land, and that the product they raise on that land sometimes doesn't make them enough money to pay the mortgage.

A family rancher is usually land rich and money poor. His bank account is his land. It's what he survives on. It's what he borrows on. It's what he depends on. When the day comes that he is too old to ranch, he can pass it on to his heirs if he has any who want to work hard; he can put the land in a conservation easement, to prevent it from ever being subdivided; or he can sell the land to those who are willing to pay for it, the developers. Selling to developers may be the only way he'll ever see any real money from the land, and it may be the only way he'll ever be able to leave any money to his children. A family rancher only becomes rich if he sells off the fundamental asset that makes him a rancher.

For many ranchers, selling out is the last resort. These are people who love their rural lifestyle and the solid American values that it fosters. They love working hard, they enjoy working with animals, they treasure the opportunity to be their own bosses and to live off the land. There are many rancher/cowboys who would rather live poor on their own land than live rich anywhere else.

In the modern world there is a hunger for land. Everyone wants his thirty-five-acre ranchette, and every individual or company with a lot of extra money will eagerly invest in land purchases so that the land can be subdivided for those eager new landowners. It is a threat to ranching that will never subside as long as America is rich and prosperous and its population continues to grow.

To wrap it all up, then, the single biggest problem facing the twenty-first-century cowboy will be the availability of land on which to ranch. It is estimated that by the end of this newest century, the population of America will double. Those people will require someplace to live.

At the present time, nine of the ten fastest growing states in America are in the West. Of course, there are some large tracts of land that are generally undesirable, even to developers. Many of these are in northern states, where weather reduces its desirability as a dwelling place for people. The windier, colder, less scenic parts of Montana, Oregon, Washington, Idaho, Wyoming, North Dakota, South Dakota, Nebraska, Colorado, New Mexico, Arizona, Nevada, Utah, Oklahoma, and Texas, for example, may well endure as ranching land for another century. Much of the land in those states is harsh and still remote, and cattle ranching may be the only common-sense way to use it.

But much of the rest of the West may soon be lost. There isn't an undeveloped ranch in any pretty mountain valley in the western United States that isn't being eyeballed by some subdivider for future development. And when a struggling rancher stands to make millions on land that barely provides him a subsistence living, the temptation to sell out is enormous.

Add to this the fact that ranchers are constantly having to defend against the efforts of people both inside and outside of land management agencies to remove cattle from all public lands. Presently, there are about 26,000 ranchers in the West who use federal permits. If those permits are pulled permanently, then the millions of acres the ranchers now live on and protect will be paved over. And it is those mountain valleys that provide critical wildlife habitat, especially in winter.

Many people think driving out the rancher will save the land, but, actually, it will do just the opposite. Running off the ranchers will hasten the destruction of the land by turning ecologically productive mountain valleys into dead zones. The rancher has to find a way to show the public that his fenceline is the only thing holding back the subdividers. Fragmentation of our last open spaces will be the ultimate destroyer of western ecosystems.

For all of that, it is possible there still will be cowboys at the beginning of the twenty-second century. The West is a vast place. It's not unreasonable to believe there will still be uninhabited land only suited for grazing. And such land will probably be rough land, hard land, land only a man on horseback will be able to traverse.

Never in the history of cowboying has money been the motivating factor. Cowboying, and by extension, family ranching, have, historically, been among the lowest paying jobs in America. Cowboying isn't about money. It's about doing work a man or woman can love. It's about being horseback in wide open country. It's about freedom. It's about being your own boss. And it's about performing a task that requires expert and finely honed skills. Further, it's about honor. Much of cowboy work is purely miserable and hard work. There is nothing fun about fourteen-hour-long horseback days in cold, wet, windy weather. But there are men and women who know it's worth it. And as long as these men and women seek that kind of life, the cowboy tradition will remain alive in America.

A MEDICAL NECESSITY

Allen P. Bristow

THE FIRST TWO HOTCHKISS howitzer rounds bracketed the cave. A strong stench of cordite filled the humid Kalalau Valley as the gun crew turned to Major James Pratt for his orders. The choice was between bombarding a family with artillery fire or exposing his troops to further loss of life. He ordered the shelling to begin.

Major Pratt's agonizing decision was the result of a medical necessity created by an arbitrary government policy. One tragic chapter in Hawaii's history concerns the diseases brought to the native population by the rush of discoverers, settlers, and missionaries. Syphilis, smallpox, cholera, plague, and leprosy seriously affected the native population by the end of the 1880s. Leprosy most resisted control efforts and King Kamehamea V established a quarantine colony at Kalaupapa on the Island of Molokai. Many lepers took their families along to provide nursing care. Relatives could remain with the patient until death and then leave if not infected. The volume of quarantined lepers gradually increased to an average of five hundred a year and by 1890 almost all lepers in Hawaii were at Molokai except for those living in remote areas.

It was coincidental that in this period the government became unstable. Pressures were strong for annexation by the United States. In January 1893, Queen Liliuokalani abdicated and a provisional government was established to rule Hawaii until annexation was completed. In an attempt to make Hawaii more attractive to the United States, all elements of the provisional government strove to showcase their activities, particularly in the public health field.

Thus, what had previously been a medical necessity for the Board of Health became a political necessity. In early 1893, a ship arrived at Waimea on the Island of Kauai. Aboard were health officers and a doctor whose purpose was to examine all residents in the remote mountain areas of the island, identify those with contagious leprosy, and remove them to Molokai. They sought the aid of Francis Gay, owner of the largest Waimea ranch, to accomplish their task. Cattle raising was a major Hawaiian industry by 1890 and the ranches were patterned after those in the American West. Their beef was shipped throughout the Pacific export market.

The health team needed a guide that knew the inaccessible areas of Kauai and a thirty-one-year-old cowboy was recruited from the Gay ranch for this purpose. His name was Kaluaikoolau, popularly called Koolau. He was a valued employee and was also known as a skilled rifleman and a hunter of boar and wild cattle in the island highlands.

Koolau and his family were well liked by the native Hawaiians on Kauai. Unfortunately, he had been infected by leprosy. The authorities felt that these two factors would make him a perfect emissary to the island lepers.

Led by Koolau, the health officers began to visit every isolated valley to convince lepers that removal to Molokai would be in their best interest. All lepers were advised when the ship would leave and what personal property they could bring. When the task was complete, the health officers told Koolau that his own leprosy had advanced to the point that he too must go to Molokai. Koolau agreed to accompany them only if he could bring his wife, Piilani.

On the appointed day many of the island lepers and their families came to the pier at Waimea and began the loading operation. Koolau set the example by being the first to board. His wife was to follow but she failed to make her way through the crowded dock. When the last leper was boarded the ship left the pier for Molokai. Koolau, in a state of panic over his wife, dove into the sea and swam back to the pier.

Once ashore he collected his wife and ten-year-old son, Kaleimanu, and struck out for Kalalau in the Kokee forest. They traveled an exhausting route up Waimea Canyon, over Lookout Ridge and down into the Kalalau Valley where they joined Judge Kaukai and other lepers refusing quarantine.

Koolau was now a fugitive. He violated an ordinance of the Provisional Government when he left the quarantine ship and fled inland. The dramatic nature of his escape and defiance made apprehension a high priority. It was feared that his example, if successful, might be followed by other lepers.

At inception, the Provisional Government established a law enforcement structure similar to that of the United States. Police departments were established in the cities, and a marshal was appointed to administer rural and outer-island law enforcement. A sheriff was appointed for each island, and deputy sheriffs were assigned to geographic areas. Deputy Sheriff Louis Stolz was responsible for the district of Kauai, which included Waimea and Kalalau. He was Koolau's friend and in past years they worked together in several ranching endeavors.

When Deputy Stolz was notified of Koolau's flight, he immediately launched a search. Accompanied by two native assistants, he went by boat to the beach near Kalalau and sent word up the valley that all lepers were to report to him at the beach camp or they would be arrested. This was the first threat of force made in the leper roundup. All previous attempts had been through persuasion and voluntary compliance.

The next night a group of lepers and their families arrived at Stolz's camp and he convinced most of them to disregard Koolau's example and take the next leper boat from Waimea. Judge Kaukai was present and stated that a small group would return to the interior with him to join Koolau. They would remain in the Kalalau Valley and in complete isolation until death. Judge Kaukai cited as a precedent that both the Royal and Provisional Government permitted lepers to remain on the remote islands of Niihau and Kawaihoa. Deputy Stolz refused their plan and ordered them to Waimea with the rest of the lepers.

On June 5, 1893, Deputy Stolz went to Honolulu for a conference with Marshal Edward Hitchcock. It was his purpose to resign and return to San Francisco for family reasons. Marshal Hitchcock persuaded him to remain until the Koolau matter was settled. Believing that native police could not be trusted in such activities, he advised Stolz to delay any operations in the Kalalau Valley until more Caucasian deputies were available to help.

Meanwhile Koolau and Judge Kaukai convinced the lepers remaining in the valley that Stolz was wrong and they should not go to Waimea for exile to Molokai. When Deputy Stolz returned to the beach at Kalalau he found that the lepers were not going to live up to their agreement. Against the advice of Marshal Hitchcock he began a hunt for Koolau using native assistants.

On the evening of June 27, a leper informant contacted Stolz and led him to Koolau's hiding place. Two other lepers were eating dinner with Koolau and as Stolz approached, they fled. It was later claimed by witnesses that Deputy Stolz aimed his rifle at them with an order to stop. Koolau fired his .44/40 Winchester rifle and Stolz fell wounded. As he struggled to rise, Koolau killed him with a second shot.

Koolau and Piilani immediately fled higher into the wilds of the Kalalau Valley while a frightened leper rushed to the beach camp with news of the murder. When advised of Stolz's murder, Sheriff George Wilcox first notified his superiors in Honolulu and then commandeered a coastal steamer for Kalalau. His deputies recovered Stolz's body and took many frightened lepers aboard. The native population was terrified by the shooting and its potential for further violence. Sheriff Wilcox and his deputies then established a cordon of all the trails leading out of the valley. They realized that a search for Koolau was too dangerous for so small a posse and requested assistance from Marshal Hitchcock's office at Honolulu.

In addition to its civilian police organization, the Hawaiian Provisional Government established a militia system to preserve order during the transition. Staffed by a cadre of officers appointed by President Sanford Dole, the militia consisted primarily of former servicemen from the United States who worked or lived in Hawaii. A quantity of surplus U.S. Army uniforms and equipment were obtained for militia use. Armament included rifles, pistols, and several Hotchkiss mountain howitzers. President Dole declared martial law on Kauai and activated the militia to quell the perceived leper revolt.

A combined force was dispatched at once to Kalalau. It consisted of fourteen militiamen as well as one mountain howitzer and twelve special deputies. The exact composition of this mixed force becomes confusing because it was swelled by those deputies already at Kalalau and depleted as manpower was siphoned off to transport surrendering lepers.

On July 1, 1893, the mixed force arrived at Kalalau and began the manhunt for Koolau. In command was Major James Pratt who obtained horses from a nearby ranch. The operation took on the appearance of a posse hunting a western outlaw. The troops organized random patrols in the valley and soon captured Judge Kaukai and many of the hideout lepers. They then closed in on a high ridge where Koolau, Piilani, and their son were hiding.

The troops deployed to search the ridge, and as one soldier crept up to the ledge, Koolau killed him with a single shot. The rest of the unit fled back down the ridge, surrounded the area, and sent back for reenforcements. The next day a patrol again attempted to gain the ledge, and Koolau shot another soldier. As the troops sought cover, a second soldier accidentally shot himself. The balance of the patrol retreated to lower ground, leaving one dead and one fatally wounded.

To avoid further casualties, and recognizing that Koolau was in an impregnable position, the militia brought up their howitzer. After calling on Koolau to surrender, they shelled the ridge and cave where they believed the family was hiding. The high explosive shells caused a landslide over the cave area. Following the barrage, the troops advanced to search the debris, but found no bodies.

Major Pratt and Sheriff Wilcox assumed that Koolau and his family were killed when the landslide covered the cave, and since the troops had no more stomach for the operation, a withdrawal was ordered. The mixed force returned to Kalalau and sailed back to Honolulu.

Unknown to Pratt and Wilcox, Koolau and his family escaped from the ridge before the shelling began and found their way to a more remote sanctuary. For over three years, they lived a fugitive existence and had little contact with others. Koolau's son was seriously infected with leprosy and died during this period of isolation. Koolau followed his son in death within two months. Piilani sealed his body in a cave with the assistance of her old friend, William Kinney.

Piilani returned to Kekaha, her original village. She remained in good health and later remarried. Although the islanders claim that she never revealed the location of Koolau's grave, it is widely held that several years later William Kinney took Sheriff Wilcox to the gravesite. It is said they exhumed the body for identification and then reburied it, removing only Koolau's Winchester .44/40 rifle.

The annexation process ground to a standstill in the aftermath of the 1893 manhunt for Koolau. President Grover Cleveland opposed the action and blocked approval in spite of strong pressure by the sugar interests. It was not until 1898 that President William McKinley, mindful of the need for a naval base in the Pacific, encouraged Hawaii's annexation as a Territory.

The leper colony on Molokai was continued in various configurations and is now a modern medical facility and home to about eighty remaining patients. Mandatory commitment of approximately eight thousand infected Hawaiians to the colony occurred from 1866 to 1969, when the medical necessity was held to no longer be appropriate.

DID LAMBE LEAD MARY TO SLAUGHTER?

Larry K. Brown

Mrs. [Mary] Lambe is tall, and perhaps the spareness of her frame accentuates her height. Her face is by no means unattractive. Her eyes, when she looks directly at you, have a deep shade of brown. Her mouth and chin are well shaped. Her cheek bones are inclined to prominence and undoubtedly aid at times in giving a hard expression to the eyes. Her hands and feet, although well shaped are large and the former indicate that the owner has come in contact with the harder side of ranch life.

. . . People have said that she would have a fondness for the society of women, would like pretty clothes and the many things that appeal to the feminine mind and would want to come to town and mingle with her kind as often as she could, if there wasn't something "peculiar" about her.

CONTINUING, THE *CHEYENNE* [WYOMING] *Daily Leader* scribe observed that the twenty-three-year-old woman ". . . was clothed in a dark blue skirt of a fashion in vogue several years ago and a simple [shirt] waist with her dark brown hair combed back in the plainest possible way." But he found it strange that this wife of one of the wealthiest of Converse County's ranchers did not wear a wedding ring.

Just three weeks earlier—at about 9 P.M.—Mary or "May," as her husband and in-laws called her, said she sat alone in a room at Hiram R. Daniels's South

Third Street rooming house in Douglas, Wyoming. There, as she dozed in a chair, snug in the coat to ward off the chill of that Friday night, March 13, 1914, she said, an odd noise caught her ear. When she stood to check it out, however, a man's hard hands snared her arm and looped her neck. She screamed and strained until, with her free hand, she pulled a small automatic pistol from her pocket. *Crack! Crack! Crack!*

Drawn by the noise, proprietor Daniels burst through the door to find Zeb Bumgarner, a well-known man-about-town, dead on the floor. Although the facts would not be officially known until after an autopsy took place the next day, each slug had taken its toll. The first shot, which struck the man's neck "would have been fatal, the second entered and broke his arm and the third passed through his head and . . . twice through his hat."

Although the jury for the coroner's inquest cleared May of crime, the victim's brother, Kay [sic], and their friends, did not buy the verdict. In fact, they sought out C. L. Rigdon, a U.S. district attorney in Cheyenne, Wyoming's capital, and convinced him to investigate further.

Due to such unusual interest in the case and the introduction of an outside authority, local officials put May in the custody of a special deputy at the home of her uncle, Daniel Schofield, who lived in Douglas. There, the good Mr. Rigdon paid her a call. But his visit proved to be all business as he soon peeled back her earlier lies and forced her to tell the truth about Bumgarner's death. Worse, some thought, his deft interrogation rolled back a rock to reveal one of the most heinous, sex-inspired crimes in the Cowboy State's history.

What Led to Zeb's Demise

IT ALL BEGAN THE previous December when May's spouse, Tom, helped his mother and younger brother move to Panama City, Florida, where they would make a second home for the sibling, who had been ill for some years. Doctors advised that a lower elevation might improve his health.

Not long after Tom left on the train his father, George, who knew well of May's weak will, decided to move in for the "kill," so to speak. The mustachioed, fifty-seven-year-old rancher, May swore later, "kept putting his arms around me every time he would be close to me." Sex? "Well," said the gray-haired George, with a spark of new-found youth in his pale blue eyes, "a person ought to if they wanted to, there was no harm in it, all the harm there was in it was in the telling." "So," said May, "I did it to get rid of him, I guess." But that would not be their last tryst.

As the adage goes, the apple did not fall far from the tree. Still one more of George's sons—Albert—had followed his dad's lead. And so did Bumgarner, who worked at the Lambes' ranch. All three, it seems, had found May's charms and lithe five-foot, seven-inch frame more than a mere mortal man could do without.

Regrettably, May soon found herself pregnant as well as infected with a venereal disease. Thus, torn with guilt, as well as worn from loneliness, worry, and desperation, she poured out her wrongs—that told only of the hired help's role, of course—to her spouse when he came home two months later. Tom roared back with anger and recrimination. Worse, he told her to pack her clothes and leave. The young rancher also said that he should kill "the villain," who had so defiled his wife. But May begged his mercy. She also asked if she might not win his forgiveness if *she* would shoot Bumgarner. Though she later claimed he answered, "maybe," she said, too, "he did not think in his own mind that I would do it."

In the meantime, when George Lambe learned that his daughter-in-law had so bared her soul, he fired Bumgarner and sent him packing. Later, at May's request, the elder Lambe warned his former employee that he should "get away out of the country," because his son knew of his fling with May as well as of her resulting "delicate condition." The ex-lover fired back that Tom "couldn't shoot any quicker than I could." And, as if to prove his disdain for the Lambes, he not only refused to flee, but he even found a new home in Douglas.

As for Tom Lambe, when his wife asked him to get her medical treatment, he refused. So, May's father-in-law stepped forth and offered to take her to town. Their horse-drawn wagon trip that day, she later said, came to be the incubator in which they hatched a plan to kill Bumgarner. Such a fate would serve him right, they reasoned. It also would keep him from telling others—most specifically, Tom and his mother—of their—lust-stained lives.

So their plot went as planned. Once in Douglas, George and May rented a room at the Daniels's place and shamelessly spent that night together. The next day, as George left for home, May sought out Bumgarner and asked him to come to her room as she had "something important to tell him."

George soon learned en route back to his ranch what had happened as he sat near a phone in the home of a friend with whom he spent that same night.

Each time the phone rang—it was on a party line—he was unable to conceal his agitation. Finally his own number was rung, and he leaped for the instrument. The call was from the sheriff of Converse County. He was calling up May Lambe's husband to notify him that she had just shot Baumgarner [sic].

"Mayme" Schofield

SO, FROM WHOM AND from where did this flawed *femme fatale*, with her deep dimpled chin, spring forth? May—or "Mayme," as her family called her—came into this world on August 2, 1891, as one of nine children born to William M. and Sarah Schofield. This child of the wind and sage, who loved the outdoors and rode with grace, would grow up in the mountainous Cold Springs area southwest of Douglas on La Bonte creek.

By all accounts, a happy home life filled her early years. And, at least one who knew her claimed she ". . . always was a good girl."

Then, in her teens, she met Tom Lambe, a "catch" by most young girls' standards of that time, and on May 19, 1909, they tied the knot in an Episcopal rite at Christ Church in Douglas. Following the ceremony, they returned to his family's ranch, where they made their home in his parents' first house on "the upper spread" of the Lambes' original place on the La Prele.

But the life that followed not only required her do the customary womanly chores, she also rode on roundups and helped the men care for some five hundred head of stock. And, in their first five years together, neighbors noted that Tom let his spouse go to town "but a few times."

The Trials Begin

IT SEEMS CLEAR THEN that May's lack of wile and worldly ways left her easy prey to attorney Rigdon's probe for the truth. And so, following her confession to Rigdon, the law swooped in to lock up George and Tom in the Converse County Jail. There, they cooled their heels until the trio went before Justice of the Peace John D. O'Brien on March 28 for their preliminary hearing. The county prosecutor and attorney Henry C. Miller, aided by Rigdon, represented the State of Wyoming, while Fred D. Hammond of Casper defended the Lambes. Though scant evidence made its way to the bench, Judge O'Brien deemed May's admission enough to send all three men to trial that fall at the Sixth Judicial District Court. Facing the charge of murder in the first degree, each pled "not guilty" without much show of emotion, except for May, whose voice "was tremulous."

With no women's ward in his jail, Sheriff Albert W. Peyton kept May in custody at her uncle's home until he could send her to the Laramie County Jail in Cheyenne for safe keeping. In the meantime, George and Tom went back to their cells, where they stayed until Hammond got them out that April 4 on bail bonds, respectively, of $25,000 and $15,000.

Five months later, the three defendants appeared at district court in Douglas, where, again, each pleaded innocent. They also asked for separate trials, a request the judge immediately approved.

Tom would not have to wait long to learn his fate, and he regained his tattered life that same day—September 8—when the court dropped his case due to lack of hard evidence.

As the trial for her life began the next week, a svelte May and her attorney took their seats at the defense table. But, based upon her "revolting" admission, as well as new, related facts that the prosecution presented to the court during the next six days, it took the jury but a few hours to deem her "guilty of murder in the second degree." It could have been worse. Had May been convicted of first degree murder as first charged, she might well have worn a hemp "necklace."

Although presiding Judge Charles E. Winter might have taken more time, it is clear he resolved to be swift with his just sword. And so, he sentenced her to a term of "not more than twenty-one years and not less than twenty years" in the Colorado State Penitentiary. Wyoming officials sent their convicted women criminals there at the time, because they had no adequate facilities in their own state.

As escorts hauled May off to Cañon City, where she would serve her time, the court granted George's request for a change of venue, so that he would be tried in Casper, Wyoming, the Natrona County seat. He and his attorney took that tactic, it is believed, because they felt sure the people there would be more sympathetic. Back in Douglas, more than a few had loudly voiced that if the court did not hang him, it should lock him away for life.

Sign of the Beast

GEORGE'S HOPE FOR RELEASE, however, proved short-lived. When authorities called him to trial at 9 A.M. on October 29, he found May at the prosecutor's table. In a surprise move, she had been brought back from prison to testify as the state's principal witness. Defense attorney Hammond immediately asked for and received permission to speak privately with her. Although no one knows what went on in that long, secretive session, most speculate that when George and his attorney heard May say she would tell *all* about their crimes, the men knew the course they must take.

To avoid the noose, they called for Prosecutor Miller and told him that, if he would agree to a lesser charge, they would end their fight. With that deal struck, they went back to Judge W.C. Mentzer's bench, where Hammond said his client "would enter a plea of guilty of murder in the second degree. The judge dismissed the many witnesses who had been brought to testify and sentenced George to serve "not less than twenty-five years and not more than thirty years" in prison. He also ordered him to pay a fine of $1,000, plus all costs of his trial.

The following day, after a swift trip southwest to Rawlins, George's armed escort led him through the barbed-wire gate at the south side of Wyoming State Penitentiary and into the administration building, where he signed in as Inmate #2103.

So Much Promise; So Many Problems

SO, WHAT IS KNOWN of George Irving Lambe? This is part of what he wrote on an inmate form:

> . . . employed in one provision store, from 9 yrs 7 mo of age till 14 yrs of age, then worked at carpentering till coming west in the winter of 80 & 81 ran a place of my own 15 miles from Sherman till 1889, came to Converse County in 1889 and lived [there at his ranch] till put in here. My wife had seven children, five of which were born in Converse County, was married May 24 1879.

Lambe family records help flesh out that past. They tell, for example, of his birth on December 31, 1856, in "North England"—most probably in Ulverston—to Thomas and Betsy Lambe. He also attended school for eight years, more than most men of his time. And, he gave thanks to his "Christian parents that tried to do their duty" in teaching him the ways of the Church of England [Episcopal]. Even while in prison, he said, he attended religious services "fairly regular till put on Duty Sundays" as a "prison gate opener."

Thanks to his progenitors, too, we know that George married Anna R. Redhead Lother, a twenty-three-year-old he may have known from childhood. Not long after their wedding took place at the St. Nicholas's Church in Liverpool, England, the newlyweds sailed for America.

From New York City, the pair took the train west to Fort Collins, Colorado, to be near some of George's relatives. There, he first made his way as a carpenter until an uncle convinced him to take up ranching and helped set him up a small spread in the Cherokee Park area northwest of Livermore, Colorado. With the help of a younger brother, who had joined them from England, the Lambes began to raise cattle and horses. They cultivated potatoes for which they found eager markets in Fort Collins as well as in Laramie and Cheyenne. The Lambes also raised a family as their first two sons, Robert R. and Thomas Henry, sprouted and took root there.

Then, in 1889, the Lambes moved north into Wyoming's Converse County. They homesteaded and began to ranch about twenty miles southwest of Douglas and some ten miles due east of Boxelder. There, they produced three more sons and one daughter.

From that point on, George's prosperity soared. Not only did his stock grow sleek and fat on the fine, green grass near La Prele Creek, but he added sheep to the mix. He also bought some grain threshing equipment that he rented out to reap his neighbors' crops. He put in a small sawmill operation. And, as the cash flowed forth, he poured it out to those in need and leveraged the loans by foreclosing on those who failed to pay back what they owed.

Consequently, those folks and their friends would call George such things as "ruthless," "conniving," and worse. He also had to defend his name and wealth in seven civil actions, plus three alleged crimes, not including the one that had put him in prison.

But through luck or wile, George had skated over most of those bumps. How, then, did he fail in the Bumgarner fiasco? Well, when asked, George held that, "My side of the case was never heard." Then why, one might ask, did he plead "guilty" to those charges that had sent him to the pen? Depending on his frame of mind, he said either that he "was a ninny" or "deranged."

May and George might well have spent the rest of their lives behind bars had it not been for Wyoming's then Acting Governor Frank L. Houx. After each had served but fifty months in their respective prisons, the state's chief executive officer pardoned the pair, in December 1918.

The public, however, would not learn that news until a month later. That is when they also found out that Houx, as the State Board of Pardons chair, had failed to consult with any other board members before he turned loose the principals of one of Wyoming's most sensationally sordid crimes. And he did so just ten days before he left office and the state. Then, with but three hours left before Houx not only retired as Acting Governor, but as head of the State Land Board, he also "granted to himself a half interest" in oil-rich state property valued at some fifty-thousand dollars. It came as no surprise then, when many cried out that the Lambes must have "bought" him.

Trial's End

HOUX'S GENEROSITY COULD NOT restore the Lambes' lives to their once-happy state. Tom, for example, had divorced May soon after she went to prison. And though, after she left the pen, she married John Krebardis, a railroad "gandy-dancer" with whom she had a son and a daughter, the couple's strong differences caused them, too, to split. So, May made her way by cleaning the house and caring for an elderly, prominent rancher in Converse County until he passed on. Then, his appreciative family took pity and hired her to care for their place at Ten Sleep, Wyoming. That is where she died on November 4, 1971, at age eighty. Her family took her remains back to Douglas for burial.

George would live no better. Set free from prison, the once-rich rancher rejoined his wife at the home they built some ten miles south of Marianna, Florida. But Annie saw to it that he did enjoy his stay there. After money from the sale of their Wyoming ranch went to Annie, "she handled the finances from that time on . . . he was left out." In fact, claim their kin, if he ". . . wanted anything to eat, he had to prepare it himself, he was denied the use of a bed and slept on a cot in the back hallway near the porch." And, with their divorce in 1925, she moved him out of their house once and for all.

In 1928, George tried to reinvent himself by investing with his son, Albert, in a Pontiac-Oakland car dealership. But he learned for the last time he no longer would hold the reins. Albert managed their business while George "kept books" and served as a "secretary" until June 7, 1929, when he died at the age of seventy-two years and seven months.

What can be learned from this case? Who is to be believed? Did Mary . . . May . . . Mayme . . . "have," not one Lambe, as the nursery rhyme tells us, but two: her husband and her father-in-law as well as the hired hand? And did *she,* as George claimed, seek revenge and lie under oath to taint him with her crime?

Or, did *he,* as May swore under oath, lead the way as they planned Bumgarner's death so that the hired man could not tell George's wife and sons of his dalliance with his daughter-in-law, thus saving his marriage, his home, and his rich lifestyle?

The real truth may never be known. But as vile as May's sins may have been, most tend to agree that she must have paid her price by now. And George? Well, there are still those who say the hounds of hell have yet to catch their prey.

MUGGINS TAYLOR:
THE MAN AND THE MYTH

Robert Casemore

THE MAN, DESPERATE IN his haste, dug spurs into his mount. Then with his boots solid in the stirrups he half rose in his McClellan saddle and with a score of Sioux and Cheyenne in hot pursuit galloped unknowingly at the age of forty-six into the pages of history.

He carried a message destined to stun the then thirty-seven states and territories, a jubilant nation that was set to blow out one hundred birthday candles to celebrate its independence that centennial summer of 1876. If, a few days earlier, he had thoughts of a century of life, liberty, and the pursuit of happiness, they did not ride with him that night.

He set out straight from the bloody battlefield, an area where the Little Big Horn River joined the Big Horn in Montana Territory, to bring the news of the massacre on June 25th of Lieutenant Colonel George Armstrong Custer and over two hundred members (the body count varies) of the famed Seventh Cavalry. He found that a peaceful, verdant valley had been transformed into a scene of crimson carnage.

He dared not linger if he wanted to avoid an arrow in his back or gain a hatchet haircut, yet he needed to fix the dreadful sight in his mind, then get word of what happened to military authorities as quickly as his horse could carry him.

Without dismounting, he scanned the site, saw that he was spotted by the enemy, set off on his mission, urged his horse on in a race for survival and, due to his horsemanship, soon shook his pursuers.

The slaughter he had come upon occurred when over five thousand Sioux and Northern Cheyenne braves, under the leadership of Sioux chiefs Crazy Horse and Sitting Bull, trapped Custer and his men on that midsummer day. Giving the soldiers of the Seventh no quarter, the Sioux and Cheyenne killed every man jack in the company. It is worthwhile to refresh one's knowledge of Custer in order to put in proper perspective the rider who discovered the debacle and galloped away with the news.

He was H. M. Muggins Taylor, an army scout who may or may not have known Custer personally, but who probably knew a great deal about him. Custer was a West Point graduate who served under General Phil Sheridan in the Civil War. He later earned fame as a military leader in campaigns designed to control Indian uprisings. Like most everyone in the young nation, Taylor knew that Custer was a seasoned Indian fighter, though often a rash, egotistical, and unpredictable military leader. Taylor would find it hard to believe that Custer would meet his match at the hands of Sioux and Cheyenne that fateful June day.

Taylor, well known and respected in his prairie community, scouted for troops in Montana under the command of General John Gibbon, today a commander nearly forgotten. Gibbon had maneuvered his force in the Big Horn River valley to provide "cover my back" protection for Custer. The tactic failed.

Taylor, being an army scout, was at the right place at the right time to discover the disaster and report it. Of course, the nation would in time learn of Custer's defeat, but Taylor rode away with the news first. How much Taylor knew of Custer's reputation for recklessness is unknown. Yet, he must have admired Custer's bravado, and to find him slaughtered was sure to have been a devastating blow.

George Armstrong Custer still maintains a well-established foothold in the legendary annals of the American West. Muggins Taylor, who brought news of the tragedy to America and the world, remains a solid historical footnote to the accounts of western exploits in the late 1800s.

THIS BEGS THE QUESTION: Who exactly was Muggins Taylor?

A phrase coined by Winston Churchill and uttered in a different context nearly sixty years after Taylor's death, fits the news bearer like a hip-hugging holster fits a .45.

"... *A riddle wrapped in a mystery inside an enigma.*"

Many facts are known about Muggins Taylor. There is also a saddle bag of half-truths, conjectures, and myths.

His remains, lying probably in a pine box, are buried in Boothill Cemetery, a spot high and lonely on the eastern edge of the Rim Rock that overlooks present-day Billings, Montana. A few interested visitors check out the site each day and most of them have a devil of a time trying to find it. At approximately 28,000 square feet, Boothill is not large when compared to most cemeteries, even those found in small towns. Yet it contains scores of wooden crosses that mark known and unknown graves. Along a worn footpath between them, is a stone encased bronze headstone that reads:

H. M. (MUGGINS) TAYLOR
BORN 1830
DIED OCT. 1, 1882
RESULT OF GUNSHOT WOUND
IN COULSON SEPT. 27, 1882

Chapter one in the extraordinary life of this man of the west is cited in an understated inscription on an impressive plaque at the entrance of the grave yard. The heading on the plaque is BOOTHILL CEMETERY. The inscription below it reads:

"Named Boothill because so many of its occupants went to their deaths with their boots on. This cemetery was the burying ground for Coulson, a Yellowstone River town existing from 1877 to 1885 on the edge of what was to be Billings. Most famous buried here was H. M. (Muggins) Taylor, the scout who took the news of Custer Massacre, June 25, 1876, from the battle area to Bozeman."

There is more to the Boothill inscription just quoted but that is chapter two, which was also the final chapter in Taylor's life.

Let's backtrack to the many facts as well as conjectures and myths that lie behind the inscription's brief phrase "took the news." Much lies behind those three words.

Taylor set out from the Little Big Horn battlefield, a scene of unbelievable carnage, for Fort Ellis, a frontier post near Bozeman, where he knew a telegraph station existed. Telegraph wires had been strung in Montana from Virginia City to Helena by way of Bozeman.

On the trail and after hours of hard riding, Taylor stopped to rest at the spread of a known rancher, Horace Countryman, who lived near present-day Columbus, Montana. Countryman was a weather-beaten, elderly, transplanted

Californian who came initially to Montana to mine and mill quartz. Taylor rested briefly before pressing on with the report of the slaughter.

At Fort Ellis he was dismayed to find the telegraph out of order because, it was alleged at the time, the telegrapher may have been drunk. Undaunted, Taylor rode on to Bozeman where he delivered the news. From there the word passed on to Helena.

An avalanche of dispatches from the press in Salt Lake City and Helena gave credit to Muggins Taylor for arriving with the tragic news. Between the third and sixth of July, the fate of Custer and his detachment of the Seventh Cavalry was relayed to Newspapers in St. Paul, St. Louis, Bismarck, and many other cities both west and east of the Mississippi. The account spread with lightning speed across the shocked United States.

Reaction from the eastern press was a mixture of skepticism and outright denial. After all, editors agreed, the report of the Little Big Horn slaughter came only from an unknown frontier scout.

The military high command in Washington, including General Sheridan and General "War is Hell" William Tecumseh Sherman, concluded that the news of the massacre of Custer and his men was improbable, likely untrue, and far-fetched, despite the fact that the news was literally "fetched far" by an army scout, not just an unknown frontier scout. The reports were a blow to army pride.

The army based its conclusions on the fact that the news did not come from an accredited newspaper reporter who was supposedly at the site of the battle. That reporter was a capable and reliable journalist, Mark Kellogg of the *Bismarck Tribune,* who had been assigned to accompany Custer and his detachment. There was good reason the army did not receive an official dispatch from the reporter. Kellogg, like Custer, was killed in the massacre.

Then, to give the military pause, a telegrapher in Bismarck, Dakota Territory, settled the matter. The rapid Morse code tapping began. The transmission key danced like the boots of a cowboy doing a grand right and left at a lively hoe down.

First *Dash dot dash dot,* then *two dots and a dash,* then *three dots,* followed by a *dash,* a *dot,* and *dot dash dot.*

CUSTER.

After those six letters of the dashing cavalry officer's name, the frenetic tapping continued, officially confirming the news of the Little Big Horn battle, the deaths of the widely admired Custer, all his officers, more than ten score of the Seventh's men, and the journalist Mark Kellogg.

The people of the hundred-years-old United States and its territories were plunged first into nationwide grief and then anger over what was ultimately to become known as "Custer's Last Stand."

The Centennial Exposition centered in that cradle of independence, Philadelphia, was particularly affected. No other event of that type had been seen in the world thus far in the eighteenth and nineteenth centuries. The Custer defeat dampened the Exposition's activities for weeks to come.

Regardless, Muggins Taylor, the bearer of the news of the Little Big Horn disaster to America and the world, became, over night, a *bona fide* hero.

His midnight ride that began in late June 1876, deserves comparison to the midnight ride of Paul Revere on April 18th a century earlier. They equate in significance if not in purpose. Revere's midnight gallop through colonial villages was a warning to a yet-to-be nation to prepare for disaster at the hands of the British. Taylor's dogged dash on prairie turf brought somber news to a then-growing republic that a disaster had occurred at the hands of (to be politically correct today) Native Americans.

THERE ARE ALWAYS SOME people who lose little time in trying to lasso a hero from his pedestal. They asked, "Did Taylor really bring the news of the Little Big Horn massacre to Bozeman?" as is now stated on the Boothill inscription.

Conjecture about Taylor's feat continued for over a quarter century after his death. In Coulson and neighboring communities some people believed Muggins Taylor did not ride on alone to Bozeman after reaching Fort Ellis. Others suspected that at Fort Ellis the inebriated telegrapher simply passed on the news by mail.

Many were of the opinion that Taylor, while at the Countryman ranch, decided that he and Horace Countryman should ride on to Bozeman together, and jointly deliver the appalling news. An equal number believed that Countryman took over and alone delivered the news to Helena.

Bolstering the latter view, one of Countryman's sons, Dan, who was thought to be mentally impaired, claimed that Taylor rode only part way with the message, and that his father continued on to Helena.

An Associated Press representative in Helena, a Mr. Fisk (or Fiske) reported that it was Horace Countryman who brought the news to Helena on the Fourth of July.

IN 1911, TWENTY-SEVEN YEARS following Taylor's death, a rancher separated fact from conjecture and changed the latter to pure myth. He was the late W. H. Norton, a partner with Horace Countryman and his son, Henry. Norton remembered well the night of July 1, 1876, when Taylor galloped in, saddle sore, out of breath, and on a mount whose flanks and chest and neck were foaming with sweat.

Norton, Countryman, his two sons, Dan and Henry, and a man named Ben Gardiner, referred to at that time as a "colored man," were present when Taylor arrived. They were surprised because of the midnight hour and shocked at the man's appearance. One can imagine their responses to Taylor's appeal for assistance and for a chance to rest briefly.

Norton recalled that if anyone had taken over for Taylor that night it would not have been Horace Countryman, a man too advanced in years and unfamiliar with the Montana trails. He also thought that Fisk, the Associated Press man at Helena, was thoroughly off canter in his account because Countryman most certainly did not ride there on July 4th. In fact, Countryman didn't visit Helena for well over a month following the massacre and when he did, he drove a team of four mules to get there, "and then had to prod their asses with a hickory stick to beat the stubbornness out of them."

From Norton's revelation it appears obvious that Taylor rode on alone.

At any rate Horace Countryman, his kin, Ben Gardiner, and Norton, are lost in the dusty pages of history while Muggins Taylor lives on.

With conjecture raging about the hero up to his death, Taylor might well have asked himself, "Who the hell am I?"

JUST WHO WAS THIS legendary hard-riding man of the western frontier, whose life is both known and unknown, with a blurred dividing line. The seventeenth-century Shakespeare, had he met the nineteenth-century Taylor, might have observed ". . . the elements so mix'd in him . . ." as he had written in *Julius Caesar*.

First the known facts:

His surname really was Taylor.

His nickname without a doubt was Muggins.

He was Irish but whether by ancestry or by birth in the Emerald Isle is unknown. Many Irishmen fled the potato famine and many emigrated to America to help build the railroads, but neither of those events produced Taylor in Montana.

Although Irish, he was not of the Roman Catholic faith.

He came from Utah but he never claimed to be of the Mormon persuasion. This was something of a surprise at that time. When a man hailed from Utah he was presumed to be a Latter-Day Saint. Close friends might add he was neither early nor latter.

He was probably Protestant because Reverend Shuart, who preached Taylor's burial service, was a Congregational minister.

Historians are aware of Muggins Taylor, but a physical description is nonexistent. Height, weight, color of eyes and hair, mustache or beard—all unknown. It is odd that during an era when photography was already in vogue no one took a picture of Taylor, not even Matthew Brady, the American pioneer portraitist who photographed so many personages during the Civil War and postwar years.

A painting by a Billings artist, J. K. Ralston, now in private hands, purports to contain the figure of Muggins Taylor. In the foreground a cluster of uniformed men and a dog stand in the presence of a mounted, stalwart scout. In the background are more men in uniform, some military tents, and rough buildings. The mounted man is alleged to be Muggins and although the rider sits tall in the saddle and keeps tight rein on his well-muscled horse, the painting is not considered an accurate likeness of Taylor.

With no existent portrait, one might romanticize Taylor as a typical hero of the Old West; tall, rangy, weather-beaten, laconic, shoulder-length hair, quick on the draw, and eyes that could bore right through you. To so fantasize him might be a mistake, yet that romantic view is what Ralston might have had in mind—then called the man Muggins Taylor.

Taylor came to Coulson from Salt Lake City. He became a rancher who raised sleek thoroughbred race horses, and he enjoyed racing them at Helena.

He knew horses like a prairie sodbuster knows the land he tills, and he was very much at home in the saddle. That quality served him well as the rider who bore the Little Big Horn tidings.

In addition to a rounded education gleaned no one knows where, he also appeared to be of a literary bent. It is reported he named one of his horses Oscar because the stallion was "wilde" and unpredictable. The spelling was intentional and the inspiration for the horse's name and disposition was Oscar Wilde, the young unpredictable Irish poet, playwright, and storyteller who, at that time, was already famous (or infamous if you prefer) in both England and America.

Taylor's peers knew him to be an honest man with integrity, an inveterate gambler, a practical jokester, fun-loving, easy-going, a lover of women but not a womanizer, an accomplished dancer who appreciated a well-turned ankle, fearless, a hard drinker but level-headed, a sharpshooter, and altogether a man well thought of in Coulson on the Yellowstone.

WHAT ABOUT CONJECTURE, MUCH of which became myth?

The initials at his grave site are *H. M.* although some accounts say they should rightfully be *W. H.* No one knows what the *H* stands for whether in *H. M.* or *W. H.* Harry, Herbert, Henry, Howard? Who knows? Same with the *W* in *H. W.* William, Walter, Wesley, Woodrow? Again, who knows? Some say the *M* actually stood for Muggins. Probably pure myth. Why?

Muggins was a popular card game in the late nineteenth century, a game now largely forgotten and one that Taylor enjoyed playing. Many of his gambler friends claimed his nickname came from that, and they are probably right. On the other hand, muggins was also a form of dominoes, but it is unlikely that this frontier army scout ever played with the white dotted black tiles.

Concerning the matter of the intoxicated telegrapher at Fort Ellis mailing the news of the disaster. How and to where? Only the legendary Pony Express, were it still in existence in 1886, could have delivered the mail as fast as Muggins rode with it.

Although he was a man's man, some women said he was handy with needle and thread and adept at sewing outfits of fur and leather for soldiers in the area. That's why he was called Muggins the Tailor, a combination of his nickname and a play on his surname.

Some said he never married.

Some vowed he wed in Salt Lake City and either abandoned or divorced his wife.

Some believed he murdered his wife and fled to Montana to escape the law in Utah. Others swore he killed a man during a jealous rage over his wife and then headed for Coulson.

There is no record of children born either in or out of wedlock. It is rumored he once said, "I have no children—to speak of."

Such are the myths that, along with facts, combine to take the measure of a man and a legend.

AS INDICATED EARLIER THERE is a chapter two in Taylor's life as testified in the latter part of the inscription on the plaque at Boothill. It relates to Muggins Taylor's death and reads:

"Taylor, later a Deputy Sheriff, was gunned down in 1882 in Coulson's laundry as he attempted to stop the laundress' drunken husband from beating her."

Following his acclaim as the news bearer of Custer's massacre, Taylor relished the role of hero. Custer County (later to be called Yellowstone County) was proud to see him become a Deputy Sheriff stationed at Coulson.

Like most bachelors in frontier towns he used the services of a Coulson laundress named Mrs. Henry Lump. Whether he was enamored with her is unconfirmed, but it is known that he was shot endeavoring to protect her from her husband who was drunk and enraged by jealousy. Deputy Sheriff Taylor lived for four days after the shooting. He became the first sheriff in Coulson to lose his life while on duty. Practically all the citizens of Coulson gathered on the Rim Rock to attend his funeral at Boothill.

The fate of Henry Lump, Taylor's killer, is unknown.

Today, Taylor is not only commemorated in Boothill for those two chapters in his life, his name also adorns the two-column Mavity Law Enforcement Memorial that stands proudly in front of the Billings City Hall.

Muggins Taylor . . . a western hero and much more than a footnote to an event that climaxed America's first hundred years.

But he still remains ". . . a *riddle wrapped in a mystery inside an enigma.*"

"IS NOT THIS THE RED RIVER?"
ZEBULON PIKE, JAMES WILKINSON,
AND THE SEARCH FOR THE
FAR SOUTHWEST

James A. Crutchfield

LIEUTENANT ZEBULON MONTGOMERY PIKE was a tired man as he entered his modest quarters at Fort Bellefontaine, located a few miles up the Missouri River from St. Louis. The army post, the first military structure to be built in the newly acquired Louisiana Territory, had only been activated the previous year, and Pike considered himself lucky that he had been able to bring his family with him when he was assigned there nine months previously.

The date was April 30, 1806, and Lieutenant Pike had just returned from an exploration of the upper Mississippi River, under orders of James Wilkinson, the governor of Louisiana Territory and the ranking general of the United States army. His mission, in addition to performing a general survey of the region, was to acquire from the local Indians suitable sites for the construction of army posts and government trading houses. A secondary goal, if time permitted, was to locate the source of the Mississippi.

When Pike left St. Louis on August 9, 1805, Meriwether Lewis and William Clark were somewhere on the upper Missouri River trying to find a water route to the Pacific Ocean. It was a time of great exploration for the United States and its curious president. Indeed, Thomas Jefferson wanted to discover everything he could about the vast Louisiana Territory that he had only purchased recently from the French for a mere three cents an acre.

Pike's mission was mostly successful, although he failed to find the exact source of the Mississippi. He did, however, obtain from the Indians a large tract of land surrounding the Falls of St. Anthony, which eventually became the site of Fort Snelling, and later, Minneapolis–St. Paul.

Pike was hoping for a long, well-deserved rest when he arrived home from his upper Mississippi River explorations. As events turned out, however, he was able to spend precious little time with his wife and small daughter before he was pegged by General Wilkinson for another important assignment. Within two and a half months of his return, the young lieutenant left Fort Belle-fontaine once again, this time on a mission far more dangerous and meaningful than his previous one.

IF ANYTHING, JAMES WILKINSON, the new governor of Louisiana, was an enigma. A longtime army officer who was also highly successful as a merchant in the private sector, Wilkinson had within the last few years become a close friend and confidant of Aaron Burr, Thomas Jefferson's first vice president. Of late, Burr had championed a course of destiny for some of the new western states that would alienate them from the central government and possibly even lead them to form their own confederation. Now, the onetime popular, former vice president was much maligned across the nation, even to the point of being burned in effigy on numerous town squares.

At the time Wilkinson issued orders to Pike for his second mission, he was Burr's enthusiastic disciple—and a willing advocate of his scheme to separate some of the western states from the Union, as well as to "liberate" distant Spanish colonies in the far Southwest. But, as bizarre as this elaborate proposal sounded, it was old hat to Wilkinson who had, himself, secretly attempted to orchestrate a similar scenario almost twenty years earlier.

As governor of Louisiana and army commander, Wilkinson was now in a perfect position to further Burr's plans. He would dispatch Lieutenant Pike on a combination exploring and spying mission to the distant Southwest, that region still owned by Spain and encompassing much of present-day Texas, New Mexico, Arizona, and Colorado. Pike would not only learn the lay of the land and collect data about the various Indian tribes, flora, and fauna, but at the same time, he would gather intelligence about the "settlements of New Mexico" in the event information of this nature might be needed in furthering Burr's scheme. Of course, since it could be dangerous to Wilkinson's career if these espionage activities were ever made public, the alleged primary purpose of the mission was defined to be the return to its village of an Osage Indian deputation that had recently visited Washington, D.C. It was also hoped that

Pike could establish a permanent peace between the Osages and their neighbors, the Kansas.

GENERAL WILKINSON'S ORDERS TO Lieutenant Pike were dated June 24, 1806, and were later complemented with a few additional instructions on July 12. In addition to the fifty-one Osages whom he would transport to their home villages, Pike was accompanied by twenty-one soldiers, including Lieutenant James B. Wilkinson, the general's son, an interpreter and Dr. John H. Robinson, who would serve as the party's physician, completed the expedition's roster. Two large river boats were outfitted, each carrying portions of the supplies and equipment. On July 15, 1806, the two vessels and their human cargo pushed off from the pier at Fort Bellefontaine, as Pike's pregnant wife and daughter waved a tearful good-bye.

Wilkinson's orders called for the expedition to proceed up the Missouri River to the mouth of the Osage. The party would then go up that stream until they came upon the Grand Osage villages, situated near the present-day border between Missouri and Kansas. There, the Osage group would be left. A circuitous overland trek across Kansas would then bring Pike and his men to the northern bank of the Arkansas River. If circumstances permitted, the group was to split into two parts. One, with Lieutenant Wilkinson at the helm, was to descend the Arkansas River to its confluence with the Mississippi at Arkansas Post.

The other party, under Pike's command, was to explore the Arkansas to its headwaters (in the area of today's Canon City, Colorado) as well as to make an attempt to locate the headwaters of the Red River (Pike had erroneously been led to believe from a study of Baron Alexander von Humboldt's map that the Red's source was located in the highlands near Taos, New Mexico, when in reality it begins far to the east in the Texas Panhandle). Then, Pike and his command were to descend the Red River to Fort Claiborne at Natchitoches, at the time the nation's westernmost army post; there they were to await further orders from General Wilkinson.

It was while on this mission that Pike observed climatic conditions on the southern Great Plains that compelled him to write in his journal that the region was "parched and dried up for eight months in the year," and that "not a speck of vegetable matter existed." These vivid remarks were augmented by the prediction that because of the severe climate and uncompromising geography of the region, American settlers would "be constrained to limit their extent on the west, to the borders of the Missouri and Mississippi, while they leave the prairies incapable of cultivation to the wandering and uncivilized aborigines of the country." Thus, with these words, later published in Pike's official record of the expedition, the young explorer created the "Great American Desert" myth, which discouraged American immigration across the Great Plains for years.

Soon after Pike and his entourage left the Pawnee villages situated along the Republican River near the present-day Kansas-Nebraska border, they picked up a portion of what a few years later became the Santa Fe Trail. At this point, as ordered, Lieutenant Wilkinson and his small command left Pike and the others and headed down the Arkansas for Arkansas Post. Pike's group turned west and followed the river upstream. Along the way, they spotted enormous herds of bison and other wildlife, causing Pike to write that "I believe that there are buffalo, elk, and deer sufficient on the banks of the Arkansas alone, if used without waste, to feed all the savages in the United States territory [for] one century." Crossing the future Colorado-Kansas border, the exploring party arrived in the vicinity of present-day Pueblo, Colorado, on November 23, 1806. Unbeknown to Pike, his infant child, whom he had never seen, died back home at Fort Bellefontaine on the same day.

THE WEATHER WAS NOW turning frigid, and Pike ordered his men to build a small, makeshift stockade for protection from both the elements and marauding Indians. When the structure was completed, Pike, Dr. Robinson, and two privates left camp to hike to a huge mountain that appeared to be located only a few miles northward. As it turned out, they were gone from camp for six days, but the summit of the mountain was eventually reached. From its top, another peak, even higher, was spied. The freezing weather and lack of adequate supplies prohibited a serious attempt at climbing this second mountain, although years later, it would be named Pike's Peak in honor of the young explorer.

The men of the expedition were now literally about to freeze to death. Temperatures hovered between nine above zero and seventeen below. To make matters worse, no one had packed traditional winter clothing when they had left Missouri. "I wore myself cotton overalls, for I had not calculated on being out in that inclement season of the year," Pike wrote later. Added to the discomfort was the fact that game was becoming scarce, all drinking water had to be thawed from ice, and forage for the horses was nonexistent.

Much of December 1806, and January 1807, were spent by Pike and his men endlessly wandering in the Colorado mountains searching for the source of the Red River. Their travels carried the cold, weary, and hungry explorers as far north as the South Platte River and as far west as today's town of Buena Vista.

Finally, they headed south and on January 30, they reached what they thought was the Red River. In reality, they had arrived at the headwaters of the Rio Grande. Nearby, about twelve miles south of present-day Alamosa, they built another stockade of cottonwood logs and measuring thirty-six-feet square. "Thus fortified, I should not have had the least hesitation of putting the 100 Spanish horse at defiance until the first or second night, and then to have made our escape under cover of darkness . . . ," Pike later wrote, referring to an elusive Spanish cavalry troop that he and his men had been tracking in the mountains for days.

Upon completion of the stockade, Dr. Robinson set out on his own for Santa Fe. His visitation there was part of a scheme devised by Pike and Robinson to allow him to gather intelligence about Spanish troop strength and facilities in the city. The ploy was structured around the fact that, before he departed St. Louis, Pike had promised a merchant in Illinois that, on his behalf, he would attempt to locate an errant trader. The missing agent had gone to Santa Fe with his employer's goods and while there had liquidated the inventory and absconded with the proceeds. Allowing Dr. Robinson to investigate this incident provided a quasi-legitimate reason to visit Santa Fe and one that would not attract as much attention as the lieutenant would, decked out in an American army uniform. "Our views were to gain a knowledge of the country, the prospect of trade, force, etc. whilst, at the same time, our treaties with Spain guaranteed to him [Robinson], as a citizen of the United States, the right of seeking the recovery of all just debts and demands before the legal and authorised [sic] tribunals of the country . . . ," Pike later explained.

On February 16, nine days after Dr. Robinson had left Pike and the others, a Spanish dragoon and an Indian scout surprised Pike and a companion while they were deer hunting in the woods near the stockade. Despite the language barrier, Pike learned from the two that Robinson had already arrived in Santa Fe. Knowing that they must be wondering who he was and why he was encamped nearby, he told the pair of puzzled strangers that if the colonial governor would dispatch an interpreter to him, he would gladly reveal his plans. The dragoon and Indian rode away.

ON THE MORNING OF February 26, the inevitable occurred. Pike and his men peered through the stockade's rifle ports to observe about one hundred Spanish dragoons and mounted militia approaching. Their commander was Lieutenant Ignatio Saltelo, who, along with Lieutenant Bartholemew Fernandez, was invited to breakfast inside the stockade. After the meal, Lieutenant Saltelo told Pike that the New Mexican governor had sent him and his soldiers to provide assistance to Pike and his men who had obviously lost their way in the mountains. Saltelo offered "mules, horses, money, or whatever you may stand in need of to conduct you to the head of Red river." Pike stared at Saltelo in disbelief and exclaimed, "What, is not this the Red River?" Saltelo assured Pike that the stream upon which they were camped was not the Red River, but rather a tributary of the Rio Grande.

The fact that the Americans had arrived on the Rio Grande meant that they had illegally crossed the international border into Mexico. Whether or not Pike already knew that he was trespassing—and whether the entire incident was merely a ploy to get as close to Santa Fe as possible in order to spy without getting caught—will probably never be known. In any event, Saltelo persuaded Pike that he and his men must accompany him to Santa Fe for an interview with the governor. Because of inclement weather, a few of Pike's entourage and some of the horses had previously been left behind in the mountains, so he requested that two members of his party be allowed to remain behind at the stockade to receive the frostbitten men and weather-weary animals when they arrived at camp.

Pike and the soldiers who were to accompany the Spanish dragoons to Santa Fe moved their camp to the one Saltelo's men had established about twelve miles away. The following day, from this location, Lieutenant Fernandez and fifty of the Spanish troops led Lieutenant Pike and his small contingent of men due south. They generally followed present-day U.S. Highway 285, passing through the pueblo towns of San Juan and Tesuque, before reaching Santa Fe in early March.

UPON FIRST SIGHTING SANTA Fe from a distance, Pike remarked that the town of some "4,500 souls" reminded him of "a fleet of flat bottomed boats, which are seen in the spring and fall seasons, descending the Ohio river." He found that the village stretched along the banks of a small stream for about a mile, but that it was only three streets wide. Two churches dominated the skyline, and formed "a striking contrast to the miserable appearance of the houses." A palace, or government building, which housed official offices and provided quarters for soldiers, was situated off the plaza.

Nearing the palace, Pike was confronted by a crowd of curious onlookers who had seen few Americans before. Although his uniform, consisting of "blue trowsers, mockinsons, blanket coat and a cap made of scarlet cloth, lined with fox skins," was badly damaged and in disarray by his months of travel, the young lieutenant still cut a dashing figure. Dismounting at the palace, Pike was escorted into an anteroom where he awaited the governor's appearance.

Upon Governor Joaquin del Real Alencaster's arrival, the interview began. "Do you speak French?" asked the governor. Pike replied that he did, so the ensuing conversation continued in that language. Pike got an early impression from the nature of Alencaster's questions that the governor was trying to trick him into admitting that his mission was really one of intelligence gathering and espionage. However, after reading Pike's army commission, the governor moderated his tone somewhat and extended his hand to the American, telling him that he was "happy to be acquainted with me as a man of honor."

On the next day, March 4, Alencaster examined the contents of Pike's trunk and found what he thought to be incriminating documents. He informed Pike that he must send him to Chihuahua for detention and further questioning. Following a finely fashioned dinner at the palace, consisting of "a variety of dishes and wines of the southern provinces," Pike rejoined his men, and the party was escorted to the edge of town where they began their long journey to Chihuahua, engulfed by a blinding snowstorm.

Pike's trip to Chihuahua carried him first to Albuquerque, then to El Paso del Norte—located on the south side of the Rio Grande across the river from today's El Paso, Texas—thence to his destination. The party generally followed present-day Interstate Highway 25 from Santa Fe to El Paso and Mexico Federal Highway 45 from El Paso to Chihuahua. The route used was an ancient one, El Camino Real, New Spain's royal highway that linked Mexico City with Taos. Dr. Robinson, who was being held under house arrest in Albuquerque, joined Pike's entourage there and accompanied them to Chihuahua. Taking command of the group at Albuquerque was Lieutenant Facundo Melgares, who, the previous year, had been dispatched from Santa Fe in search of Pike's expedition while it was traversing the Great Plains. With so much background and experience in common, Pike and Melgares soon became good friends.

The caravan reached El Paso on March 21, and after spending several days there, being entertained "in a very elegant and hospitable manner," the party was off for Chihuahua, reaching the city on April 2. Upon entering the office of Governor Nemesio Salcedo, Pike was surprised at the governor's bluntness. "You have given us and yourself a great deal of trouble," Salcedo declared. Pike replied boldly, "On my part entirely unsought, and on that of the Spanish government voluntary." Salcedo then asked for Pike's papers, had them translated over the next several days, and eventually concluded that Pike's real mission had been one of espionage and not scientific exploration. However, fearful that a vigorous prosecution of his charge might push the United States to the brink of war, he dismissed the entire Pike affair by writing a few letters to American officials expressing his indignation. He then released Pike to return to the United States.

In one of his missives to General Wilkinson, the disgruntled Spanish governor told the general that Pike's "documents contain evident, unequivocal

proof that an offense of magnitude [spying and trespassing] has been committed against his Majesty [the King of Spain], and that every individual of this
party ought to have been considered as prisoners on the very spot." He also
told Wilkinson that all of Pike's documents would be confiscated, but that
Pike and his men were free to proceed home. In an aftermath of the incident,
Valentin de Foronda, the Spanish charge d' affaires in Washington, D.C., advised Secretary of State James Madison several months later that although Pike
might really have been lost when he accidentally crossed the border into Mexico, "it may also be a pretext, and the latter is more probable."

Pike and his men, escorted by a troop of Spanish dragoons, departed Chihuahua on April 28, following a circuitous route deeper south into Mexico.
They then turned generally northeast, crossed the Rio Grande into Texas, and
arrived in San Antonio on June 7, and at their destination of Natchitoches in
Louisiana on July 1. "Language cannot express the gaiety of my heart when I
once beheld the standards of my country waved aloft," Pike declared.

ON JUNE 11, 1806, shortly before Zebulon Pike and his small command began
preparations for their long journey to the Southwest, General Wilkinson had
received orders from Secretary of War Henry Dearborn. Wilkinson was instructed to proceed to the lower Mississippi River Valley and to fortify the
army command in the South for a possible conflict with Spain. Because at the
time of his receipt of Dearborn's letter, he was planning feverishly for Pike's
departure, Wilkinson intentionally disregarded the orders. Not until nearly
three weeks after Pike and his expedition had departed did he respond. Along
with his apologies, Wilkinson sent Dearborn a copy of his June 24, 1806, instructions to Pike. Wilkinson eventually left St. Louis and arrived at Natchitoches on September 22, there to assume his new command.

A short time after reaching Natchitoches, Wilkinson received two disturbing
letters. One, from a confidant in Washington, D.C., warned the general that

> It is well ascertained that you are to be replaced at the next session. Jeffer-
> son will affect to yield reluctantly to the public sentiment, but yield he will.
> Prepare yourself, therefore, for it. You know the rest. You are not a man to de-
> spair or even despond, especially when such prospects offer in another quarter.
> Are you ready? Are you numerous associates ready? Wealth and glory!
> Louisiana and Mexico!

The other letter was from Aaron Burr himself, and its contents revealed that
the former vice president was ready to put his filibustering scheme into action.

He told Wilkinson that he would be in Natchez in mid-December in order to meet with him and discuss plans.

When he finished reading the two letters, Wilkinson began to brood. This was not the time to be plotting against the United States government, he thought. He considered the frightening situation in which he found himself and wondered how he might escape from it unscathed. The facts as he saw them were obvious: he might soon lose his position as commanding general of the army, thus ending his military career; the war clouds with Spain had dissipated with the recent American fortification of the Texas frontier, thereby minimizing the chances of a confrontation; Burr's scheme for creating a separate empire in the Southwest had been exposed on the front page of practically every newspaper in the country and American citizens everywhere were howling for his blood; and he [Wilkinson] still had not heard from Lieutenant Pike about what was going on in New Mexico. Clearly, if Wilkinson was ever going to make an effort to salvage his career, now was the time. He must distance himself from Burr and his cohorts.

It took Wilkinson a little more than a week's time after the receipt of the two letters to decide what he must do to get back in the good graces of President Jefferson and other officials in Washington. He wrote the president a personal letter in which he described, "in a dramatic, even hysterical, manner," according to one of his biographers, his "discovery" of a serious plot underway to destroy the integrity of the United States. Having learned of the situation, he wrote, he was prepared to patch up the peace with the Spaniards in Texas and to devote his full energies to destroying this sinister conspiracy. Since "a numerous and powerful association, extending from New York through the western states to the territories bordering on the Mississippi, has been formed with the design to levy and rendezvous eight or ten thousand men in New Orleans," he declared that he would proceed to the city at once to defend it from the filibusterers. President Jefferson swallowed Wilkinson's lies hook, line, and sinker. Later, when the general arrived at New Orleans, he speedily set about creating an air of hysteria among the residents, most of them totally frightened out of their wits about the nonexistent invasion of their city.

President Jefferson soon issued what would today be called an "all points bulletin," for the arrest of Aaron Burr. On January 17, 1807, Burr surrendered to the acting governor of Mississippi Territory. He was taken to Washington, the territory's capital situated on the Natchez Trace, examined by the grand jury there, and released on bond. He immediately fled Washington, but was arrested again by soldiers from Fort Stoddard. Under armed escort, he was then transported to Richmond, Virginia, to stand trial, arriving there on March 27.

With Burr's arrest and trial, his notorious scheme to alienate the western sections of the United States from the rest of the Union was over for good.

ZEBULON PIKE WROTE A letter to General Wilkinson in late April 1807, bringing him up to date on his capture, arrest, march to Chihuahua, and interviews with the Spanish officials there. From New Orleans, on May 20, Wilkinson replied to Pike, who by now had been promoted to captain. He told Pike that, upon his return to the United States, "you will hear of the scenes in which I have been engaged, and may be informed that the traitors whose infamous designs against the constitution and government of our country I have detected, exposed, and destroyed." He confided that these enemies were "vainly attempting to explain their own conduct by inculpating me." He then proceeded to tell Pike that "among other devices, they have asserted [that] your's and lieutenant Wilkinson's enterprise was a premeditated co-operation with Burr." His letter also warned Pike that he "must be cautious, extremely cautious how you breathe a word, because the publicity may excite a spirit of adventure adverse to the interests of our government. . . ." In other words, Wilkinson was telling Pike to keep his mouth shut about any secret conversations the two may have had about the purpose and objectives of the expedition.

When Pike returned to the United States, it was under a pall of suspicion that he had, indeed, been associated in some manner with the Burr conspiracy. It is unknown to this day whether or not he really was. The important documents that were confiscated from him by the Mexican authorities in Chihuahua were discovered in 1907, and scholars everywhere hoped that they would reveal some new insight into the question. Unfortunately, the lost papers disclosed nothing that was not already known.

The mystery lives on. Did Pike conspire with Wilkinson, and thus indirectly with Burr, to betray the United States government? Or, was he a helpless pawn merely going about his life's work, following orders, although those orders were issued by a conspirator? Only two people knew for sure: Pike himself, and Wilkinson. Pike continued his army career, eventually attaining the rank of brigadier-general, but his voice was silenced when he was killed during the War of 1812. Wilkinson went on to testify against Burr at his former associate's trial in Richmond. He served several more years in the army and was honorably discharged in 1815. He died as a land speculator in Mexico in 1825, carrying his secrets to an unmarked grave in Mexico City. If Aaron Burr ever had knowledge of Pike's complicity, he failed to reveal it as well. He survived two trials for treason and one for "misdemeanor" and died, tired and impoverished, in 1836.

WESTERN TRAILS

David Dary

THERE IS A CERTAIN fascination about trails in woodlands, mountains and even on the open prairie and plains. Unless you know where they lead, you have the urge to follow them to satisfy your curiosity. Long before Europeans arrived in North America, Indians followed animal trails, especially those made by buffalo. The Indians learned that buffalo trails were best because the shaggies chose the line of least resistance in their travels.

The longest and perhaps the oldest Indian trail in the West, which today is called the Old North Trail, no doubt included some buffalo trails. The trail stretched for perhaps three thousand miles from northern Canada deep into Mexico and ran along the eastern side of the continental divide between the mountains and the plains. For thousands of years Indians traveled this trail on foot and in time on horseback crossing streams, going around buttes and traveling over low ridges. Still other Indian trails crossed, joined or branched off from the Old North Trail including the Ute Trail in modern Colorado.

When the first white men settled along the Atlantic Coast, they followed Indian trails including those first made by the buffalo that once ranged as far east as Pennsylvania and south through the Carolinas. After the American Revolution, when a new spirit of freedom spread across the young nation, settlers began crossing the Appalachians looking for land to farm and where they could build their homes. Many settlers followed old buffalo trails, but found them too narrow for wagons in heavily forested areas. They could only use pack animals to negotiate such trails.

Because overland travel was difficult, the settlers moving west turned to the major waterways including the Muskingum, Hocking, Scioto, Miami, Wabash, and Ohio rivers. The rivers provided faster transportation, and the Ohio River became the settlers' main westward route flowing nearly a thousand miles from its origin in Pennsylvania through the rolling country of Ohio, across Indiana, and along the southern edge of Illinois, to where it runs into the Mississippi at Cairo. Settlements developed rapidly along the Ohio between the Appalachian Mountains and the Mississippi.

In 1803, President Thomas Jefferson purchased Louisiana Territory and with one swoop of his pen doubled the size of the nation. The following year Jefferson sent Meriwether Lewis and William Clark and their Corps of Discovery westward to explore the new territory. When they returned east twenty-eight months later after traveling about eight thousand miles, they reported among other things that they had found the new territory rich in furs. The news triggered the beginning of the western fur trade and the age of the mountain man.

Meantime, settlers were crossing the Mississippi River and pushing westward, especially up the Missouri River. By 1821, the year Missouri became a state, there were many settlements along the Missouri River, which flows into the Mississippi north of St. Louis. The Missouri, the longest river in North America, flows about twenty-five hundred miles south from the Bitterroot Mountains in Montana. To the west of a north-south line along the western border of Missouri, where the Missouri River turns and flows east, the major rivers were too shallow for most steamboats. Only a few especially constructed steamboats with shallow drafts could negotiate a short distance up the Kansas, Platte, and Arkansas rivers. After decades of relying on the waterways for travel, settlers hesitated to travel overland across the prairie and plains.

Between 1820 and 1840, only rugged mountain men, traders, explorers, and adventure seekers ventured onto the prairie and plains where Indians made their homes. While some traders traded with the Indians, other traders sought to open trade with Santa Fe, but the ruling Spanish blocked their way until 1821 when the Mexican Revolution occurred. William Becknell and a handful of Missourians were the first Americans to reach Mexican Santa Fe. They were welcomed, and the traders found a waiting market for American goods. The route Becknell followed across modern Kansas and Colorado and south through Raton Pass became known as the mountain route of the Santa Fe Trail. The following year, 1822, Becknell took wagons loaded with trade goods toward Santa Fe. Knowing the wagons could not traverse Raton Pass, Becknell turned southwest in what is now western Kansas and blazed what became known as the dry route across the tip of the present-day Oklahoma Panhandle into northeast New Mexico.

Crossing the mountain route of the Santa Fe Trail was the Taos Trail, which stretched from the vicinity of an early trading post near Fort Laramie, Wyoming, and ran south to the Arkansas River east of the Rocky Mountains and then passed north of the Spanish Peaks along the Huerfano River, up Oak Creek and over Sangre de Cristo Pass to the San Luis Valley. From there it ran south to Taos located north of Santa Fe.

Still another trail from Santa Fe was the lesser known Old Spanish Trail that never was a single well-worn route. It may very well have been the longest and crookedest pack-mule trail in the West. It ran northwest of Santa Fe up the Rio Chama Valley to the village of Abiquiu and then wove through a spur of the Rocky Mountains while crossing the Continental Divide into modern south-west Colorado. The trail forded the Colorado and the Green rivers above their junctions and swept northwest to avoid the rugged Grand Canyon region. The trail went over the rim of the Great Basin into modern Utah near Castle Dale and then went southwest through stretches of desert in Nevada and California, through Cajon Pass before reaching Los Angeles.

The Old Spanish Trail was first blazed by Spaniards in 1776 seeking to supply their missions in California without sailing around Cape Horn. Likewise they did not want to use the route west and southwest of Santa Fe across the deserts of modern Arizona and California. The trail saw little use until the 1830s and '40s when annual pack trains carried woolen blankets from New Mexico to trade for California horses and mules. It usually took the annual caravans eighty-five days to travel the trail from Santa Fe to Los Angeles.

A slightly older Spanish trail in California was El Camino Real (The Royal Highway), linking Franciscan Father Junipero Serra's twenty missions, which he founded between 1769 and 1779 from Velicata in Baja California north to modern San Francisco.

When William Becknell opened trade with Santa Fe in 1821, he started west from the town of Franklin in central Missouri, which became the trail's eastern terminal. But by the late 1820s the eastern end of the trail had moved west to Independence in far western Missouri. Located near the Missouri River, Independence became a trading and outfitting center. Meantime the government had surveyed the route as far west as the Arkansas River in modern southwest Kansas, which was then the international boundary between the United States and Mexico. Government surveyors marked the trail with mounds of earth, but within a few years they were eroded by rain, snow, and wind. Still an increased number of traders found the trail to Santa Fe. Between 1830 and 1839 the amount of merchandise carried by traders over the trail increased from $120,000 to $250,000. The traders turned a good profit.

By the 1840s travel over the Santa Fe Trail increased and included Mexican traders carrying goods to Missouri. After the Mexican War began in 1846, American soldiers bound for New Mexico and other points west began traveling over the trail. The military continued to use the trail through the Civil War, but the Santa Fe Trail was primarily a route for trade until the arrival of the railroad. The iron horse could haul more goods faster than the trader's slow ox-drawn wagons that averaged about fifteen miles a day. The Santa Fe Trail soon passed into history.

By the early 1840s as the fur trade was dying in the West after the beaver trade had collapsed, missionaries carrying the gospel to the Indians were already in the West. They first came with the Spanish explorers, and the oldest trail in middle America to be used by Europeans was the Franquelians Trail named for Franciscan Monks. The trail ran from northern Louisiana north across what is now Arkansas to where Mountain View, Missouri, presently stands. There the early Franciscans would strike the Osage Trail and follow it west across what is now southern Kansas to the junction of the Little Arkansas and Arkansas rivers on the site of modern Wichita, Kansas, where they would visit the villages of the Wichita Indians. This area was also the hunting grounds for the Osage Indians.

When missionaries ventured beyond the plains and prairie carrying the gospel beyond the Rocky Mountains into Oregon Country, they were impressed with the land. When they returned east Americans heard their glowing reports about Oregon Country. Compared to the region of middle America that explorer Zebulon Pike had earlier labeled a desert, Oregon sounded like paradise. Land was free, and it was rich, well watered, and forested.

There were two ways to get to Oregon: one was by ship, the other by traveling overland. Ship passage was too costly for most emigrants so beginning in 1840 the first party of thirteen emigrants began to push west from the Missouri River to Oregon. The first large party of nearly nine hundred emigrants left Independence, Missouri in 1843 and crossed modern northeast Kansas and struck the Platte River in what is today Nebraska. Continuing west they crossed the modern states of Wyoming and southern Idaho to Oregon. Much of the route had been blazed earlier by traders and mountain men, but as emigrants made their way west it became known as the Oregon Trail.

The emigrants did not worry about the Rocky Mountains blocking their way because in 1812 Robert Stewart had discovered South Pass while returning east from Astoria, John Jacob Astor's fur trading post, which was located near the mouth of the Columbia River on the Pacific Coast. Wagons could easily traverse South Pass located nearly sixty miles northeast of modern Rock Springs, Wyoming, and then cross into modern Idaho traveling north into eastern Oregon.

Emigrant travel over the Oregon Trail was limited to the period of spring through early fall. The earlier their departure from the jumping-off towns along the Missouri River, the better chance they had of reaching their destinations before fall and early winter storms. The emigrants tried not to depart until grasses along the trail were greening up to provide feed for their oxen and other livestock. It took most emigrants four to five months to reach Oregon. Their goal was to reach their destinations before winter weather arrived.

When Oregon-bound emigrants and their wagons reached The Dalles—French for the rapids of a river through a narrow gorge—they could not take their wagons any farther. The Dalles were seventy miles east of modern Portland, Oregon. The emigrants had to leave their wagons and travel down the Columbia by raft or follow nothing more than a footpath west. In 1845 emigrant Samuel Barlow decided to correct the problem and build a road around the south side of Mount Hood to the Willamette Valley. He completed the road in 1846—it was actually a wagon-wide trail cut through the forests—and charged a toll.

The year the Barlow Road was finished, two other emigrants, Lindsay and Jesse Applegate, laid out what became known as the Applegate Cut-Off. It ran from near modern Dallas, Oregon, south to what is now Humboldt, Nevada, where it joined a trail to California that came from Fort Hall in Idaho. The Applegate Cut-Off became known as the southern route to Oregon.

By then some emigrants, who had heard glowing reports about Spanish California, had followed the Oregon Trail into what is now southern Idaho, and then blazed trails southwest across the Sierra Nevada into California. This California Cut-Off or California Trail, as it became known, had several variants, but all of them angled southwest from modern southeastern Idaho to the Humboldt River which was followed until the river disappears underground. From that point it turns and goes over the Sierra Nevada into California.

Between 1841 and 1849, nearly three thousand emigrants traveled to California, many following this route. But after gold was discovered in California in late 1848, the rush began in the spring of 1849. From that year until 1860, more than 200,000 people followed the Oregon Trail west and then followed trails to California. Aside from the California Trail already described, other trails were blazed supposedly to save traveling time. They included the Truckee Route, first blazed in 1844, which left the Oregon Trail at the Raft River in modern Idaho and went south to the Humboldt Sink and then over what is now called Stephens Pass in the Sierra Nevada.

That same year emigrants followed for the first time a trail mountain man William Sublette had blazed about 1826. Now known as Sublette's Cut-Off, it was a shortcut between South Pass and the Bear River, saving perhaps seventy miles of travel. When emigrants first used it in 1844 it became known as the Greenwood Cut-Off because a former mountain man, Caleb Greenwood, led the first emigrants over the route.

Another trail was the Hastings Cut-Off named for Lansford Hastings, who led the first emigrant wagons over this route in 1846 from near Fort Bridger in southwest Wyoming, south through Weber Canyon to Salt Lake Valley. The route then went around the south side of the Great Salt Lake and across what are today the Bonneville salt flats. The infamous Donner emigrant party followed the Hastings Cut-Off in 1846, but what was supposedly a one-week journey took four through Weber Canyon. By the time they reached the Sierra Nevada, it was fall and the party got caught in early winter snow storms and became trapped in the mountains. Only forty-five of the eighty-nine emigrants survived, some by eating the bodies of those who died.

Another trail called the Carson Route was blazed in 1848. The trail ran from the Carson sink up the Carson River passing the site of modern Carson City, Nevada, crossing the Sierras south of Lake Tahoe and continued westward to Placerville and on to the American River and Sutter's Fort at Sacramento.

In 1849, the year of the gold rush, gold-seekers sought the shortest route possible to California. Benoni Hudspeth thought he could shorten the route and with the help of John J. Myers blazed a cut-off that left the California Trail near modern Soda Springs, Idaho, and rejoined the California Trail about 130 miles later near present-day Malta, Idaho. Known as the Hudspeth Cut-Off, the route neither saved much time, nor was it much better than the California Trail.

About three years later, in 1852, another cut-off was blazed from the Oregon Trail at Fort Hall across the Snake River plains to Lost River and then west, rejoining the Oregon Trail near Ditto Creek south of modern Boise, Idaho. Although it followed an old Indian trail, the route became known as Gooddale's Cut-Off, named for the old mountain man Tim Gooddale.

The only portion of the Oregon Trail constructed with government help was the Lander Trail, a short-cut laid out in 1858 between South Pass and the Snake River region. The trail passed north of modern Big Piney, Wyoming, and went up South Piney Creek through Snyder Basin and Star Valley, into present-day Idaho to Fort Hall. It was named in honor of Frederick W. Lander, an engineer with the U.S. Department of Interior.

The Oregon Trail corridor along the Platte River also carried more than forty-five thousand Utah-bound Mormon emigrants between 1847 and 1869. They started from the Missouri River at what is today Council Bluffs, Iowa, and followed the north bank of the Platte River across Nebraska into Wyoming where they crossed South Pass. They then turned south to Fort Bridger and continued south into present-day Utah. Today the Mormons call their route the Mormon Trail.

West from Salt Lake City ran another important trail called the Central Overland Road. It ran west of Salt Lake City until it met the California Trail coming down from southern Idaho.

Until 1869, when the Transcontinental Railroad was completed, thousands of emigrants, gold-seekers, land speculators, businessmen, and others traveled the Oregon Trail either to Oregon or California or points between. In contrast to the Santa Fe Trail, the Oregon Trail was primarily a trail for emigrants. (While some emigrants did travel the Santa Fe Trail, it was mainly a trail of commerce.) By 1850, however, other trails had developed in the west for other purposes. The Shawnee Trail, which developed during the 1840s for driving cattle to northern markets, ran from South Texas, north into Indian Territory, and northeast into Missouri. Thousands of Texas longhorns were driven up this trail destined for eastern markets.

Beginning in 1857 another important western trail was the 2,800-mile Butterfield Overland Mail route, often called the "ox-bow route" because of the semicircular path it followed. The Butterfield Overland Mail was established to improve communication between California and the East. The influx of gold-seekers mushroomed California's population and it became a state in 1850.

In 1849, the United States Mail Steamship Company started carrying mail by ship between the East Coast and California. The many months it took for the mail to get through were shortened when trails were established across the Central American isthmus, but high postage rates and excessive time to deliver the mail remained a problem.

Sending the mail overland was faster than by ship, and John Butterfield signed a six-year contract with the government for a semi-weekly mail service between St. Louis and Memphis, Tennessee, to San Francisco. Coaches from St. Louis and Memphis met at Fort Smith, Arkansas, where the mail and passengers changed coaches and then followed a trail that had been blazed earlier by Captain Randolph B. Marcy to El Paso, Texas.

From El Paso the Butterfield route followed the Gila Trail, which followed rivers across New Mexico and Arizona to Los Angeles and then continued north through the San Joaquin Valley to San Francisco. The Gila Trail may be the oldest trail in the Southwest. Stations were constructed along the entire route. At first some stations were forty or fifty miles apart. This meant that the coaches had to travel that distance without changing teams. But eventually there were 142 stations ranging from eight to twenty-five miles apart. Coaches stopped in the morning, at noon, and evening for meals at selected stations. It cost $200 for a passenger to travel west from St. Louis to San Francisco but the return fare was only $100. Passengers had to buy their own meals costing 75 cents to one dollar at specified stops. Most trips were made in twenty-one to twenty-three days although the schedule called for twenty-five days. The stagecoaches carrying the mail over this trail were also seen as giving emigrants a new route to follow in going west.

But then, in March 1861, Texas withdrew from the Union. On government orders from Washington, the Butterfield Overland Mail service was stopped since the South deemed it a Yankee enterprise. The overland mail route was soon shifted north to the Oregon Trail where it remained during the Civil War and until the completion of the Transcontinental Railroad in 1869.

When gold was discovered in the Rocky Mountains of modern Colorado late in the 1850s, a new trail developed from Leavenworth and Atchison in eastern Kansas Territory. It was called the Smoky Hill Trail, and it ran through the Kansas River Valley to where the Smoky Hill River flows into the Republican River near modern Junction City, Kansas. From there it followed the Smoky Hill River west to Cheyenne Wells in modern eastern Colorado and then northwest to Denver. It became the route for the Leavenworth and Pikes Peak Express.

Far to the northwest another trail was blazed by necessity. The military needed a road from Fort Walla Walla, in eastern Washington Territory, to Fort Benton, Dakota Territory. During the years 1859 to 1862, John Mullan, an Army-trained engineer, laid out the 624 mile route used first by the Army and later as a trail for emigrants to follow. There are accounts of wild horses having been driven over the trail and even camel trains carrying supplies from the west to Montana Territory.

The discovery of gold in western Montana created the need for a new trail to the diggings. Gold seekers could reach the gold fields by traveling the Oregon Trail to Fort Hall and then going northeast in Montana, or they could travel up the Missouri River by steamboat to Fort Benton and go overland by horseback. Both routes were long, and the Missouri River route was expensive.

John M. Bozeman, a native of Georgia, who had followed the Oregon Trail route in 1862, was convinced he could find a shorter route. The following year he blazed what became known as the Bozeman Trail from the Oregon Trail in central Wyoming, northwest along the Bighorn River and through what is now called Bozeman Pass in Yellowstone National Park and through the Gallatin Valley to Bannack.

Before gold was discovered in Montana, Colorado, Idaho, and Oregon during the late 1850s, most Indians in the West tolerated the seasonal passage of emigrants with their wagons and livestock. Occasionally a few Indians might steal from the emigrants or drive off their horses and cattle, but there were few real hostilities. The Indians also accepted the construction of military forts and private trading posts because these places provided the Indians with places to trade. But when gold-seekers began to veer off the established Oregon Trail and cross territory claimed by different tribes, the Indians' view of the white man changed. Indians became more resentful of whites and occasionally attacked them. Soldiers were then sent to punish the Indians. As more and more whites intruded on lands claimed by Indians, the hostilities increased and before the Civil War ended, travel over many trails was seriously affected. It was not until the Fort Laramie treaty of 1868 was signed that emigrant safety over the trails improved, but that was only a year before the Transcontinental Railroad was completed.

When many Texans went off to fight for the Confederacy during the Civil War, vast numbers of Texas cattle were left unattended on the open ranges. They multiplied in number, and when Texans returned home following the war there were so many longhorns that an animal's hide was worth more than its meat. But in New York City sirloin steaks were selling for 25 to 35 cents a pound. The Civil War had drained the North of its cattle. Texas cattlemen again began driving herds of longhorns over the Shawnee Trail into Missouri, but were either robbed by Jayhawkers or turned back by farmers because the longhorns infected domestic cattle with what was called Texas Fever. Later it was learned the longhorns were immune to a tick they carried that was responsible for the sickness.

Two Texas ranchers, Charles Goodnight and Oliver Loving, decided to try and sell their cattle in New Mexico. In 1866, they blazed a trail from northwest Texas to Fort Sumner, New Mexico, which became known as the Goodnight-Loving Trail. In 1875 it was extended from New Mexico northward into Colorado. It was important as a cattle trail, but not as significant as what became known as the Chisholm Trail.

When Joseph McCoy, an Illinois stockman, established the railhead cattle town of Abilene, Kansas, on the Union Pacific Railroad, Eastern Division line, Texans found a place where they could sell their cattle. It was then that the Chisholm Trail was born. It was named for Jesse Chisholm, an Indian trader, who earlier blazed a trail from modern Wichita, Kansas, south to the Red River. The various trails from South Texas northward across Indian Territory into Kansas became known as the Chisholm Trail, and it was the principal route followed by drovers first to Abilene, and later to Newton and Wichita in Kansas.

As settlers in Kansas pushed farther west and state lawmakers passed laws prohibiting Texas cattle from being driven across settled areas for fear they would infect domestic cattle with Texas Fever, new Kansas cattle towns were established on the rail line or farther west. One such town was Dodge City, in southwest Kansas. Beginning in 1877 and lasting until 1886, Dodge City was the state's last cattle town. Since it was far to the west of the Chisholm Trail, cowmen blazed a new trail called the Great Western Trail from Fort Griffin and Fort Belknap in northwest Texas across far western Indian Territory to Dodge City and to points north in Nebraska including Ogallala in western Nebraska.

An unusual trail blazed exclusively to accommodate trade with buffalo hunters was the Jones and Plummer Trail first used in 1874. It followed the Great Western Trail south of Dodge City to what is now Beaver, Oklahoma. There, it heads off due south and southwest to where Charles Edward "Dirty Face" Jones and Joseph H. Plummer established a trading post on Wolf Creek. To the south was the settlement of Mobeetie, Texas. Between 1880 and 1886, the Jones and Plummer Trail not only carried supplies to buffalo hunters, but also materials needed to built Fort Elliott near Mobeetie.

Two years after the Jones and Plummer Trail was opened, Dodge City merchant Charles Rath took a train of freight wagons loaded with supplies south to Fort Elliott and implemented another trail farther south across the Salt Fork, across the Red River, over the Brazos, and up the Double Mountain Fork near the Double Mountains. There, Rath established a trading post for buffalo hunters known as Rath City or Camp Reynolds. The Rath Trail remained in use for two years, from 1876 to 1878. By then most of the buffalo on the southern plains had been slaughtered.

After George Armstrong Custer and every officer and enlisted man in five companies of the Seventh Cavalry were killed in the battle at the Little Big Horn and Indians on the northern plains were moved to reservations, new trails developed on the northern plains as buffalo hunters and then cattlemen moved into the region. And after gold was discovered in the Black Hills of modern South Dakota, entrepreneurs blazed the Cheyenne Black Hills Stage Road between Cheyenne in southeast Wyoming and what is now Deadwood, South Dakota. From there another trail ran northeast and soon divided, with one branch running to Medora, the other to Bismarck, both in modern North Dakota.

About this time another trail developed in the northwest. It was the Nez Perce (Nimiipu or Nee-Me-Ooo) Trail used only once in 1877. When the Nez Perce Indians refused to sign a treaty with the government, they fled and headed for Canada. The route they took was actually composed of many old trails used by Indians for generations, but it became known as the Nez Perce Trail. It started at Wallowa Lake, Oregon, crossed the Snake River River at Dug Bar, and passed into Idaho at modern Lewiston. From there it ran across north-central Idaho and entered Montana near Lolo Pass, then traversed the Bitteroot Valley. The trail eventually ended at Bear's Paw Mountain near the Canadian border.

To the east of Dakota Territory there also was an important circular trail between modern St. Paul, Minnesota, and Pembina, North Dakota. The western leg of the trail was called the Red River Trail and it ran parallel to the Red River, while the other was the Pembina Cart Trail, which ran east of the Red River to the south before crossing the Mississippi River and going to St. Paul. Pembina was a meeting place for Indians and hunters who carried their pelts including buffalo robes to St. Paul, about 470 miles away. The furs were carried in what became known as Red River carts, a two-wheeled vehicle usually pulled by one ox. The trip took twenty-three to fifty days depending upon trail conditions and the weather.

Countless other western trails were blazed during the latter half of the nineteenth century as the west was being settled. Some were branches off the major trails that rapidly declined in use after the Transcontinental Railroad was completed in 1869 and numerous other railroads moved into the West. One such railroad was the Atchison, Topeka and Santa Fe, which followed much of the route of the Santa Fe Trail, and the Missouri-Kansas-Texas Railroad (KATY) which shipped many cattle from Texas north. These and other lines carried people, freight, and mail, which were once hauled in wagons and stagecoaches over the trails.

By the early twentieth century many of the old trails were fading into history, but others had been turned into modern roads and highways that exist today. In some areas travelers still follow the routes of the early trails first made by buffalo. They were the best.

THE TOUGHEST TOWN IN TEXAS

Riley Froh

SEVERAL TOWNS IN TEXAS have historically taken on a distinct character just as certain individuals do in life, and sometimes a slogan springs up to characterize the place and set it apart. For example, Fort Worth is commonly known as "Cowtown." The saying, "Where the West Begins," has become synonymous with the city. A catchword does not always last—since Snyder and Cuero have long ago ceased to be shipping centers for buffalo hides, they are no longer referred to as "Hidetown"—but when the nickname does stick it can be good for the community. San Antonio will always be "The Alamo City," which is quite a distinction and one worth keeping. The title, "The Bayou City," adds a certain charm to Houston, even though Buffalo Bayou is unrecognizable now since it has become the Ship Channel, waterway to the largest inland port in the world.

When cities lose a colorful and descriptive phrase that was once linked to the history of the spot, there are usually definite reasons for the loss. Obviously, the taming of the frontier may make a saying obsolete. This is the case for Luling, once called "The Toughest Town in Texas," which is a hard name to live up to in the Lone Star State, a territory known from coast to coast for its rough and rowdy ways. But when Luling did bear the distinction of being a risky spot to dwell and an easy place to die, it lived up to its billing.

Geographically, Luling was founded on dark and bloody ground. The site of a terrific Indian battle is only six miles north of the town, and the scene of a terrible Indian massacre lies barely seven miles to the east.

The massacre occurred in 1825 when a large force of Comanches attacked a party of Mexican silver miners who had hidden forty-three silver bars in their secret cache. The Indians soon overwhelmed the smaller band of Mexicans. Only fourteen-year-old Pedro Gomez, who was out foraging for firewood, survived to tell the tale. Pedro stayed concealed in the rocks and woods until long after the sounds of slaughter had ended. What he saw when he returned to the mine shocked him into flight south on foot. He grew to manhood along the banks of the Rio Grande, always fearful of returning to Central Texas and the site of such a traumatic experience.

Never a wealthy man, Pedro Gomez did possess information about a small fortune in rich silver. When Pedro's son was murdered, he presented a map, as a token of gratitude, to Texas Ranger A. S. Lowry, who tracked down the murderer. Lowry put little stock in the information until he retired; then, just for a lark, he sought the mine, locating the actual shaft and smelter furnace in 1875. But he and his nephews searched for years in vain for the hidden silver and legions of Luling citizens to the present day have prowled and dug without success. The smelter, though crumbling, was still easily recognizable in the 1950s, but souvenir hunters have since chipped it down to the ground. Searchers who have spent the night at the place claim that they have reason to believe the spirits of the dead miners are still guarding their secret.

If the Comanches emerged victorious over the silver miners in 1825, when the Luling area was a part of Mexico, the warriors' descendants suffered their worst defeat only a few miles to the west on August 12, 1840, when Texas was an independent republic. This large war party raided all the way to the Texas coast, burning and pillaging Linnville and Victoria. A smaller but determined group of Texans took a stand on Plum Creek at the crossing the Indians always used when returning to the safety of the rugged Texas Hill Country. Led by such notable Indian fighters as Felix Huston, Ed Burleson, and Old Paint Caldwell, the Texans and their Tonkawa scouts devised a battle plan and stuck with it throughout the day, inflicting heavy losses and soundly defeating the enemy. The great Baptist preacher, Z. N. Morrell, who at great risk was able to rescue one of the female captives by killing two Comanches, demonstrated the frontier adage that the Sixth Commandment did not apply to Indians. The surviving braves retreated westward, and neither they nor their brothers ever ventured east of the Balcones Escarpment again, although they continued to defend their hunting grounds from the Hill Country westward until the 1880s.

The Tonkawas, cannibals to the core, feasted on leg of Comanche until dawn, and the blood ran red for six miles along Plum Creek to the site upon which Luling would be founded thirty-four years later. The town was planted in the midst of several winter camp sites of various tribes of Indians. Who knows what sacred Indian burial grounds were disturbed by the coming of these white men, for the Native Americans had long enjoyed the well-watered, heavily-wooded, game-filled locale near Plum Creek's confluence with the beautiful and pristine San Marcos River. These two streams mark today's eastern and southern city limits of Luling.

The Galveston, Harrisburg, and San Antonio Railroad stopped at the spot in 1874, not for the beauty of the place, but because the advance work crew had difficulty constructing a bridge over the steep banks of the forever-winding San Marcos River. Not until 1876 did the railroad move on toward San Antonio. Luling sprang up overnight and for two years lived up to its deadly reputation as "The Toughest Town in Texas."

Legend has it that the town was named after the Chinese laundryman, Loo Ling, who followed the construction crews and settled in Luling when the train stopped. Actually, the fellow's name was Ling Loo, and the similarity of the reversed name is merely a coincidence. Luling was given the maiden name of the wife of Colonel Thomas Wentwerth Pierce, the president of the railroad. That's why there is a Luling, Louisiana, on the same line.

The town's christening ceremony in September of 1874 was led by Lady Leah Cahar, a Scotch noblewoman and large stockholder in the company. Wearing her riding habit of short green skirt, black jacket, derby hat, and high-topped laced boots, Lady Cahar drove the silver spike, proclaiming, "This is the center of the town I name Luling." After taking a riding tour of the area to explore the country, she returned to her homeland.

The executives set the town a mile west of the tents and temporary shacks housing the bridge builders, pick and shovel men, teamsters, and other members of the construction crew. This shantytown quickly took on a reputation of an area to avoid because of the rough nature of the men who followed the railroad.

No place along the railway became as tough and murderous as Luling, Texas, and, other than the traditions of the violent past the locale enjoyed, there was one simple reason for the lawlessness. Law enforcement was nonexistent. The town just appeared out of nowhere when the track temporarily stopped on the southern edge of Caldwell County. The county sheriff had plenty to do in the county seat of Lockhart, sixteen miles to the north, and never ventured to check on this new community in the outlying area of his jurisdiction.

History has shown time and again that where there is no legal authority, the lawbreakers will be happy to "police" the area in their own way—with six-gun law, where the strong survive. Or, if not the strong, the cunning, the mean, the underhanded.

Neutral ground always attracts the criminal element. Luling proved a good magnet for these low types, drawing desperadoes, gunmen, outlaws, bandits, cardsharps, cutthroats, and other felons. These were characters gifted with great fortitude in bearing the evils they inflicted on others.

These parasites must have something to feed on, and the business trade of the honest and productive citizenry of Luling generated the money. As a terminus of the Galveston, Harrisburg, and San Antonio Railroad from 1874 to 1876, Luling became a popular crossroad and a shipping and trading center for a large market in all types of goods and services. For example, the Chihuahua Trail, popular as a freight wagon route, picked up at the railhead in Luling. This was the link between Northwestern Mexico and the port of Galveston and provided a connection to all parts of the globe. Valuable minted silver creaked out of Chihuahua on huge wagons, drawn by large teams of mules. Cargoes would be exchanged at the railhead in Luling. The Mexican goods would depart by rail for the Gulf of Mexico while the mule wagons returned with coffee, machinery, and other needed products for the Mexicans. Much money exchanged hands in the process, and some of it found its way into the dens of iniquity lining Luling's main street.

A branch of the Chisholm Trail also ran by the town, and many cattle from South Texas passed on their way to the main trail at Lockhart. Cowboys are not going to pass by a row of saloons without at least one drink. And then maybe one more. They bedded down the cattle east of town and slaked their thirsts—or urges—in Luling. For some, it was their last hurrah, as some unmarked graves testify today.

There were forty saloons from which to choose for a night on the town, a number contrasting sharply with the twenty other types of business houses opening their doors to trade daily. Walking westward down Main Street one would first pass a rooming house decorated with the unlikely sign, "Squar Meals at Reasonable Figgers, Bord by Day or Week." Ling Loo's laundry was next door. Then came a saloon followed by a bakery. Two more saloons lined up next, one with billiards. A lumberyard broke the usual pattern, which picked up again with a dance hall, a restaurant, another saloon, a shooting gallery, a gambling house, a grocery, another saloon and hotel, a ten-pin alley, a concert hall, a saloon, and a gun shop. The same types of irregular businesses were mirrored on another street directly across the railroad, which ran down the center of town. All was hustle and bustle.

The infamous gambler and gunman, Rowdy Joe Lowe, built the first saloon, and his dance hall stood out as the most popular and famous gin mill of them all. His equally notorious paramour, Rowdy Kate, wearing full evening dress throughout business hours, dealt the cards at the faro table and even occasionally acted as bouncer.

Joe and Kate landed in Luling, fresh out of Ellsworth, Kansas, where the Lowes declared they had maintained their livelihood in "the entertainment business." The authorities in Ellsworth perhaps described the entrepreneurships more fittingly as saloons, dance halls, gambling parlors, and brothels—undertakings not welcome within the city. The sheriff and city marshal sent them packing off to Texas, but, other than the inconvenience of the move, the two felt right at home in the new railhead settlement. Emerson Hough, in *The Story of the Outlaw*, describes Rowdy Joe's Luling Saloon as "the toughest dancehall in America," which fits in perfectly with the author's characterization of the town itself as "the worst place in Texas."

Regulars at Joe Lowe's included petty criminal and gambler Joel Collins, professional cardsharp Joseph P. Maxwell, and local gunman Texas Jack. More famous badmen such as Ben Thompson and John Wesley Hardin were occasional visitors. The former would drop in from Austin when slumming. The latter would ride up from DeWitt County in between rounds of the Sutton-Taylor Feud.

Rowdy Joe had his competitors, all vying for top honors in rough and wild entertainment. The Sunset, The How-Come-You-So, The Panther's Den, The Road to Ruin, and The Dew-Drop-In were a few of the other noted enterprises dedicated to the sale of intoxicating liquors. Ordinarily, beer cost a nickel and whiskey went for twenty-five cents a shot. At eating establishments a cup of coffee sold for a quarter, and one could dine on a poorly prepared plate lunch for a dollar. Mainly, though, strangers and the residents from the workers' camp came to Luling not for the cuisine but to drink, gamble, and carouse.

Certainly, young men didn't intend to reside permanently in Luling's boot hill but the odds were against leaving town in one piece. A typical shooting played out like the one recorded in the spring of 1875 at the Dew-Drop. A drunken cowboy shot out a lamp and a mirror behind the bar. While he was taking wavering aim at another lamp, the barkeep drilled him in the leg, lung, and neck. Spectators carried the bleeding man to the street where he expired. "He never knew what hurt him," a witness sagely remarked. No trial ever ensued and nothing came of the matter. Within several days, talk ran to the more recent gunplay which killed two men and badly wounded one woman.

As a point of comparison, one may rate Luling's violence by contrasting it with other well-known towns punctuated by frequent gunplay. For example, Wyatt Earp testified in the Lotta Crabtree Estate Trial that, other than the 1881 gunfight at the O.K. Corral, there were only four homicides in Tombstone that year.

Caldwell County authorities may have looked the other way when news of shootings in Luling reached them, but that does not mean some men did not pay for their transgressions. Area rancher Bill Gatlin shot one horse thief and hanged another a day's ride south of town during the same week of the three Luling killings. Of course, the culprits the rancher dispatched did steal horses, an unforgivable offense not only in Texas but in much of the West as well. And anyone who took a horse knew full well the harshness and the expediency of the penalty if apprehended.

When a soul did depart in Luling's early days, no minister was available to send it on its way with prayers and supplications. But the frontier had its share of pioneering preachers and it was only a matter of time until some felt called to deal with the evil blatantly challenging the Lord's ways in the little railroad community. Staunch Southern Baptist R. M. King, who had actually been trained for the ministry at Concrete College in Cuero, set his mind on founding a Baptist church even as he was establishing the township's first grocery store. Eventually, King was instrumental in starting the First Baptist Church but he fulfilled his spiritual calling as a deacon rather than pastor.

The first church service in Luling took place because one could ride the train as far westward as the terminus, and this put Episcopal Bishop Robert Elliott right in the middle of town while on his way to a Bexar County meeting. Before starting on horseback to San Antonio, Reverend Elliott put out the word that he would preach a sermon in the railroad car. This was a record of another sort, for only on rare occasions did a rival denomination beat the Southern Baptists to the punch in Texas, and for the Episcopalians to upstage the Baptists was news indeed.

Elliott spoke to a full house, although he did have to raise his voice at the last to compete with the riotous celebrations on both sides of the track. "An abomination calling itself the Celebrated French Can-Can was in noisy operation at the Headquarters Saloon, within a stone's throw of our chapel on wheels," the bishop complained.

The bishop was deeply impressed by how the law-abiding citizens were thrown together right next to the rowdy element of the town, where contact between the two groups was "close and almost imperative," and where "those who struggle in the midst of such hastily gathered populations are compelled to live in dangerous and daily proximity to temptations which elsewhere are not so incessantly and shamelessly advertised."

A Galveston *Daily News* reporter journeyed down the same tracks the bishop rode to see what was at the end of the line that began in his city, and he echoed the same observation as the churchman. In spite of the obvious "cesspools of iniquity" and the general "vice and immorality of the city," the newsman found many "good people" coexisting with the "bad element."

Certainly the boom-town conditions weighed heavily on the upstanding townspeople. A group of community leaders petitioned the state legislature for relief from the gunplay in the summer of 1875. "Bad men, by their vicious acts are daily and hourly rendering unsafe the lives and property of peaceful citizens," their letter stated. "The continual rattle of firearms upon our streets every night reminds us of a real war." Typically, the legislature was slow to act, and Luling remained wild and woolly with the historic excesses of the frontier until after the railroad moved westward.

Commerce went on regardless of the circumstances. Businessman August Santleben risked the untamed climate to carry on his successful wagon freight operation between Luling and Chihuahua, and he wrote about his varied experiences at the railhead. Santleben witnessed a knifing that actually brought the Lockhart sheriff's deputies to town looking for the killer, so the deceased must have been somebody with connections. Although Santleben does not name the parties involved, he does mention that the people of Luling thought the stabbing was justified and that they "enabled him [the killer] to escape the clutches of the law." Santleben's sympathies also lay with the young man, and the wealthy freighter provided him with a horse and a saddle on which to make his escape. One of Santleben's associates presented the youth a Winchester rifle and shells and pointed him "towards Mexico, which was a place of refuge for all such fugitives." Santleben's concluding remarks about the affair speak volumes about conditions of the Texas frontier: "He ought to have felt grateful when he parted from us that night, and I suppose he did, but we never heard from him afterwards, nor do I know what became of him."

According to Santleben's memoirs, the most anxious time he ever spent with a cargo were the two days and a night in 1876 when he camped in Luling with $200,000 in Mexican silver coin waiting for the train bound for Galveston. He knew that surrounding him were "all sorts of people, including many rough characters who were capable of committing any crime." Here was a man who had just traversed some of the most dangerous ground in North America by first moving across bandit-infested northern Mexico before crossing the territory of the dreaded Comancheros of the borderlands and finally venturing through Comanche country running from the Pecos River to Castroville, forty miles west of San Antonio. Yet, one night in Luling caused the most apprehension for this tough-minded businessman. "I felt a natural uneasiness," he said. He and his men stood on armed guard all night around the wagons. Based on the town's record, his anxiety is understandable.

August Santleben hauled his silver into Luling openly, but because the place was an outlaw hangout, criminals often slipped into town with their ill-gotten gain concealed on their person. According to legend, some of it still lies hidden there. Curious markings adorning the ancient oak tree that stands on the corner of Bowie and Pecan Streets supposedly represent a map that points out the location of the buried treasure.

Will King, son of pioneer grocer R. M. King, conducted a thorough search in the early 1900s based on additional firsthand information he had obtained. A blind ex-slave told King he had overheard the outlaws talking behind the livery stable about hiding gold south of town in the dense grove of large oaks on the deep gully which runs into the San Marcos River a quarter of a mile from the trees. Armed with this extra intelligence, King was able to read the tree's crudely carved map. However, King's search was unsuccessful, and as far as anyone knows the money is still there, resting in the shade of the mighty oaks right across from the Luling Hospital.

Along with the tales of hidden treasure are stories of romantic figures who create the stuff of legend. One example is the gambler Joseph P. Maxwell, or Monte Joe as he was known about town, who stepped off a railway car immaculately dressed and holding the hand of his five-year-old daughter, Little May. May was a precious child who won the hearts of all who saw her. Although Joe never spoke of his past, his associates learned from the little girl that her mother was deceased and that her father grieved steadily over the loss.

Joe maintained two separate personalities. One was the loving, caring father of Little May; the other, the cool, detached individual who earned his living at the card tables. Joe never let the two entities intermingle.

Once a man harboring a grudge over an earlier gambling loss accosted Joe on the street and cursed and slapped him in the presence of his daughter. Flushed but otherwise unruffled, Joe returned his child calmly to the hotel before seeking out his assailant and killing him on the spot, a homicide the citizens endorsed as justifiable.

Little May never saw the violent side of her unusual father. To her, he was the man who took her on walks and picnics to the banks of Plum Creek to gather wildflowers. He also told her stories, particularly Bible stories. An agnostic himself, Joe taught May as much as he could of her mother's Christian faith.

The idyllic life of the gambler and his daughter was not destined to last. Little May returned from an outing to the creek with a chill and fever, which grew worse the next day. She lingered nearly a week before succumbing to whatever the malady was which the town doctor could not identify at the time. The figures on childhood mortality reflect that for the children of nineteenth-century America, life was as much a gamble as the games of chance by which Monte Joe earned his living. Legend has it that Little May aroused from a feverish delirium, told her father that she would be waiting for him in heaven, and then died.

Grief-stricken, Monte Joe eventually moved on with the railroad and is lost to history. One must assume that just as others who follow the profession, he ultimately struck a streak of bad luck and cashed in his chips somewhere in time. Little May rests in Lone Oak Cemetery just east of Luling. The stone once marking her grave has crumbled into ruin, but her touching story lives on in Luling folklore.

Monte Joe was not the only Luling character to move west with the railroad, for once the builders got across the difficult San Marcos River crossing, they made record time over the fifty miles to San Antonio. The Alamo City became the next terminus in 1877, marking the same date Luling began its transformation from "The Toughest Town in Texas" to a strictly law-abiding community.

Rowdy Joe closed shop and set up in San Antonio where lucrative pickings seemed a little more opportune. Soon he was off to Fort Worth. He made other changes in his life, leaving Rowdy Kate for Mollie Field. Kate established a house of prostitution in Weatherford in Northwest Texas before following the Texas and Pacific Railroad to Big Spring to continue her career as madam. Her last stop in the world's oldest profession was San Angelo, Texas, where she died in the late 1880s, modestly well off financially at the time.

Joe Lowe's crony Joel Collins left Luling and teamed up with the legendary Sam Bass. The two contracted to drive a herd to Nebraska but neglected to return to Texas with the $8,000 profit. After squandering the money in gambling halls, they robbed a bank to refinance their extended vacation. Nebraska authorities gunned down Collins after a two-week manhunt. Sam escaped back to Texas and his celebrated and famous rendezvous with death at the hands of the Texas Rangers in Round Rock.

Meanwhile, back in Luling, the bad men who remained began to find life as risky as Collins and Bass did, for in time the better element outnumbered the lawbreakers. After a vigilante committee lynched a troublemaker under the bridge over Salt Branch on the edge of town, other undesirables began to drift on. Fearless and outspoken newspaperman J. P. Bridges founded the Luling *Signal* in 1878, and his editorials demanded reform. The Caldwell County sheriff found the time to station some no-nonsense deputies and constables in Luling, and law and order became commonplace for the first time in the town's history.

Outlaws found that Luling was no longer a safe haven when fleeing from peace officers. For example, when stagecoach robber Ham White, known as the "knight of the road" for his refusal to steal from women passengers, held up the regular stage between Austin and San Antonio in March 1877, he rode off toward Luling with his loot from the U.S. mailbags. Captain Lee Hall and two other Texas Rangers trailed him to his destination by the tracks of a broken shoe on the getaway horse.

The three Rangers were searching the township for White when Captain Hall jumped him in the livery stable. Before White could pull his pistols, Hall subdued him with his fists and relieved him of his sidearms and his plunder. The gallant stage robber had found no one to harbor him in town. Gone were the days when a fugitive could locate any number of his fellows in crime in the Toughest Town in Texas to conceal him from the law.

The lawmen then transported Ham White to San Antonio for trial before a tough federal judge who gave the stylish stage robber ninety-nine years. But White had relatives in high places. His cousin, Secretary of the Navy Nathan Goff, interceded on his behalf, and the last official act of President Rutherford B. Hayes was to pardon Ham White, who, true to form, returned to his former life, robbing stages from Colorado to California until he faded from recorded history in 1892.

Luling completed the gradual transformation from tough to tame rather quickly. Curiously, the decent element of Luling always liked and admired the place. Pioneer businessman Kosiusko Keith even named his daughter Merri-anne Luling Keith because of his high regard for his new home. She was the fourth child and the first girl to be born in the new community.

Thomas Wilson, immigration agent for the railroad, funneled a growing number of responsible settlers from his native England into the area, and Wilson settled in Luling himself, becoming a solid businessmen as well as a community supporter. A Baptist and Methodist church soon proved stabilizing influences, and Luling reached the stage of development that reflected the end of the frontier experience.

From age nine to twelve, Annie Huff watched Luling grow from its inception on the edge of her father's four thousand acres that bordered the town, and she noticed great changes over the three-year period. She recorded that by 1877 women no longer needed an escort when walking down Main Street. She watched as the cowboys began to drive the trail herds by without stopping for entertainment, for most saloons and dance halls had closed their doors. Once, while gathering eggs near the ancient oak that marked the trail north after the San Marcos River crossing, she got a bird's-eye view of the work. The trail boss lifted her into the fork of the tree, safely out of harm's way, and passed the word back from point man to swing men to the drag men bringing up the rear. One of the drag men took her back down out of the tree, placing her carefully on the ground. These cowboys seemed much gentler to little Annie than the wild sort that first hit town.

Actually, the new city government of 1877 became reactionary about any wild behavior, and troublemakers soon regreted calling attention to themselves. City fathers hired only rough and rugged types to enforce the law, and county deputies and constables have traditionally borne the same stamp. Where once miscreants determined their own degree of conduct, it became advantageous for them not to cross the line within the city limits. Violence tapered off. Certainly criminals continued to make attempts to ply their trade, but these efforts met with little success, as the files of The Luling *Signal* reflect, and this law-and-order mood has prevailed down to the present.

DANCING IN THE EYE OF THE STORM

Carmen Goldthwaite

SOPHIA SUTTONFIELD AUGHINBAUGH RODE into Texas, a harsh foreign land percolating for war, in July of 1835. If any teenage bride could thrive in the Mexican province of *Tejas* in the 1830s, it was Sophia. She overcame a sullied reputation to become a Texas legend and to be crowned a Civil War heroine.

Reared on an army post, a saloonkeeper's daughter, Sophia itched to leave Fort Wayne, Indiana's frontier compound. Her black hair, buxom build, soldier-gawking good looks and high spirits tattered her reputation. Flirtatious and perky as a colt in spring, she married the post's schoolteacher, Jesse Aughinbaugh, and coaxed him into the Texas adventure. The post turned out in full for the bon voyage party that Sophia's parents hosted.

Lured by broadsides sent across the nation touting land, free or cheap, Sophia and Jesse embarked, entering *Tejas* at Nacogdoches. They received a grant of a league of land on the Trinity River in exchange for promises to develop it and practice Catholicism, Aughinbaugh's faith.

Already, though, winds of change blew across the sprawling *Tejas* landscape like the famed Texas northers. Outraged by taxes and frustrated by *El Presidente Santa Anna's* bureaucracy, Texans gathered in "consultations' that fall. They recruited emigrants to fight in exchange for free land. On March 2, 1836, representatives signed the declaration severing Texas from Mexico. Earlier that year, Texans, Indians, and the Mexican Army's peasant soldiers had skirmished. Crowing with confidence born of easy victories, Texans enlisted by the scores. But now, following the Declaration of Independence, General Santa Anna threatened Texans. He crossed the Rio Grande with thousands of professional Mexican troops, vowing to kill all Anglos in his path.

Fear strode through the province. Texans—largely women, children and the elderly—streamed into Louisiana to huddle under United States's protection. The mass migration became known as the "Runaway Scrape" and it lasted for weeks. One who vanished during this time was Sophia's husband, Aughinbaugh. Whether he abandoned Sophia, or she dumped the quiet teacher, preferring instead, Texas' hard-charging revolutionaries, never has been learned. But, she did not flee.

Under Mexican law there would be advantages for her. With Jesse gone, she would be the recognized landowner since Mexican law acknowledged women. Instead of joining the Runaway Scrape immediately, Sophia sallied into Washington, a small settlement located west of her on the Brazos River and later called "Washington-on-the-Brazos." In that cold, wet winter of 1836, Sophia arrived without home, family, or husband at a time when prostitution was about the only known occupation for women. She entered a hamlet where rivers thundered at flood stage, panic raged, and the new government's officials met at a tavern to draft petitions for arms, ammunition, and men.

The raw little village on the banks of the swollen Brazos hosted the government. The Texas Army camped in a copse of trees nearby. The leader, General Sam Houston, rode in and out of Washington. Couriers galloped with word of Santa Anna's march, his victories at the Alamo and Goliad, and his fulfillment of the pledge to kill all Anglos in his path. The advent of war heightened gatherings in the village saloons for Texas's leaders. Charged with prestige, power, danger, politics, dancing, wealth, and drinking, the saloons' environs melded into a force that would draw Sophia. She would dance in the eye of many storms in the coming years in Texas.

Accustomed to men away from home, with too much time on their hands, too much whiskey, and not enough women—the milieu she grew up in—Sophia not only tolerated, but flirted with soldiers and politicians. The innocence she had stitched back together on the trek to Texas as a married woman sloughed off on the muddy shore of the Brazos. Tales of illicit love swirled around her like ruffles on a petticoat for as long as she possessed her uncommonly good looks. One oft-told account of an affair featured Sam Houston at Washington, where they met. Known for his eye for the ladies and a taste for whiskey, he would figure in Sophia's life for years, both in gossip and in friendship, in triumph and tragedy.

Soon though, Houston led his troops out of Washington on a march to San Jacinto, the Plains of St. Hyacinth. The government fled. Whether Sophia left earlier, became mired in the Runaway Scrape, or whether she tagged along behind the Texas Army, known to Mexicans as the *soldades goddammed,* is not known. However, weeks later, after the Texans' victorious Battle of San Jacinto, April 19, 1836, Sophia claimed, "I was the first one to him," meaning the wounded Houston. Texas folklorists acknowledge that she did practical nursing, like "sponge-bathing Houston's face and combing his hair."

But, Republic of Texas documents note that Houston oversaw the mop-up of the battle, ordered Santa Anna's life spared, and negotiated a treaty for the independent republic after being shot in the leg during battle. No mention of Sophia.

Sophia, though, had a way about her that defied official reports. If the facts needed a boost for a better story, she obliged. In Washington, for instance, she reported that her father was colonel and post commander at Fort Wayne, not saloonkeeper. Now, instead of being abandoned by the schoolteacher, Aughinbaugh, Sophia suggested he was a "high ranking Prussian officer," missing in action.

So, whether Sophia reached Houston first, or nursed him at all, is conjecture, or perhaps is one of the many Texas brags commenced on this battlefield. But, no doubt they became friends. After the battle, Houston arranged for her to return to Washington to stay with his friends, America and Sam Lusk. A friend of theirs, Holland Coffee, visited often, both before and after the war.

Coffee had been in Texas since 1833, when he led a trapping expedition to the upper reaches of the Red River. Previously, he had supplied such expeditions, settlers, and Indians from his trading company in Fort Smith, Arkansas. There, he first met Sam Houston in 1829, while Houston lived with the Cherokees. Returning from the expedition, Coffee set up a trading company, with one of his Arkansas partners, Silas Colville, along the north shore of the Red River where he negotiated the Camp Holmes treaty, authorizing the relocation of eastern Indians to lands west of the Mississippi. This area became known as Indian Territory. Coffee was respected by the Indians, fluent in their languages, and indulgent of their customs, and often they brought in their captives for trade with him. Many white women and children were returned to their families from the Coffee Trading House.

Coffee moved his post several times, the last location on a bend in the Red River that became known as Preston Bend, or Preston Point. In these early years, the town that grew up around his Trading House was ribald, boisterous, and profane. During the consultations leading toward revolution, and after-

ward in the Republic's government, Coffee served as a Representative of this
frontier region. It was during these visits to Washington, that he met Sophia.
After signing the Declaration of Independence, March 2, 1836, Coffee had led
troops into battle as a colonel in the Republic of Texas Army.

When victory opened the republic's doors to increased Anglo occupation,
settlers streamed across the Red River via Coffee's and George Butt's ferries.
With the increase in population along the river, criticism of Coffee and his
Trading House mounted. Critics accused him of trading guns and alcohol with
the Indians. He argued his denial successfully in the House of Representatives
in 1837, and Republic president Sam Houston authorized Coffee's post to become a mail station, and named him the Indian Agent. The name was changed
to Coffee's Station.

Immediately after the Texans' victory at San Jacinto, development sprawled
northwards. Speculators laid out town lots, and a boisterous, tawdry village
soon rose on the banks of Buffalo Bayou. Named in honor of Sam Houston,
now president of the Republic, the legislature designated Houston as the capital. Builders and opportunists quickly cobbled together saloons, prostitution
houses, hotels, and boarding houses on the site where the "Houston Ball" was
held commemorating the Texans' success a year after the war.

Sophia arrived with Coffee to dance through the night with him, and all the
noted dignitaries, including President Houston, at the ball. On this first an-
niversary of the "Battle of San Jacinto," Coffee and Sophia paraded across the
battleground with a host of early settlers, celebrating Independence and spin-
ning stories of heroic actions and legends of love and sacrifice.

The next year, Coffee was elected to the Republic's House of Representatives, requiring him to visit the new capital often.

Since war-torn Washington days, Coffee and Sophia had been attracted to
each other, but her marriage to Aughinbaugh had crimped any wedding plans.
And with Texas under Anglo land laws, she could not claim her league of land
on the Trinity. She moved to Houston to run a hotel.

Since Aughinbaugh could not be found, she was having trouble gaining a
divorce. Despite her dogged efforts, the judges refused to grant the divorce. In
Houston, she would be close to the power center to push it through. The Republic had recruited soldiers and boarded them in a hotel, or boarding house,
that Sophia ran. The government paid the troopers' keep and made no complaints about her, though many ventured that she rented more than rooms.

Determined to win her divorce, Sophia sought an Act of Congress to termi-
nate her first marriage. Convening in Houston, the House met, delayed, and
finally passed the decree. Newly elected Representative Coffee voted "aye."

But, the Senate squashed the bill. Sophia called on her friend, Sam Houston. The president pushed it through the upper chamber, freeing her to marry Coffee on January 19, 1839, at Washington.

A military escort from another trader's Red River post, Old Warren, rode to Washington to escort the newlyweds. They safeguarded Sophia and Coffee along the six-hundred-mile overland journey through hostile Indian lands to the Red River. They traveled along the Old San Antonio Road to Nacogdoches, then took Trammel's Trace, an old Caddo and Cherokee trail, to Clarksville, and then the Chihuahua Trail to Warren's Trading House. This settlers' community welcomed the handsome wedding couple with a grand ball at the post before the final twenty-five-mile leg of their journey to their new home where Sophia would begin her near sixty-year reign as hostess, heroine, and alleged trollop.

Tall poles, trimmed and shaped from native *bois d'arc* saplings—treasured by the Indians for the straight, hard wood that made strong arrow shafts—protected the hundred-square-foot log building that served both as house and trading post. Coffee's Station, Sophia's new home, perched on a bluff, overlooked the Red River and the ferry down below. Within its walls, she described, "a lap board house with puncheon floor . . . our table consisted of a dry goods box with legs in it." A rag rug warmed the floor, made from cotton Sophia grew and picked. Another dry goods box held her clothes.

In 1839, the Preston Point region was still a rowdy frontier, on the western end of settlement along the Red River Valley. Roving Texas Rangers guarded the post. Raids during which Indians stole horses and captured and murdered settlers might have terrified some, but not Sophia. She had grown up among the tensions of warring Indians and settler encroachment in Indiana. Years later, she would say of these times, "I was the happiest woman in Texas."

While Coffee operated the ferry and trading post, negotiated releases of captives, and developed a town-site of Preston, Sophia devoted her attention to the land and what it could produce—cotton and cattle—marshaling slaves to herd and plant.

Within their first year of marriage, Texas General Albert Sidney Johnston recommended the construction of a new line of forts be built on the western frontier and a military road to connect them. The line would stretch from Austin to Coffee's cut on the Red River. The army stocked up at Coffee's Station, from clothes to food. Instead of growing prosperous, however, the Coffees, like many in Texas at that time, were land rich and cash poor, since most of the Texas army's provisions were paid for in land script, not cash. During this time, General Johnston became friends with the Coffees and admired the hospitality Sophia offered.

Eventually, the army pulled out, and Coffee joined James Bourland's militia company to protect the frontier and to build the forts and military road. At Bird's Fort, near present-day Birdville, a small lake, as "beautiful and curvaceous as Sophia," he dubbed "Sophia's Lake." Cash from his Army work helped Coffee's Station stay open until the military road was completed, which rejuvenated business. Trade prospered with wagon trains of soldiers and settlers entering Texas and needing supplies, as the country approached statehood.

With the new prosperity—from his trading and her cattle and cotton—Sophia badgered Coffee for a new home. He built her a two-story dog-trot. The dog-trot, two log rooms separated by a covered walkway, was popular on the frontier. It offered shade and a breeze during Texas's simmering summers. Normally the two chimneys consisted of grass and mud. But those in Sophia's new home were made from fieldstone. Painted white, she called her new house, the "finest in the area," and named it Glen Eden. Later it would become Glen Eden Plantation. She furnished the house with goods brought by steamboat upriver to the port of Jefferson, in East Texas. She and Holland hosted a ball to show off Glen Eden. Proud of her growing reputation as frontier hostess, Sophia received travelers in style, with dinners and balls. She favored men in the know, but never hesitated to include handsome young officers from military wagon trains that rolled through, a hospitality that spiced her reputation, especially in Coffee's absence, when he was gone for politics or trade, or when he was negotiating treaties with Indians.

One favored visitor was the Coffees' old friend, Sam Houston. However, one such visit led to tragedy. People talked. Rumors of Sophia having an affair with Houston flourished. Tired of these tainted tales, Sophia demanded Coffee avenge her honor. "I'd rather be a widow of a brave man than the wife of a coward," she said. To squelch the rumor and defend his wife's honor, Coffee called out one of the tale-spinners, Charles Galloway, a nephew by marriage. Galloway killed Coffee with his Bowie knife in a fight to the finish, on October 1, 1846.

Widowed now, Sophia found herself with a 5,000-acre spread to run, along with nineteen slaves, herds of cattle and horses, Coffee's trading post business, and a large debt to take care of. Yet, she continued to entertain, and her parties, by now had become a highlight in the Valley. Always, prominent Army men gathered at Glen Eden. In addition to Albert Sidney Johnston of the Texas army, young United States officers like Robert E. Lee and Ulysses S. Grant frequented her home early in their careers. Adventurers like Randolph Marcy visited and resupplied their outfits. Those invited to Sophia's parties considered themselves fortunate and would ride a couple of days to attend.

To help manage Glen Eden and the trading house, and to shore up its solvency, Sophia brought in one of Coffee's business partners, George Butt, another Red River ferry operator. Within a year they negotiated a marriage. He paid off her notes, gave her cash, and she gave him land and three slaves.

Texas statehood, in 1848, brought the advent of another string of military forts to protect the growing settlements. A thousand wagons a year rolled through Preston Point. Trade climbed. Cotton production soared, and Sophia and George Butt voyaged often to their favorite port city, New Orleans, to trade their cotton and beeves, party, and acquire the latest fashions, fine china, and furniture. They enlarged her beloved home place, Glen Eden, blanketed the logs with siding, and added galleries the width of the house front and back, a kitchen, and a wine cellar. The cellar served to enhance Sophia's well-established reputation for entertaining Texas notables, but inflamed the stories and scorn that circulated about her.

With Butt engaged in the business, Sophia dwelled in the garden, growing the first roses in Grayson County. More than a hundred fruit trees dotted the hill behind Glen Eden. Grape and berry vines snaked across the side yard. A magnolia tree shaded the front lawn, grown from a seedling Sam Houston gave her. Catalpa trees arched the long drive up to the front of her house, the seeds a gift from General Johnston, shipped from a federal posting to California. A frequent guest of Sophia and her husbands, Johnston enjoyed Sophia and Glen Eden. However, when his wife joined him on the move from Missouri to San Antonio, Mrs. Johnston chose to remain in her cold, wet military tent rather than visit "the settlers," in pre–Civil War Texas.

When secession fever seeped into Texas, prosperous plantation owners joined the southern sympathizers. Sophia and George supported the Confederacy in a region split in its sympathies. Midway during the Civil War, Quantrill's Raiders wintered nearby Glen Eden—ranging back and forth across the Red River between the renegade-populated Indian Territory and Preston Point, plundering and killing. These troops contributed to another Sophia story of grit, on Christmas Eve, 1863, and caused another tragedy.

Sophia and George, who had confronted William Clarke Quantrill about his tactics, danced at a ball at the Ben Christian Hotel in Sherman. Some of Quantrill's men, drunk, spurred their horses into the hotel. One of them spotted Sophia dancing. She ignored them and kept on dancing. The raider bet his partner he could shoot the tassels off her hat. He did. Sophia kept on dancing. Partygoers vouched that she never stopped dancing, a tale recounted in North Texas papers for decades.

But, after the New Year, George rode into Sherman to sell cotton and did not come home. A week later, searchers found his body on the Sherman-to-Preston road, shot. Days later, Sophia glimpsed his watch on a guerilla and hounded Confederate officials until they ran Quantrill and his men out of the area.

Widowed again, Sophia operated Glen Eden with her slaves. At times, they stacked cotton bales two-stories high on the galleries to ward off Indian bullets and arrows. Another danger lurked. Federal troops patrolled the area. One of Coffee's army friends, James Bourland, commander of Texas's Frontier Regiment, stopped to warn Sophia that Union soldiers neared. She prepared for them, an event that would polish her reputation and alter her fame from vamp to heroine.

When the Federal dragoons arrived, she invited them in for "home cooking," maintaining her role as social hostess. After dinner, she offered a tour of her famous wine cellar. Officers and men trooped downstairs and sampled her wines until they were drunk. Sophia scampered upstairs, locked the door, ran outside, and grabbed a mule tied near the house. She slipped through the night, past the ferry so not to awaken the ferryman, who might sound an alarm, and swam the January-cold Red River. On the other shore, Indian Territory, she sent word to Bourland that the "Yankees" were snared in her wine cellar. He and his men returned, collected Sophia's prisoners, and dubbed her "the Confederate Paul Revere."

Now fifty years old, Sophia gained hero status along the Red River Valley, but it was time for her to leave. Even for her, long accustomed to Indian raids on the frontier, it had grown too dangerous. A heroine to the Confederates, her fame targeted Sophia as an enemy of the Union. Together with her slaves, she hung buckets of gold coins, topped off with hot tar for disguise, beneath a wagon and set off for Waco, the nearest refugee town, two hundred miles south.

After the War, on the way from Missouri to Mexico, a trek made by many weary rebels, Confederate cavalry officer, James Porter, a former judge, also stopped in Waco. In a town that throbbed with the ache of war, brimming with refugees, Sophia and Porter met. He became her fourth and final husband on August 2, 1865, married by the president of Baylor College. That fall, they returned to Glen Eden to begin the task of rebuilding.

A religious man, Porter encouraged Sophia to find religion. Although more at home on a dance floor than in a sanctuary, she tried. One day, during a camp meeting, Sophia decided to attend, or so she reports. She donned a bright orange satin dress. When the altar call came, she ran down the aisle, crying and shouting, professing her sins, and prostrated herself at the minister's feet. Instead of accepting her, he said, according to Sophia, "the sun, the moon and the stars are against your being a Christian." This hell-fire and damnation preacher had known her for a quarter of a century, and knew about her wine cellar and the dances at Glen Eden.

Never deterred by another's opinion of her, Sophia next tried Sherman's First Methodist Church where she found both a friend and a minister in Rev. J. M. Binkley. Porter and the church mellowed Sophia's behavior, but the frisky temperament of youth, now aged, whipsawed from courteous to curt. She and Porter gave money and land for churches. Her last marriage would be her longest, the least tempestuous, and perhaps most loved. Like with Sophia, civilization settled in along the Red River while Texas recovered from the Civil War.

She and Judge Porter continued Glen Eden's popular dinners and gatherings, but now, no dancing or wine. This area near Denison grew. No longer in the trading house or ferry business, from their bluff, Glen Eden's proprietors saw the influx of cattle being driven north to market, crossing the Red at the Preston cut. Their prosperity was enhanced from the buying and selling of land to the new arrivals in post–Civil War Texas.

When Porter died in 1886, she had him buried near Glen Eden, like Coffee had been. For the last eleven years of her life, Sophia continued to entertain, "the notable persons of the day," to learn of "the state of politics and social life of Texas, what she had been apart of for sixty years."

A woman friend who stayed with her in her waning years said, "She was as changeable as the Texas winds . . . a tempest of temperament but altogether lovely and loveable."

On August 27, 1897, Sophia died, at eighty-one. The Methodist minister, her friend, Reverand Binkley, who accepted her in the church thirty years before, sat by her bedside. He conducted the funeral at Glen Eden, a service likened to a camp meeting for hundreds who thronged to mourn the grand old lady of the Red River Valley.

Sophia Suttonfield Aughinbaugh Coffee Butt Porter spent the first part of her life scrapping for what she wanted; during her later years, she repaired her reputation, dancing in the eye of the storm, aided by a late night January swim across the Red River, earning her burial site marker, "The Confederate Paul Revere."

THE LAST WAR CRY:
BATTLE BUTTE, JANUARY 8, 1877

Janet E. Graebner

"A people without history is like the wind on the buffalo grass," the old man said over his paint stones and his quill and bone brushes.

"Hou! That is true!" Crazy Horse agreed.

Crazy Horse: The Strange Man of the Oglalas,
Mari Sandoz

BY THE END OF 1876, the opportunity for the Teton Lakota (Plains Sioux) to direct their own destiny was drawing to a close. The nation's centennial summer had been marred by news from Montana Territory of General George Crook's failure to win a decisive victory against an alliance of Northern Cheyenne and Lakota on June 17 at Rosebud Creek. This indignity to the American frontier army was compounded eight days later by the annihilation of Lieutenant-Colonel George Armstrong Custer and 231 men of the Seventh Cavalry, in the valley of the Little Bighorn.

The outraged response from the eastern establishment and the U.S. government guaranteed that the non-reservation Indians would be forced by whatever means to surrender and become "good" Indians. The public was especially irate at those thousands led by Sitting Bull, Crazy Horse, and the Cheyenne leaders Two Moons and Dull Knife, who steadfastly refused to submit to the government's authority.

Colonel Nelson A. Miles was the prominent figure engaged to subdue the roaming, recalcitrant Sioux. In fact, he had asked for the task, stating unequivocally that "the Indians should be disarmed, dismounted, and taught trades useful in white-dominated society."

Ambitious, brash, and determined, Miles had served during the Civil War, and had been in various Indian campaigns since 1866. His unorthodox decision to campaign on the western plains all winter, in severe minus-degree temperatures that froze the mercury thermometers, set him apart from the earlier failed winter strikes under the command of Colonel Joseph J. Reynolds and Brigadier General Alfred Terry.

The half-day's battle at the Tongue River on January 8, 1877, which brought Miles's troops face-to-face with Crazy Horse's warriors, was seldom treated by early historians as more than a footnote, if mentioned at all. But there is evidence to support the idea that this fight was a significant factor—the last war cry—in ending the Sioux war of 1876–77, thus advancing America's western frontier.

Neither the fight nor the location was well known at the time, leading historians to erroneously call it the Battle of Wolf Mountain. But the Wolf Mountains lie west of the Tongue River and are situated between Rosebud Creek and the Little Bighorn. Today, southwest of Birney, Montana, five miles upstream on the Tongue, the area is called Battle Butte.

An east/west gravel road bisects the bluffs and an eroding rocky ridge that extends about nine hundred yards from the hills on the south end to the Tongue on the north. This ridge and the pyramid-shaped butte in the center (about seventy feet high with steep sides) is where the Lakota and Cheyenne initiated their defense against Miles's Fifth Infantry. The ridge and crumbling breastworks occasionally still yield ancient shell casings.

The Indians whom the army was attempting to subjugate between late 1876 and spring 1877 were hounded forth and back through the Powder River country. They were devoid of shelter, already starving, and poor in spirit. Their desperate condition raises several questions: What prompted such strong military action against these people during the winter, a time of respite, usually, from army troops scouring the country? Of what significance is this particular conflict at an obscure butte located on the Tongue River in southeastern Montana? Was Miles's penetration into the Indians' winter camp on January 8, 1877, retaliation against the Sioux and Cheyenne for hostilities committed towards miners and emigrants invading the Black Hills and the Powder River country? Were there additional factors emanating from the government with a more serious intent?

The Backstory

PERSPECTIVE IS GAINED BY recalling that for three decades after the Civil War the surge of people over the trans-Mississippi West was unprecedented.

The government and the Indian nations alike were alarmed at the rapid advances of miners, cattlemen, traders, freighters, farmers, and business opportunists. In their wake came demands for a transportation network (roads, railroads, and overland carriers) that would criss-cross the country from the East to the Pacific coast.

The 1860s and 1870s were especially charged with conflicts between whites and Indians. In an attempt to placate the Indians and to provide safe passage for emigrants, the government offered the treaty of 1868, which gave to the Sioux the Black Hills and Powder River country. The government at the time considered the region worthless; too hilly to attract settlers and too far from transcontinental transportation routes.

The treaty of 1868 stated that "no white person or persons shall be permitted to settle upon or occupy any portion of the territory, or without the consent of the Indians to pass through the same." It also called for the abandonment of the army forts on the Bozeman Trail; the creation of the Great Sioux Reservation (west of the Missouri River in what is now South Dakota, including the Black Hills, which held religious significance for the Indians); and that the lands north of the North Platte River and east of the summits of the Bighorn Mountains would be unceded Indian territory prohibited to whites, which permitted the Sioux to continue to hunt one of the last remaining buffalo herds on the northern plains.

On November 6, 1868, after two years of resistance, Red Cloud, Spotted Tail, and other Indian leaders signed the treaty; they did not, however, speak for the whole Sioux nation. The holdouts were the northern Lakota and their Cheyenne allies, absent from all negotiations.

A tentative peace prevailed for several years after the treaty signing, but Crazy Horse and his followers remained openly contemptuous and suspicious of Red Cloud and others who had acquiesced to the U.S. government's demands and given up their nomadic ways for life on the reservation.

In 1872 and 1873, Northern Pacific Railroad survey crews, under military escort, entered the unceded Indian territory, sending the non-reservation Sioux into fresh turmoil. As it became more apparent that westward-moving whites would continue to breach Indian territory, General Philip Sheridan got permission in 1873 from the Interior Department to conduct a reconnaissance of the Black Hills, with the intention of building a major fort there. Sheridan appointed Lieutenant-colonel George Armstrong Custer to lead an expedition in 1874 to gather military and scientific information about the region. Excited messages sent back said there was gold in the Black Hills "from the grass roots down."

From then on, treaty obligations began to crumble as hunting and religious grounds were invaded, and neither the army nor the Indian Bureau effected any restraint on the trespassers.

By 1875, angry Indians and determined encroachers were at severe logger-heads, and Indians from the agencies began to slip away to the north country to support the resisting bands.

Alarmed at the army's failure to protect Indian territory, Red Cloud and Spotted Tail protested to Washington officials, which resulted in a series of government commissions arriving to persuade the Sioux to relinquish the Black Hills. Runners were sent to invite Sitting Bull, Crazy Horse, and other "wild" chiefs to the council, writes Dee Brown in *Bury My Heart at Wounded Knee,* but they adamantly refused to cooperate. At one point, the commission-ers offered payment for the Black Hills, which was rejected. (Today millions of dollars from that period, plus interest, remain in escrow, unclaimed by the Sioux nation.)

As 1875 rolled into 1876, hostilities between whites and Indians increased. The military assumed control of the reservations in Sioux country, Brown says, and a new law (without regard for the 1868 treaty) dictated that Con-gress would make no further appropriations for supplies to the Indians unless they complied with three provisions: "First, that you shall give up the Black Hills country and the country to the north; second, that you shall receive your rations on the Missouri River [which meant the Indians would have to move]; and that the Great Father [President Ulysses S. Grant] shall be per-mitted to locate three roads from the Missouri River across the reservation to that new country where the Black Hills are [called the Great American Desert at the time and belatedly recognized as mining country and a cul-tivable resource]."

On hearing these demands, one of the chiefs, replied that since the Great Father promised them that they would never be moved they had been moved five times. "I think you had better put the Indians on wheels," he said sardon-ically, "and you can run them about whenever you wish."

The leaders present at these councils accused the government of betraying the Indians and breaking promises; and, they pointed out, the 1868 treaty re-quired the signatures of three-fourths of the male adults to change anything in it. Since half the warriors were in the north with Sitting Bull and Crazy Horse, they were not included in the discussions. The commissioners prevaricated, Brown says, by explaining that "the Indians off the reservations were hostiles; only friendly Indians were covered by the treaty."

Since many of the Indian leaders could not accept this, the commissioners dropped strong hints that unless the Indians signed the new law all rations would be cut off immediately; they would be removed to Indian Territory in the south (present-day Oklahoma); and the army would take away their guns and horses.

The Indians were stymied. The Black Hills were stolen; game in the Powder River country was gone; without agency rations the people would starve; the thought of moving away was unbearable; and if the army took away their guns and ponies, they would no longer be men.

Again, Red Cloud and Spotted Tail signed first, the others followed, and after that, Dee Brown writes, "the commissioners went to agencies at Standing Rock, Cheyenne River, Crow Creek, Lower Brulé, and Santee, and badgered the other Sioux and Cheyenne to sign."

The Sioux War 1876–77

THE CAUSES OF THE 1876 Sioux war will probably always be in contention. In *The Great Sioux War 1876–77* (ed. Paul L. Hedren), Harry H. Anderson, for example, challenges Mark H. Brown's view. Brown takes the military's side and says that "it has been fashionable to make U.S. government the whipping boy for what occurred." He emphasizes the hostile actions by what he calls "renegade Sioux" and focuses attention on geographic factors of the Yellowstone Basin and the Powder River country that were paramount to settlement and construction of railroad routes. An additional problem, Brown says, was the proximity of the Crow reservation to the unceded Indian territory, hence a source of constant warfare between the Sioux and Crow.

For his part, Anderson claims "important errors of both fact and interpretation" in Brown's argument. Blaming the Sioux, he says, was *de rigueur* for the time; both the military brass and certain government officials did so. The difference in their official approach by 1876 was to eschew peace commissions and use military force, which signaled for Anderson a definite relationship (denied by Mark Brown) between the Black Hills gold rush, trespass by railroad survey crews, the incursion of settlers, and Indian hostilities; a relationship that General George Crook, Commanding General of the Department of the Platte, had formally denied in an annual report dated September 23, 1876: "The occupation by the settlers of the Black Hills country had nothing to do with the hostilities which have been in progress."

Crook's statement supports the belief at the time that Indians in general were savages intent upon attacking whites without provocation. More important, it ignores westward-moving economic opportunities in goods and services that followed the gold seekers. Everyone was clamoring for safe passage, and, once settled, for security from roaming Indians who had become barriers to an advancing white frontier.

The Indians themselves were being destabilized within their own culture as political factionalism raised its head. To their personal advantage, leaders like Red Cloud and Spotted Tail negotiated with Washington officials and eventually gained their own agencies in 1871 in northwestern Nebraska. With U.S. government approval, they regularly sent emissaries to the non-reservation Sioux to encourage them to surrender; a tactic of divide and conquer, hostiles versus friendlies.

Sitting Bull, Crazy Horse, Lame Deer, Two Moons, and Dull Knife continued to refuse interaction with whites and became heroes for their resistance. As ill-will fomented between Indians and settlers, it became common for agency Indians to leave the reservation during the spring to spend the summer with the resisting bands, enjoying the last vestige of old-way freedom, including swelling the ranks of warriors, which created a perplexing problem for the Indian Bureau.

In James O. Gump's comparative study on the subjugation of the Zulu and the Sioux (*The Dust Rose Like Smoke*), even formerly sympathetic white administrators finally yielded to the idea that political expediencies in the 1870s dictated that total war against the Sioux was a necessity.

President Grant came to the same conclusion *as early as November 3, 1875,* in a secret meeting with Secretary of War W. W. Belknap, Secretary of the Interior Zachariah Chandler, Assistant Secretary B. R. Cowan, Commissioner of Indian Affairs Edward Smith, and generals Sheridan and Crook. The outcome: Unable to halt white trespassers on Sioux lands, and unsuccessful at purchasing the Black Hills, the U.S. government decided to escalate military involvement.

It was necessary, however, according to John S. Gray (*Centennial Campaign*), "to devise some smoke-screen to cloak such naked aggression from political opponents and the public . . . [and] shift the onus to the Indians, especially the 'hostile' bands. This would demand a little ingenious conniving," Gray continued, "inasmuch as the Sioux had chosen to remain so peaceful in the face of outrageous provocation."

President Grant had no dissent from his cabinet or the generals concerning his decision to resort to war. The plan would commence in two phases, one public, one secret: 1) public notice would state "that the orders forbidding trespass into the Black Hills would no longer be enforced, though they would not be rescinded"; 2) preparations would be initiated, in secret, "for a punitive campaign against the [Indian] winter roamers in order to subdue them."

Some newspaper reporters suspected more than the government's public information offered; most notably, William E. Curtis of the Chicago *Inter-Ocean*, who wrote several articles speculating that the military would be more involved with Indian matters than it had been in the past.

In addition, George W. Manypenny, a former Indian Commissioner, either knew personally or suspected, Gray says, "that this decision had been reached at the [November 3] White House conference." General Crook's aide, Lieutenant John G. Bourke, also knew of the meeting and mentioned it in his book *On the Border with Crook*.

The other army generals were informed once the plan was in place. Nearly all sided with General Sherman's attitude that "the Sioux must be made to know that when the Government commands they must obey." Only General Alfred Terry demurred, saying that any attempt to trample the rights of the Sioux that were guaranteed by the treaty of 1868 should be resisted.

Thus, by turning the resisting Indians over to the army for punishment, the major source of opposition to the Black Hills acquisition would be removed. By withdrawing military patrols from the routes leading to the gold and silver fields, the prospectors could enter in force.

The disposition of the agreed military action was then handed to General Sheridan, who immediately issued an ultimatum to the independent Sioux and their allies: Report to your agencies by January 31, 1876, or face military reprisals.

But Sheridan apparently had some doubt that they would comply, and in a report to Sherman he said that "in all probability" the Sioux would regard the ultimatum as "a good joke." He worried that "unless they are caught before early spring, they cannot be caught at all."

Sheridan's premonition gained an eerie credibility with General Crook's defeat at the Rosebud on June 17, 1876, and the wipeout of General Custer and his command eight days later at the Little Bighorn.

While the army bears significant responsibility for the war against the Sioux in 1876–77, its actions make sense only in context with the government's objectives that were decided at President Grant's secret meeting on November 3, 1875.

True, there is evidence for depredations by the Sioux and Cheyenne prior to the date of the decision to send the army after them. But questions arise when one considers that 1) none of the military commanders made any mention in their reports of the November 3, 1875, conference with Grant; 2) annuities were withheld from the agency Indians as leverage to force the independent Indians to surrender; 3) newspaper accounts directly tied corruption within the Indian Bureau to Grant's administration; 4) the scapegoat for the army's 1876 campaigns against the Sioux was Indian Bureau Inspector Erwin C. Watkins, who had called for punishment of the Sioux because of their aggressive raids and the killing of settlers.

Watkins's report, however, is dated November 9, 1875, *six days after* the White House meeting and Grant's order for the army to go out and "whip the Sioux." Watkins was a "green Indian Inspector," Gray says, on the job only two years. That he signed the report is undisputed; that he actually wrote it is questionable. Due to the "verbose and propagandistic" tone of the report, Gray suggests possible authorship by Sheridan and Crook.

Unfortunately for Watkins it was this document that Generals Sherman and Sheridan used in their annual reports to justify the January 31, 1876, ultimatum and the subsequent military move against the "renegade Sioux," especially the charismatic Sitting Bull and Crazy Horse, who had hundreds of dedicated followers.

Watkins, incidentally, was soon removed from office and dispatched to Canada as U.S. minister. Could it be that the administration was afraid he would compromise claims made in the report? Could one also then say that Custer and others were sacrificed by an engineered crisis in the cause for westward expansion?

By late 1876, as the shock of Custer's death began to wear off, some began to openly question the army's motives in the Indian wars. Indian Inspector William Vandiveer, for example, wrote to Bishop Henry Whipple, who sat on the Sioux Black Hills Commission, and urged him to expose in the commission's report the true causes of the war, that it was "unnecessary and uncalled for—that the Army and not the Indians commenced it."

It was just such an accusation as this, Anderson says, that the government and military commanders wanted to avoid becoming public knowledge, and the reason that no official record was made of the November 3, 1875, conference with President Grant. Gray concurs: "[W]ar must be justified—by illusion, if reality will not do."

Gradually, as the buffalo herds and game were being decimated, and as military patrols constantly skirmished with the Indians, always on the move, leaders like Sitting Bull and Crazy Horse were being squeezed between a rock and a hard place: surrender or die.

Battle Butte, January 8, 1877

ON DECEMBER 29, 1876, Colonel Nelson A. Miles and his troops departed the Tongue River cantonment and headed for the winter camps of the Oglala and Northern Cheyenne, said to be located 150 miles upstream at the mouth of Otter Creek. The number of remaining warriors with Crazy Horse was comparable in size to Miles' command, which consisted of five companies of the Fifth Infantry and two from the Twenty-second, a total of 436 officers and men, plus white scouts (including the famous Luther S. "Yellowstone" Kelly), several Crow scouts and a Bannock Indian. Two cannons were disguised as supply wagons.

Army shortages of mules, horses, grain, and regulation winter clothing posed a problem, as did the lack of food after a week of arduous marches over iced terrain. Snow piled several feet deep and temperatures reportedly plunged to minus 50 degrees that winter.

Likewise enduring hardships, and due to scarcity of game and forage for their horses, the Indian bands were scattered along Otter Creek and Hanging Woman Fork. As the troops moved up the Tongue River, they engaged in skirmishes with rearguard warriors on January 1 and 3, 1877. At one point, they captured several children and four Cheyenne women, relatives of prominent tribesmen: Sweet Woman; Little Chief's wife; Crooked Nose, the sister of Wooden Leg; and Lame White Man's widow, who was also the grandmother of John Stands in Timber.

On January 8, the fighting began about 7 A.M., with the Indians taunting the soldiers stationed in the valley below. The warriors' line of defense extended about nine hundred yards from the Tongue River on the north to a bluff (now called Big Crow Butte) south of Battle Butte.

The most bitter fighting took place in a snowstorm over a five-hour period as Miles's men fought for possession of the butte, a formidable task with its ice-slicked steep sides covered with snow.

By noon, out of ammunition and unable to suppress the infantry's advances, the Indians left their positions and retreated farther up the Tongue with the women and children.

Although several reports state that the troops pursued the Indians for seventeen miles, this is most likely an error. Colonel Miles himself made no such claim in his account of the fight, and distinguishing foe from friend was virtually impossible in blizzard conditions.

Miles and his men returned to the cantonment, having traveled more than three hundred miles round-trip. (Fort Keogh was built here later, where the Tongue empties into the Yellowstone River.) Crazy Horse's Oglalas and Northern Cheyenne moved west to the Little Bighorn and camped, starving now and suffering intensely from the cold, the result of having lost or abandoned their belongings as they fled the army.

An accurate count of casualties is as clouded as the weather. Miles at one time reported two men killed and eight wounded; another time, one killed and nine wounded. A scout with Miles recalled three soldiers killed and eight wounded, figures repeated by Captain Edmond Butler in his account of the campaign.

Indian casualties add up to fewer from the Indians' perspective than claimed by military accounts, which range from 10 to 15 killed and from 25 to 30 wounded. Wooden Leg recalled two Sioux and one Cheyenne killed (Big Crow, who had taunted the soldiers by dancing on the ridge until a bullet found him), and three Sioux wounded; two died later.

One could conclude that the withdrawal of both sides marks this as an inconsequential fight brought to an indecisive conclusion by the severity of a Montana blizzard. But for the non-reservation Lakota and Northern Cheyenne the conclusion was clearly decisive. They realized that the army could and would pursue them unmercifully, even through the winter.

The buffalo herds had been decimated and the hunting grounds ruined; the Black Hills region had been lost to the whites forever; the Indians no longer had access to white traders for ammunition and supplies; and their reinforcements were dwindling. Sitting Bull and Gall were preparing to lead 109 lodges to Canada, and Dull Knife's winter camp at the Red Fork of the Powder River, on November 25, 1876, had been "wiped from the face of the earth," wrote Lieutenant Bourke.

Hearing that Crazy Horse's band was attacked, many resisting Indians began to wonder how any of them could be safe. They began drifting towards the agencies, ready to recognize the inevitable: surrender.

Even some of Crazy Horse's followers, weary and despondent, departed for the agencies, persuaded by their kinsmen who acted as messengers for the army, and who conveyed promises of peace, rations, fair treatment, and their own agency. At first Crazy Horse tried to stop them, but seeing their suffering and pessimism for the future, he let them go.

His whole life had been dedicated to serving his people as a warrior, protector, hunter, visionary, and, finally, a resistance leader against white domination. But the fight at Battle Butte echoed as a last war cry and convinced Crazy

Horse that life as the Teton Lakota had known it was over. They had indeed become a people without history, like the wind on the buffalo grass.

Crazy Horse's next act was completely in character for a man who believed that he had to answer only to himself for his actions and beliefs. On May 5, 1877, in a procession two miles long, singing their peace song and moving with the majesty of royalty rather than a defeated people, he led 889 Lakota and Cheyenne and 1,700 horses to Fort Robinson, Nebraska, near the Red Cloud Agency.

"By God!" blustered General Crook. "This is a triumphal march, not a surrender!"

The only major resisters left in the north country after Crazy Horse's surrender were Lame Deer and his Miniconjou, camped near Rosebud Creek. On May 7, 1877, Colonel Miles and his command found the village. The Miniconjou raised a flag of truce, but a firefight broke out and Lame Deer and others were killed. The band broke up and fled; most surrendered soon after.

Thus ended the opposition forces of Lakota and Cheyenne, swept from the plains of Dakota, Wyoming, and eastern Montana. What the military had expected in early 1876 to be "a few weeks of easy work in the field" had stretched to eighteen months and had cost a great deal in blood and suffering on both sides.

On September 5, 1877, four months after Crazy Horse arrived at Fort Robinson, the slightly built, light-haired Oglala, about age thirty-seven (birth dates vary from 1840 to 1845), was bayoneted by Private William Gentles during a struggle in the guardhouse. (Some say Crazy Horse had a knife and accidentally stabbed himself.) His arms were pinned behind him by one of his own men, Little Big Man, bringing to a close what a youthful vision had shown: He would never be killed by a bullet or by an enemy; it was only by his own people that he could be hurt.

Crazy Horse died later that night with these words: "Tell the people it is no use to depend on me anymore now."

THE ALAMO

William Groneman III

AS WILLIAM BARRET TRAVIS lay on his cot in the pre-dawn hours of March 6, 1836, he could not have known that he was just minutes away from eternity—and immortality. He occupied the headquarters room of a makeshift fort called "The Alamo," just to the east, across the San Antonio River from the town of San Antonio de Bexar, Texas. In the same room slept Travis's slave, Joe.

Who knows if Travis actually slept? If he did he certainly deserved it. He and his garrison were going into the thirteenth day of their siege within the Alamo. On the outside was a Mexican army bent on their destruction. Besides being worn down by on-and-off cannonading and exploratory attacks, Travis's men had worked long into this twelfth night shoring up defenses and strengthening positions.

It is just as understandable if Travis could not sleep. He may have lain awake contemplating his rather unique position. Born in South Carolina, but raised in Alabama, he had made his living at times as a schoolteacher and as a newspaperman. Just a few short months ago he had been practicing law in the Texas town of San Felipe de Austin. Currently he was a twenty-seven-year-old lieutenant-colonel of cavalry in the fledgling army of Texas, engaged in an armed revolt against Mexico, of which Texas was a part. He could not complain about this situation since he had helped foment the revolt, but as a cavalryman Travis felt he should have been dashing about the plains of Texas, executing daring raids against the enemy. Instead he found himself not only boxed up in, but actually in command of a fortification—a job more correctly suited to an artillery officer.

Travis did not want command of the Alamo. He had not wanted to be there in the first place. In January he had been ordered there by Texas's ad interim governor Henry Smith, one of the claimants to authority in Texas. Travis rode to San Antonio de Bexar, or simply Bexar as it was known, accompanied by a small cavalry company commanded by Captain John Hubbard Forsyth of Avon, New York. Travis protested his orders to Smith in writing. On January 29, he explained that he was unwilling to risk his reputation ". . . ever dear to a soldier," by going off into the enemy's country with such little means, so few men, and so badly equipped. He did not mind running the risks. He just did not want to do so inefficiently. He also explained his willingness to *visit* Bexar to consult or communicate with the officers present and to execute any other commission he may have been entrusted with. He even threatened to resign his commission. However, despite his reluctance, and with no subsequent orders countermanding his original ones, he continued on to Bexar.

In the fall of 1835, Texan citizens and settlers had launched an active rebellion against the Mexican government of Generalissimo Antonio Lopez de Santa Anna. Friction had been developing for a while between the settlers, most of whom were Americans, and their host country, Mexico. On several occasions Travis had been active in encouraging this friction. The spark finally was ignited in October 1835, when a small Mexican army unit stationed in Bexar was sent seventy miles east to the town of Gonzales. They were sent there to retrieve a small cannon that had been loaned to the citizens of Gonzales for protection against hostile Indians. At Gonzales the Mexican force was met by eighteen armed citizens, the cannon, and a flag with the words "Come and Take It" emblazoned on it. The Mexican officer demanded the cannon, and the settlers refused. The eighteen negotiated and stalled while runners went for help. By the following day the Texans' numbers swelled to one hundred fifty. Gunfire was exchanged, the small Mexican force was sent reeling back to Bexar, and the Texas Revolution officially was on.

The revolution proceeded in chaotic conditions of divided leadership, no real army, and no clear-cut goals. Factions bickered over whether Texas was fighting for separate statehood in the Mexican federation (actually it was part of the larger territory of Coahuila y Tejas); independence in conjunction with other northern Mexican states; or complete independence from all ties with Mexico.

Despite the chaos, the Texans managed to assemble an armed force and mount an expedition against Bexar. They laid siege to the town and a superior Mexican force under General Martin Perfecto de Cos in November.

Cos's force was faced with defending two distinct fortifications—one in the main plaza of the town, and the other, the former mission of San Antonio de Valero (the Alamo) across the river. The mission was popularly called "The Alamo" after a Spanish cavalry unit from the town of Alamo de Parras, Coahuila, Mexico had been stationed there in the early 1800s. In a burst of sentimentality, the soldiers referred to it as "The Alamo" in honor of their home town and the name stuck.

From December 5th to the 10th the Texan force under the leadership of Benjamin Milam stormed the town. After fierce house-to-house fighting, and the death of Milam, the Texans drove the Mexican army out of the town, across the river, and into the Alamo. Cos finally surrendered and he and his men were allowed to set out for the interior of Mexico, under parole, never again to take up arms against the Mexican Constitution of 1824 (for which the Texans claimed that they were fighting).

The Texans now had control of Bexar and the Alamo. For all practical purposes the Mexican military presence in Texas had ended, at least temporarily. With the fighting over, the Texan force at Bexar began to suffer the fate of all volunteer armies once inactivity sets in. It began to dissolve. Many volunteers drifted home to families and farms. Others, bent on plunder, became involved in a wild plan to invade the Mexican border town of Matamoras. A small group of artillerymen and infantrymen (approximately eighty of them), under the command of Lieutenant Colonel James Clinton Neill, remained in Bexar.

Santa Anna was not about to let the vast territory of Texas be lost to Mexico. With the defeat of Cos, he immediately prepared for an invasion of Texas in the spring of 1836.

Neill recognized the danger. He sent a series of requests to the nascent government of Texas for supplies, ammunition, and manpower. Travis's orders to ride to Bexar were in answer to those appeals. Travis arrived there and reported to Neill on or about February 11. Within two weeks he was placed in temporary command of the post by Neill, when Neill was called away due to illness in his family.

Travis may have pondered these event, or he may have turned his thoughts to the men sharing the dangers with him in the Alamo, and for whom he was now responsible.

The original eighty or so men who were with Neill before Travis's arrival had grown to approximately two hundred fifty. This number still was not enough to defend a large complex like the Alamo. At least it showed that they were not completely forgotten by the rest of Texas. The backbone of the garrison was the artillery company of Captain William R. Carey of Virginia. They proudly called themselves "the Invincibles," and beside their normal duties as artillerymen, they had served as a sort of military police for Neill. Another mainstay of the garrison was the infantry company of Captain William Blazeby, an Englishman who had lived in New York before coming to Texas. His company was a remnant of the original "New Orleans Greys." This group was so named since they were formed up and outfitted with weapons and gray uniforms in New Orleans for service in Texas.

About one week prior to Travis's arrival, the garrison had been augmented by a volunteer force accompanying the redoubtable James Bowie. The forty-year-old Bowie had gone to Bexar with instructions from Sam Houston to destroy the fortifications in the *town*. Meanwhile, Houston, in a letter to Governor Smith offered the idea of having the troops abandon the place completely, destroy the Alamo, and remove the cannons. In the absence of a decision by Smith, the fate of Bexar and the Alamo was left up to Bowie's discretion. Bowie, with emotional and financial ties to the town, exercised his discretion and decided that it should be held. On February 2 he wrote to Governor Smith that "Col. Neill & Myself have come to the solemn resolution that we will rather die in these ditches than give it up to the enemy." [sic]

Other smaller units joined the garrison before the arrival of the Mexican army. A notable person with one of these groups was David Crockett, former Congressman from the state of Tennessee. Since the siege began, at least two other reinforcements had gotten through the enemy's lines and into the Alamo. So, while it could be done, maybe more men inside the Alamo consuming supplies and providing the Mexican soldiers with more targets was not the answer. Maybe reinforcements were now needed outside the Alamo, striking and harassing the enemy, and drawing his attention away from the fort itself. But where were these reinforcements?

Travis's thoughts may have strayed to the delicate position he held as the twenty-seven-year-old commander of a garrison that included Bowie and Crockett, two of the most famous men in the Southwest. Of course, Travis probably was grateful at having both of them to rely on. Their presence alone contributed to holding the garrison together. However, even from the beginning Bowie proved to be a handful. When Neill left the garrison he placed Travis in temporary command pending his return. His was a logical choice since Travis was the highest-ranking regular officer present. Trouble began immediately when the volunteer troops protested. Volunteers were traditionally allowed to elect their own officers. They objected to being put under Travis's command. Travis agreed to let the volunteers hold an election for an officer of their own who, of course, would be subordinate to Travis.

The volunteers elected Bowie who, in addition to overindulging in alcohol, began to take on all authority over the garrison and the civil affairs of the town, even to the point of releasing prisoners from the civil jail in order to have them available for work details and for service. The situation became so intolerable that Neill's adjutant, Captain John J. Baugh, of Virginia, protested in writing to Governor Smith. Travis actually removed his cavalrymen from the garrison for a time and camped at the Medina River. Finally, his sense of duty brought him back to town where a workable agreement was reached with Bowie. It was decided that Bowie would command the volunteer troops, and that Travis would command the regulars and volunteer cavalry. All general orders and correspondence were to be signed by both pending Neill's return.

This unusual command arraignment worked for about ten days. It began to tatter with the arrival of the enemy on February 23. At about 3:00 P.M., the Mexican army took possession of Bexar, and Travis and his men took to the Alamo. The Mexican troops raised a red flag on the bell tower of the San Fernando Church in the middle of town. The Texans answered this symbol of "no quarter" by firing a cannon. Later, Bowie was told that the Mexicans had called for a parley before the shot had been fired. He then sent the Alamo garrison's engineer, Green B. Jameson of Kentucky, out under a flag of truce to ascertain if this was so. Bowie was rebuffed with a written message from Santa Anna's aide-de-camp, Colonel José Batres, which stated that the Mexican army could not come to terms under any conditions with rebellious foreigners, and if the Texans wished to save their lives, they were to place themselves immediately at the disposal of the Supreme Government.

Travis then sent a messenger of his own, Captain Albert Martin of Rhode Island, to speak to Santa Anna's top aid, Colonel Juan Nepomuceno Almonte. Martin informed Almonte that if Almonte wished to speak to him, Travis would ". . . receive him with much pleasure." Almonte answered coldly that it did not become the Mexican government to make any propositions through him, and that he only had permission to hear the propositions of the rebels.

Travis and Bowie were beginning to take unilateral action, which may have caused a serious rift in command had fate not intervened. On the following day Bowie was felled by an unidentified illness. He remained bed-ridden and out of the action for the remainder of the siege. Obviously, Travis missed Bowie's savvy and fighting ability. However, he may have been relieved somewhat, at not having to deal with the unpredictability of their command agreement.

Crockett, on the other hand, had proven valuable. With his popularity and personality, the forty-nine-year-old Crockett could have swayed the whole garrison to any course he wished. He, however, remained in the background, exerting no influence, but pitching in whenever help was needed.

On February 25, the Mexicans launched an exploratory attack against the Alamo's walls. In a letter to Sam Houston, Travis wrote that "The Hon. David Crockett was seen at all points animating the men to their duty," during the attack. Later in the siege Crockett was called on to leave the relative safety of the Alamo's walls and go on a scouting mission to rally reinforcements. On March 4, Crockett cut his way through the Mexican lines and back into the Alamo with about fifty men. Travis could rely on Crockett even to the point of sending him out of their potential death trap with the knowledge that Crockett would fight his way back in, in order to complete his mission.

Besides Crockett and Bowie, Travis had any number of good men he knew he could rely on both inside and outside the walls. In addition of Jameson, Carey, and Blazeby, there was Albert Martin, who delivered Travis's communication to Almonte. Martin also had gone out early in the siege and come back with a thirty-two man reinforcement from Gonzales. There was John W. Smith, who had lived in Texas since 1826. Smith had gone scouting on February 23 and confirmed the approach of the Mexican army. Since then he had left the Alamo to hasten reinforcements and had led the Gonzales group in. Then, he went out again. Travis could only hope that he was leading a stronger force back. There was Amos Pollard, the New York City physician, who served as the Alamo's medical officer. His hands were full caring for the sick, including Bowie, and the wounded from the fighting back in December. There were the enlisted men and volunteers, most of whom had endured the siege for twelve grueling days. Charles Despallier, of Louisiana, and Robert Brown had sallied from the cover of the walls during the fighting on the 25th and set fire to houses that were providing cover to the Mexican troops.

Then there were the men who never ceased to surprise a commander. Sergeant William B. Ward of Ireland had been a bit of a concern during the pre-siege inactivity in Bexar, especially due to his inclination toward "the bottle." Yet, when the Mexican army occupied the town and many of the Texans were scurrying about the Alamo in confusion, there stood Ward at the artillery position covering the Alamo's main entrance—sober, confident, and calmly ready for action.

If there was one man whom Travis missed it was Captain Juan Nepomuceno Seguin, a prominent citizen and respected leader of the local Tejano troops. Travis had sent Seguin out to Gonzales on February 25 to seek help for the Alamo. Seguin was the highest-ranking officer to leave the Alamo during the siege. Travis could only hope that his influence would hasten reinforcements. Some of Seguin's reliable men remained in the Alamo. Gregorio Esparza was there with his wife and all of his children. He could not be induced to leave his post just as his family could not be induced to leave their husband and father.

Perhaps Travis's thought turned to the task ahead of him—defending a crumbling mission, parts of which were already over ninety years old. It was not much of a fort. The Alamo was a complex of walls and buildings, sprawling over three acres, and roughly resembling a capital "L." Its main plaza ran north to south and comprised the vertical axis of the "L." The longest dimension of this irregular plaza was 537 feet along its west side. It measured 503 feet along its east side. There were a series of small rooms built on the interior of its west wall. Across the main plaza, to the east, were sturdier two-story buildings known as the "long barracks." These building served as barracks for the troops during the siege and also contained the Alamo's hospital. The top of the "L" was the Alamo's exposed north wall. This free-standing wall had to be shorn up with timber and earth to withstand the Mexican cannonading. The south wall was comprised of a building known as the "low barracks." It was pierced by the Alamo's main entrance. The entrance was protected by a timber and earthen fortification outside the walls. To the east of the main gate, or along the lower axis of the "L," was a small walled-in courtyard. To the east of that, the Alamo's most recognizable building, the church, faced west. The southwest corner of the church was connected to the southeast corner of the low barracks by a wooden palisade, closing off the area in front of the church. The palisade was protected on the outside by a shallow ditch. To the north of the church and courtyard, and to the east of the main plaza and long barracks, were walled-in horse and cattle corrals. The west wall of the Alamo faced Bexar on the opposite bank of the San Antonio River. The wall itself was only about a quarter-mile from the edge of town. Most of the walls were from eight to twelve feet in height. The roofless church building had walls twenty-two-feet high.

The main strength in the Alamo was the determination and quality of the men who defended it, and the fact that the Alamo was bristling with approximately twenty cannons. However, the Alamo was a mission and not a fort. There were no interlocking fields of fire, and not all of the cannon were mounted. Just how effective they would be remained to be seen. The walls were high, but not so high that a determined attacking force could not scale them. The walls were thick, but had no embrasures. The defenders would have to expose themselves to enemy gunfire while firing over them.

Maybe Travis's thoughts strayed to his adversaries outside of the walls. Since their arrival on February 23 the Mexican force had increased in number. Travis was not even sure how many of the enemy he and his men faced. He estimated their strength, not too accurately, at anywhere from 1,500 to 6,000.

Travis may have thought back on the steady stream of communications he had been sending from the Alamo since the beginning of the siege. He tried to keep the rest of Texas apprised of the strength of the enemy, the conditions within the Alamo, and the actions and morale of the men. He also attempted to impress upon Texans the seriousness of the situation at Bexar and inspire them to action. In his letter of the 24th he was particularly eloquent, bringing to bear all his skills as a newspaperman and lawyer. In this letter addressed to the people of Texas and all Americans in the world, he called for aid, invoking liberty, patriotism and "every thing dear to the American character." If he did not receive the request aid, however, he assured all that he would "never surrender or retreat," and that he intended to sustain himself as long as possible and die like a soldier who never forgets what is due to his own honor and that of his country.

Travis's entreaties had limited results. Two reinforcements had gotten in, but they were not enough. Travis was not without hope, however. His most encouraging news came three days before with Lieutenant James Butler Bonham, of South Carolina. Bonham had been sent from Bexar before the arrival of the Mexican army. On March 3rd he returned through the Mexican lines with a letter from Travis's friend, Major Robert M. Williamson, now commanding the Texas Ranging service. Williamson wrote:

> . . . *Colonel Fannin with 300 men and 4 artillery pieces has been en route to Bejar for Three days now. Tonight we are waiting for some reinforcements from Washington [on the Brazos], Bastrop, Brazoria and San Felipe, numbering 300, and not a moment will be lost in providing you assistance. . . . For God's sake sustain yourselves until we can assist you . . .*

Obviously help was on the way. Travis could not know that Colonel Neill and Juan Seguin were among those who had assembled reinforcements and were making their way toward the Alamo.

Perhaps Travis thought of none of these things. Perhaps his thoughts drifted to his two children, Charles Edward and Susan Isabelle. Travis had abandoned his wife Rosanna, pregnant with Susan, and his son in Alabama in 1831. During the ensuing estrangement, Rosanna followed him to Texas with the children seeking a finalization of their divorce proceedings. She returned to Alabama with Isabella, leaving Charles in Travis's custody. Right now the boy was in the care of Travis's friend David Ayers. On March 3, Travis had written to Ayers asking him to "take care of my little boy." Travis added that if he should perish Charles ". . . will have nothing but the proud recollection that he is the son of a man who died for his country."

Maybe Travis finally dozed off while thinking about his son.

In the Mexican camp Travis's adversary Generalissimo Antonio Lopez de Santa Anna had no time for such sentiment. He had been up all night preparing his army for an assault on the Alamo. The forty-year old Santa Anna was the President and absolute ruler of Mexico. He had taken a temporary leave of office to personally lead his army against the ungrateful colonists and American interlopers in Texas. He considered these self-styled revolutionaries as nothing more than pirates, and he intended to treat them as such.

Santa Anna arrived in Bexar with the vanguard of his army on the afternoon of February 23. He had sent General Joaquín Ramírez y Sesma ahead with a detachment of cavalry at seven that morning to surprise the Texans in Bexar. However, Sesma halted his advance and took up a defensive position upon receiving reports that his force was about to be attacked by the Texans. The Texans finally became aware of the approaching Mexican army and occupied the Alamo. Perhaps the whole lengthy siege could have been avoided if Sesma had pressed on and attacked the unsuspecting enemy. Santa Anna did not have the luxury for idle speculation of what could have been. Accordingly, he personally assumed direction of the encirclement and planned annihilation of Travis and his men.

Santa Anna rejected out-of-hand the communications from Travis and Bowie. They had two choices open to them—surrender or die. He had artillery positions for two howitzers and two cannon set up, and he began entrenchments to the west, the south, the north, and northeast of the Alamo. He sent word back to his units, still strung out on the trail from Mexico, to hasten along certain units and more artillery in preparation for the inevitable assault. On February 29 he dispatched Sesma with his cavalry to intercept another band of rebels who were said to be on the march from Goliad, ninety miles to the southeast. This reinforcement under Fannin never materialized. After two half-hearted attempts to relieve the Alamo, Fannin decided that he could best serve Texas by returning to his own fort and waiting for the enemy. He would not be disappointed. He and his men were fated to be swept up by another division of Santa Anna's army under General Cosme Urrea, working to the south and east of Santa Anna's division. Fannin and most of his men would be caught in the open, taken prisoner, and then executed.

Sesma's mission may have been a useless exercise, but it did reinforce an important aspect of Santa Anna's campaign in Texas. Before Sesma left, Santa Anna issued him written instructions. Along with these orders he included the reminder, "In this war you know there are no prisoners."

Finally, on the morning of March 6 the stage was set. Santa Anna's requested units had arrived on March 3. The following day he had held a council of war to determine whether or not the Alamo should be assaulted. General Cos, who had been reversed in his trek into Mexico by Santa Anna, and promptly pointed back to Bexar; General Manuel Fernandez Castrillón; Colonel José Maria Romero; and Colonel Orisñuela of the Aldama Battalion all agreed that the Alamo should be attacked. However, they believed the assault should be made only after a breach was opened by their artillery, and that they should wait for two 12-pounder cannon expected on Monday, March 7. General Sesma, who would command the cavalry cordon around the Alamo during the attack, and Colonel Almonte, who would not be in the attack at all, wanted the attack made without any additional softening-up. Colonels Francisco Duque of the Toluca Battalion and Augustin Amat of the Zapadores (Sappers), and a major of the San Luis Battalion offered no opinions. Santa Anna listened to his subordinates, but failed to come to any decision at that time. By the following day, however, his mind was made up. The attack would be made on Sunday morning, March 6. There would be no more waiting, no more softening-up, no breaches, and no 12-pounders. There would be only cold steel, fire, and death.

The orders were issued at 2 P.M., March 5 by General Juan Valentine Amador, a member of Santa Anna's staff. There would be four attack columns. Only experienced troops would be used—raw recruits would sit this one out. Sesma would encircle the Alamo with his cavalry to prevent anyone's escape. Soldiers would wear shoes, have their shako chin straps down, and have their weapons, "especially bayonets," in top condition. The attack was scheduled to begin at 4:30 A.M. Santa Anna left himself the option of changing or fine-tuning certain aspects of the plan as he saw fit. The troops would begin to move into position at 2 A.M.

TRAVIS FINALLY MAY HAVE drifted to sleep. In any event his rest was short-lived. He came awake immediately as Captain Baugh burst into the room calling, "Colonel Travis, the Mexicans are coming!" Travis bolted from his cot, grabbed his double-barreled shotgun and sword, the prescribed weaponry for Texan cavalrymen, and called to his slave, Joe, to follow him. Joe took his own rifle, and both men ran out into the growing din of battle.

Travis reached the top of one of the artillery ramps at the north wall. There could have been no doubt in Travis's mind that this was no exploratory attack. Sizing-up the situation in the graying dawn, he would have seen hundreds of Mexican troops in three columns hitting the exposed north wall in a pincer movement. From his position he would not have been able to see a smaller column assaulting the wooden palisade near the church on the south side.

The garrison came to life instantaneously just as Travis and Joe had done, and the Alamo erupted with cannon and small arms fire. Travis had just enough time to encourage his men. "Come on Boys, the Mexicans are upon us, and we'll give them Hell!" He pointed his weapon over the wall and fired. Almost simultaneously he was struck by a Mexican bullet or bullets, and fell onto the earthen artillery ramp.

Santa Anna's attack had begun later than originally planned. Possibly the complexity of moving, positioning, and then launching an attack of some 1,400 men had something to do with the delay. It is more likely that Santa Anna delayed the attack intentionally so that his men would at least benefit by some feeble daylight. It would have been absurd for him to send his troops into the pitch dark and unfamiliar compound.

Santa Anna's battle plan called for three columns to assault the north wall of the Alamo (the top of the capital "L"). A total of twenty-six scaling ladders had been assigned to these columns, as well as two sets of axes and crow bars. The fourth column to the south, with only one hundred men, was little more than a diversion. They carried only two scaling ladders. Their action would prevent the Texans from releasing too many men to bolster the north wall defense.

Upon Santa Anna's signal, the attack was to have commenced rapidly and silently, so that his troops would be on the walls before the Texans knew what was hitting them. However, a unit in one of the columns to the north, caught up in the excitement of battle, began cheering for Santa Anna and the Mexican Republic. Flattering, but the cheers immediately eliminated any chance of surprise, and the Mexican troops paid dearly for this one unit's moment of recklessness.

Colonel Duque, who had offered no opinion on whether or not the Alamo should be assaulted, was felled with a severe wound. His column, with the loss of its leader, faltered. Santa Anna, observing this and seeing all three columns bunch up at the north wall, feared the whole attack was in danger of stalling. He reluctantly committed his reserve, the Grenadier companies of each battalion, which he had held out of the original attack plan, along with the Zapadores, the combat engineers.

The reserves launched themselves into the confused tangle at the north wall, giving the already overtaxed defenders more to handle. Meanwhile, the fourth column to the south diverted from the wooden palisade with its problematic ditch, veered around the works protecting the Alamo's main gate, and struck the southwest corner of the fort. There, these one hundred or so soldiers, scrambling up their two scaling ladders, quickly overcame the Texan artillery crew in that corner and gained a foothold.

In the north the Mexican troops, by sheer weight of numbers, struggled up their ladders and the uneven timber bracing the exterior of the north wall. Later, an Alamo survivor would describe the Mexican soldiers as coming over the wall "like sheep." Whether this was meant that they poured over like a flock of sheep jumping a low wall, or in the sense of "sheepishly," meaning slowly and cautiously, is unknown. However, over the wall they came.

The Mexican army's footholds at opposite ends of the Alamo compound essentially ended any strategic aspect of the battle on the part of the Texans. The Alamo's questionable value lay in the fact that it was an enclosed fortification with considerable strength in artillery. At the beginning of the siege, the best the Texans could have hoped for was to hold the Mexican force in place until enough Texas reinforcements arrived to defeat it. That hope ended with the beginning of the final battle. Once the attack was launched, the only chance the Texans had was to fight the Mexican troops to a standstill and continue to bank on the expected reinforcements. Now that Mexican soldiers were coming over the walls in ever-increasing numbers, the Alamo ceased to exist either as a fortress or as a rallying point for the Texas revolution. It merely became a killing ground.

Mexican troops fanned out through the Alamo compound from north and from the southwest corner. When they were able, they turned captured cannon around and used them against the Texans. The action moved too swiftly for Mexican soldiers to stop and reload the heavy, cumbersome Brown Bess muskets most of them carried. The real work was done with the bayonets that Santa Anna had specified be put in their best condition.

It is unknown if Travis had set up any secondary defense plan in the event the Mexicans did enter the walls. It is likewise unknown if any chain-of-command succession came into play after Travis had been hit. Company commanders could not have held any cohesiveness in their units for long.

Texans still defending the walls had three courses of action open to them. Neither of the three was very promising, and this life-or-death decision had to be made in a split second. They could: remain on the walls with Mexican soldiers closing in on them from both sides; jump inside the walls and seek dubious shelter in one of the rooms or buildings of the Alamo; or jump outside the walls and try for a clean get-away across the countryside. At least three sizeable groups of Texans went over the Alamo's walls at this stage. They did not move in blind panic. Sesma remembered that the first group "marched with organization to the plain trying to avail themselves of the adjoining brush country." This was just the situation that Sesma and his lancers had been assigned to handle. As the Texans left the Alamo, first on the east, then the center, and then the west, Sesma dispatched groups of lancers to intercept them.

Most of the Texans, cut off by the Mexican cavalry, fought and died in the ditches outside the Alamo. After organized resistance broke down, it was every man for himself. The Alamo's quartermaster, Eliel Melton of Georgia, died outside. One Texan armed with a pistol and double-barreled shotgun (probably one of Forsyth's cavalrymen) killed a corporal of the lancers before he himself was run through. Another who hid in a bush had to be shot since he could not be flushed out to the waiting lancers. Yet another was spotted under a bridge on the river and killed. A group of seven made it to the river before they were run down and killed as well.

All organized resistance inside the Alamo broke down rapidly as the Mexican troops began clearing each room and building. Travis's slave, Joe, retreated to one of the rooms, probably his original quarters, with Travis. He fired on the Mexican soldiers until his ammunition ran out, then concealed himself to await the inevitable.

In another room, two young sisters waited with uncertainty. Juana Alsbury and Gertrudis Navarro were cousins of Jim Bowie's late wife. Juana, the widow of Alejo Perez Sr., had married Dr. Horace Alsbury in January. Alsbury had gone out before the arrival of the Mexican army to find a safe haven for the young women, but failed to return in time. The sisters, with Juana's infant Alejo Jr., probably entered the Alamo under Bowie's protection. From the sounds of battle raging outside their door, Juana knew that the Alamo had been overrun. She held her son and instructed Gertrudis to open the door to allow the Mexican soldiers to see that they were the only ones inside.

The women immediately suffered the soldiers' wrath. One ripped Gertrudis's shawl from her shoulders, while others berated the women with offensive language. They demanded of Juana, "Your money or your husband!" Juana replied that she had neither. At that moment a Texan named Mitchell, who had been ill during the siege, appeared at Juana's side to protect her. He was cut down by the Mexican soldiers. Another young Texan of Mexican descent ran into the room, grabbed Juana's arm, and tried to keep her between himself and the soldiers. He was bayoneted and shot before her eyes. As the soldiers rifled the women's trunk and stole watches belonging to Travis and other members of the garrison that had been placed in the women's care, a

Mexican officer appeared and angrily led the women out into the Alamo compound. The battle still raged and the women found themselves in front of a cannon that was about to be fired. Miraculously, they were rescued by a Mexican soldier who happened to be the brother of Juana's late husband.

In an arched room on the north side of the Alamo church, another group of noncombatants huddled in fear: Gregorio Esparza's wife and children, Susanna Dickinson, wife of Captain Almeron Dickinson, and her infant daughter Angelina, and others waited for the end. Shock, trauma, and later outside influences colored much of what these women and children were to remember. In later years Dickinson and Enrique Esparza, Gregorio's eight-year-old son, gave numerous and often changing accounts.

Esparza did remember that when the Mexican soldiers burst into the room an American boy not much older than himself stood and drew a blanket around his shoulders. This action must have startled the understandably jumpy soldiers. The boy was cut down immediately.

Texan resistance in the Alamo finally ceased. One of the last aggressive acts on the part of the defenders was attempted by the garrison's master of ordnance, Major Robert Evans, of Ireland and later New York. When the Mexican troops forced their way into the Alamo church, Evans grabbed a torch and tried to fire the Alamo's gunpowder supply. He was shot down before he could accomplish this final act of desperation.

The battle of the Alamo was over. What followed was a room-by-room search by the Mexican soldiers. In the kitchen area of the Alamo, the soldiers discovered two Negroes: Bowie's cook, Bettie, and Charlie, who may also have been Bowie's slave. When the soldiers entered, Charlie tried to conceal himself, but was dragged from hiding by the soldiers. The soldiers tried to bayonet Charlie, but he grabbed the much smaller officer of the Mexican detail and successfully used him as a shield. The officer quickly became tired of this dangerous and humiliating game, especially since the soldiers were enjoying it so much. The officer promised Charlie that he would not be harmed if he would release him. Both parties honored their end of the bargain. It was just as well since the Mexican army was not at war with slaves.

In another part of the Alamo, a Mexican officer called in English through a doorway, "Are there any Negroes here?" Joe emerged from his hiding place and answered, "Yes, here's one." Perhaps Joe answered or appeared too quickly. One startled soldier jabbed at Joe with his bayonet and nicked him. Another shot at him and caused a slight wound to his side. Joe may have been killed if not for the intervention of a Captain Baragan who beat the soldiers back with the flat of his sword and took Joe into his protection. Not every slave in the Alamo was as lucky as Joe, Charlie, and Bettie. As he was led through the compound, Joe noticed the body of a Negro woman lying between two cannon.

While the cleanup operation was going on, Santa Anna entered the fort with his staff and entourage. Joe later reported that a Texan prisoner, a "little weakly body, named Warner," was brought before Santa Anna. The prisoner was executed immediately on Santa Anna's orders.

Ramón Martinez Caro, Santa Anna's civilian secretary, accompanied Santa Anna into the Alamo. He reported another incident where five survivors were brought before Santa Anna, this time by General Manuel Fernandez Castrillón. Castrillón had taken over command of Duque's men, when Duque had been wounded, and led them over the walls. Santa Anna reprimanded Castrillón severely for not having killed the men on the spot. As Santa Anna turned his back on Castrillón, soldiers fell upon the prisoners and killed them.

Susanna Dickinson later said that two of the five prisoners were pursued into her room where they were tortured and killed with bayonets by Mexican soldiers. In later statements she claimed three unarmed Texans sought refuge in her room but were killed. One of these she identified as a man named Walker, from Nacogdoches. Still later, she gave another description of a man named Wolff as having asked for quarter which was denied him. She claimed that this man's two sons, only eleven and twelve years old, came into her room and also were killed.

When the mayhem and murder finally died down, a Mexican officer appeared in the door and specifically asked for Dickinson by name. When she identified herself, he advised her that, "If you wish to save your life follow me," which she did. Dickinson had not seen her husband, Almeron, since earlier in the battle. Then he had run into her room to inform her that the Mexicans were inside the walls and that all was lost. He implored her to save their child if the Mexicans spared her, and then returned to the battle. Given the bloody scenes enacted before her eyes, she could not have held out much hope for him. She had endured a great deal up to this point including being fired at and slightly wounded as she was escorted out. Later, she spoke of seeing Crockett's body lying dead and mutilated between the church and the two-story long barracks. She even noticed his "peculiar cap" lying by his side. One scene proved to be too much for her though. As Dickinson was being led from the church, she witnessed Mexican soldiers bayoneting the Texan bodies. She fainted when they came upon the body of her husband.

WITH THE LAST SURVIVING Texans executed and the noncombatants rounded up, the battle of the Alamo was over. It was costly, but it could have been worse.

General Juan de Andrade later compiled a breakdown of casualties from each unit that stormed the Alamo. His list enumerated 8 officers and 52 soldiers killed and 18 officers and 233 soldiers wounded, for a total of 311 casualties. In his diary, Almonte numbered the Texan dead at 250, however, Santa Anna reported to the Mexican government that 600 Texans were killed in the battle.

There were still things to be done. Joe was forced to point out and identify the bodies of Travis, Bowie, Crockett. He noticed that Travis's body had many bayonet wounds. Bowie had been killed in his sickbed. Crockett's body was seen among those of a few of the men with whom he served and with a number of Mexican dead.

The women and children were taken to the Musquiz house in town to wait in fear and uncertainty for private interviews with Santa Anna. Later in the afternoon each family was brought before the general. He questioned them, finally lost his patience with the whole process, and released them all, giving each family two silver dollars and a blanket.

The bodies of the Texan dead were gathered and brought to an area called the Alameda, located just south and east of the Alamo. That evening, their bodies were placed in three large funeral pyres and ignited. The bodies burned for two to three days and still were not completely consumed. Charred bones and body parts were easily recognizable even after the fires had burned out. It was not until a year later that the remains were collected and buried in a ceremony conducted by Juan Seguin. Where the remains were actually buried is still a subject of debate.

Santa Anna continued his Texas campaign by pursuing the rag-tag Texan army, led by Sam Houston, eastward. The chase went on until April 21 when Houston's outnumbered army surprised Santa Anna's force in an afternoon attack on the banks of the San Jacinto River. Santa Anna's force was completely destroyed or captured. He was brought in the next day and held hostage by the Texans until they could negotiate a treaty that would ensure Texan independence. Santa Anna subsequently was taken to Washington, D.C., and eventually released, returning to Mexico ten months after his capture.

During his captivity and circuitous return to Mexico, Santa Anna finally may have had some time for reflection. Among the many things on his mind, he may have thought back to that terrible afternoon of the previous April 21 when the Texans' battle cry had been, "Remember the Alamo." He also may have thought with irony on how he, himself, provided the Texans with that cry when on the morning of March 6, 1836, he elevated a young cavalry officer named William B. Travis and his men to eternity and immortality.

PACIFIC NORTHWEST STEAMBOAT DAYS

Bill Gulick

THOUGH NOT AS WELL known as Mark Twain's Mississippi, the rivers of the Pacific Northwest bore a great deal of steamboat traffic in an era as colorful as any in Pioneer America. Where water flowed, bold captains and sturdy steamboats went, carrying passengers and freight to the furthest reach, the boat's bottom sometimes cushioned by little more than a heavy dew.

On the Columbia, Snake, and Willamette in the United States, the Fraser, Stikine, and Skeena in Canada, and the Yukon River in Alaska, the best and sometimes the only way to get from here to there was by riverboat.

The age of steam in the Pacific Northwest began in 1836 when the *Beaver,* built by the Hudson's Bay Company for the fur trade, was rigged as a brigantine to sail from her launching ways on the Thames to Fort Vancouver, just across the Columbia River from what would become Portland, Oregon. There, mechanics installed the engine and paddlewheels that would make her go as long as her boiler was fired by twenty cords of wood a day. She was the first of several hundred riverboats that would dominate transportation in the Pacific Northwest for the next seventy-five years.

"It is safe to say that no vessel has attracted anywhere near as much attention as this pioneer of the Pacific Ocean," the London *Times* reported in 1835. "Over 150,000 people, including King William and a large number of the nobility of England, witnessed the launching, and cheers from thousands of throats answered the farewell salute of her guns as she sailed away for a new world."

A hundred feet long, with a twenty-two-foot beam, an eleven-foot depth, and drawing eight feet of water, the *Beaver* was double-planked out of solid English and African oak, had a copper-sheathed bottom, and displaced 187 tons. Her sidewheels, when put in place, would be set well forward, and she would have a top speed of eight knots at sea, or nine miles an hour as speed was measured on a freshwater river.

An unexpected plus to the eager *Beaver* was that she proved to be an excellent sailer. Rigged as a brigantine, her 163-day passage from the lower Thames to the mouth of the Columbia set a record that would stand for many years. Ironically, the three-masted sailing ship *Columbia,* which accompanied her as her supposed escort and protector, was so much slower that time and again the *Beaver* had to shorten sail and wait for her escort to catch up, arriving at the mouth of the Columbia a week ahead of the much larger ship.

After her engine and paddlewheels had been installed at Fort Vancouver, the *Beaver*'s log recorded her first trip under steam: "Monday, May 16, 1836— Variable winds and fine weather. Carpenters shipping the paddlewheels. At 4 P.M. the engineers got steam up and tried the engines and found them to answer very well . . .

"May 31—At 9:30 A.M. a party of ladies and gentlemen from the fort came on board. At 9:45 weighed anchor and ran down the river under steam and entered the upper branch of the Willamette; ran under half power until we cleared the lower branch at 3:30 P.M., and ran up towards Vancouver."

Though Hudson's Bay Company Factor, Dr. John McLoughlin, had saluted the arrival of the *Beaver* with a volley from the post's brass cannon, he hated the stinking little steamer, for it represented a new-fangled invention in a world whose ways were changing too quickly to suit his tastes. He felt that the very idea of putting a steam engine aboard a ship was ridiculous. Designed to burn soft coal, the ship's bunkers could hold only enough of the "stones that burn," as the Indians called coal, to fire her boilers for two days. There were no coal mines in the northwest or on the high seas, Dr. McLoughlin caustically pointed out. The boiler could burn wood, of course, of which there was an ample supply ashore, but until woodlots could be established the crew had to go ashore and spend two days chopping the twenty cords of wood consumed by one day's steaming.

Still, when equipped with antiboarding nets, a couple of six-pounders, and a crew armed with rifles and pistols, the little ship made quite an impression on the natives of the lower Columbia, Puget Sound, British Columbia, and Russian Alaska. But she first proved her worth in a more mundane way.

Anchored off Fort George (formerly Astoria) the big sailing ship *Columbia* was about to depart for England when Dr. McLoughlin ordered her to come back upriver and add several packs of prime pelts to her cargo. With the wind and current against her, she could make no progress, so the *Beaver* chugged downriver, put a line on her, and gave her a tow.

Whether Dr. McLoughlin liked it or not, it had just been demonstrated that steam power would be the future of traffic on the rivers of the Pacific Northwest.

CONTRARY TO THE NOTION of many people of that day, Portland was not on the Columbia River; it was on the Willamette. Originally called "Stumptown" because so many trees had to be felled to build the city, legend has it that two sea captains from New England got into a heated argument as to whether the growing metropolis should be called Portland or Boston, flipped a coin, and Portland won. By any name, ninety miles upriver from the mouth of the Columbia, Sauvie Island Slough discharged the waters of the Willamette River into the Columbia, with that tributary flowing deep and strong twenty-five miles southeast to Portland, Milwaukee, and Oregon City.

Before 1849, all the ships in the Pacific Northwest were built on the East Coast, rigged with sail for the long trip around the Horn, then converted to steam when they reached their destination. The discovery of gold in California encouraged a regional ship-building industry. Having learned that prospectors were eager to exchange their gold dust for lumber, beef, potatoes, salmon, and butter produced in the Willamette Valley, Portland businessmen decided it would be to their advantage to acquire a steamship of their own. When a majority interest in the side-wheeler, *Gold Hunter,* which had been built by an independent company for the Sacramento River trade, came on the market, a hastily thrown-together combine of Portland businessmen raised enough money to buy a controlling interest in the the ship. Proud of the fact that they now owned what was bound to be a highly profitable steamship, the Portland merchants filled her hold with cargo and sent her on her way south rejoicing.

Unfortunately, when the *Gold Hunter* reached San Francisco, the minority stockholders residing there bought back enough shares from the ship's officers to give them a controlling interest, then put her into service between San Francisco and Panama. Quite literally, the Oregon owners had been "sold south." In response to this treachery, a group of enterprising residents of Astoria said,

"Serves you Portlanders right for trusting Californians, who are all born scoundrels and thieves. We intend to keep our money at home by building our own steamboat."

Which they proceeded to do . . .

CALLED THE *COLUMBIA,* THE homemade steamboat was framed on the bank just below the Astoria dock. Planned strictly for river use and powered by steam generated by a wood-fired boiler, its captain was an experienced riverman named Jim Frost, who had piloted boats on the Mississippi for years.

"He helped us design it," the investors said proudly. "We've got the parts for the engine ordered from San Francisco and are going to put them together when they arrive. It'll be the best darned steamboat on the river."

Since her only competition was the *Beaver,* soon to be taken into Canadian waters by the Hudson's Bay Company, the *Columbia* had the field to itself for a while. But times were changing as the country developed. Under a new law passed by the Oregon Territorial Legislature, George Flavel, a recent arrival from San Francisco, was going into the bar-piloting business. Said to be well qualified in the trade, he was in the process of forming a Bar Pilots Association, which would set standards and fees for guiding ships over the dangerous Columbia River Bar.

The builders of the home-designed-built-and-owned steamboat slid the craft into deep water in early June, 1850. Even the most loyal admitted that the boat was not much for looks.

"She's an ugly-duckling cross between a ferryboat and a scow," they said. "But she floats. Now if her engine will run and turn the paddlewheels, we'll call her a success."

The day of her maiden voyage from Astoria to Portland, July 3, 1850, was a memorable one in the annals of American steamboating in the Pacific Northwest. Never having been up the river before, Captain Frost gave a couple of Chinook Indian boys a dollar to come aboard and act as guides to show him the main channel. At first there was a communications gap, with the two Indian boys talking Chinook jargon while he spoke English with a Deep South drawl, but by using a lot of sign language, they finally managed to understand one another. Making fifty miles the first day and not wanting to risk steaming in the dark, Captain Frost pulled into the bank and tied the bow to a tree for the night. Which proved to be a mistake.

In the broad, deep lower Columbia, as Lewis and Clark had recorded in 1805, the effects of the tide could be observed 145 miles inland. When he snubbed off the boat, the tide was out. Around midnight, it came back in, lifting the stern of the boat six feet and nearly pulling her under. Waking up just in time, Captain Frost slacked off the line, then said with some embarrassment, "Never saw a tide like that on the Mississippi."

It happened here twice a day, he was told. Every day.

Other than that near-disaster, the trip to Portland went smoothly. By the middle of the afternoon, the *Columbia* was steaming along so well that Captain Frost took her into the Willamette River and chugged on up to the falls below Oregon City, her whistle tooting all the way. Along both banks, people cheered until they were hoarse, shooting off Fourth of July fireworks in celebration . . .

FROM THAT TIME ON, regional boats were designed and built locally, for the Columbia River and its tributaries—the Willamette and the Snake—had special requirements. Unlike the muddy Mississippi and the snag-filled Missouri, the hazards here were rocks and rapids, for this land had been formed by volcanic action. Though deep and quiet in its lower reaches, 145 miles inland the Columbia became swift and narrow as it entered the gorge it had carved through the ten-thousand-foot high Cascade range. In a six-mile stretch called the Lower, Middle, and Upper Cascades, the river became unnavigable and must be portaged, first by a pack animal trail, later by narrow-gauge railroads on both shores.

Passing through the heart of the mountains, the Columbia broadened and its current slowed for fifty miles, its depths showing when the light was right what was left of a natural rock bridge that had collapsed hundreds of years ago, an event noted in 1890 by a best-selling novel titled *Bridge of the Gods* and continued to the present day by a toll-bridge bearing the same name near Hood River, Oregon.

East of the Cascades, a fourteen-mile stretch of rapids called "The Long Narrows" by Lewis and Clark and by earlier French explorers "The Dalles" ("Stepping Stones"), formed a second obstacle to navigation. Dropping twenty feet at its upstream end, then roaring through chutes and channels where the mighty river literally turned on edge, the speed of the current had been measured at thirty miles an hour by Lewis and Clark. Even so, there were enough side passages, eddies, and whirlpools to let millions of migrating salmon fight their way upriver to the streams of their birth, where they would spawn and assure the survival of their kind.

Called Tumwater Falls by the Indians of the region, the area was controlled by the Celilo tribe, which exacted a tribute from all visiting natives wishing to fish there, and later from white explorers, fur trappers, and Oregon-bound emigrants. As steamboat traffic increased, an army post and a town called The

Dalles were built at the lower end of the rapids, with upriver-bound travelers staying overnight at the Umatilla House, which advertised itself to be the best hotel between St. Louis and Portland.

At 4 A.M. the portage train that would carry them fourteen miles east to Celilo Landing departed. There, they would board a steamboat for the third sector of their journey to the booming interior country five to six hundred miles inland from the mouth of the Columbia.

Variety spiced the traveler's journey in that time and place. Coming north from San Francisco for the first part of his trip, he was on a ship driven by wind power, then, as it made the hazardous crossing of the Columbia River Bar, its coal- or wood-fueled engine was fired up as it steamed upriver one hundred miles to Portland. Next morning, he went aboard a wood-burning side-wheeler that would take half a day to drop down the Willamette to its mouth, then turn east and head upriver, letting off or picking up passengers at St. Helens, Cathlamet, and Vancouver. Around noon, his upriver journey was interrupted at Lower Cascades Landing, where he disembarked and took a six-mile ride on the portage train to the Upper Cascades, where he had a couple of hours to eat, drink, and then board another boat for the fifty-mile journey on placid waters to The Dalles.

If he were traveling first-class, he stayed at the Umatilla House, rose at 4 A.M., then took the portage train for the fourteen-mile trip to Celilo Landing, where he got aboard a another boat for the remainder of his journey. In the lower and middle reaches of the river, the boat would probably be a side-wheeler, whose big metal buckets required deep water and a dock. In the upper river, the boat would probably be a stern-wheeler, for in this part of the river there was little deep water and few docks. Nosing into a sandbar, a stern-wheeler could hold the bow of the boat against the shore for loading and un-loading. If a big metal bucket on a side-wheeler was damaged, the skill of a mechanic was required to repair it, while the one-by-four slats of a stern-wheeler could be replaced by even a poor carpenter.

Upriver from Celilo Falls, white-water rapids in both the Columbia and its principal tributary, the Snake, were a danger to be reckoned with. Eleven miles upstream from the spot where the Columbia took its big bend to the north, Snake River came in from the east after its turbulent 1,036-mile journey from the southeast corner of the Yellowstone and Jackson Hole country, across the lava badlands and deserts of southern Idaho, where early explorers had suffered so much that they had named it *la maudite riviere enragee*—"the accursed mad river—" then through a hundred-mile-long gorge later named Hell's Canyon, the deepest such chasm in North America.

For most of its length, the lower Snake was filled with dangerous rapids, deadly with ice flows during spring breakup, treacherous with floating trees when in summer flood, and even more frightful when the water level dropped in late summer and the rock fangs of the river bottom were exposed. Yet it was in this stretch of river that one of the boldest of the early-day river pilots, Captain William Polk Gray, began to learn the ways of wild waters at the youthful age of thirteen.

"My father was a great believer in Manifest Destiny," Captain Gray wrote many years later. "But when President Polk reneged on his promise '54-40-or Fight,' Father got very angry. When I was just four years old, I heard him say, 'I'm so disgusted with President Polk I feel like wringing my son's neck, every time I say his name.' Believe me, when my father started arguing politics, I looked for a hiding place."

Going west with a missionary party as a carpenter-mechanic in 1836, William Gray soon gave up on religion and struck out for himself, becoming so skilled in boat-building and the ways of wild rivers that he trained four of his sons to become river captains. In 1860, he launched a keelboat upstream from Celilo Falls, filled it with merchandise for the Idaho mines, then embarked on a two-month-long trip sailing, rowing, and poling the clumsy craft upriver.

When the boat entered the Snake, it became the duty of thirteen-year-old Willie Polk Gray and his nine-year-old companion, Jimmy Davis, to get into a skiff, take a line upstream, secure it around a rock, then bring the line back downstream to be attached to a winch aboard the keelboat. After capsizing several times in a particularly bad rapid, Willie told his father, "Pa, taking a line through that rapid is impossible. It can't be done."

"My son," his father said sternly, "the word 'can't' is not in my dictionary. You and Jimmy will take the line into the skiff, go through the rapid and try again. If you capsize, you, Jimmy, and the skiff will come down through the rapids. You may not come down together, but you will come down. You will then get back in the skiff, go up the river and try again. You will keep on trying until you succeed."

Which Willie Gray did. Later, he would say, "After that experience, nothing made of wood, water, or iron has ever scared me. I learned that there wasn't a rapid in Snake River I couldn't swim."

During the next sixty-three years, William Polk Gray piloted steamboats through the wild waters of the Pacific Northwest from southwestern Idaho to northern Alaska. At the age of nineteen, he served as second mate aboard the *Colonel Wright* as it explored and charted the Snake upstream from Lewiston to see if a steamboat could go through Hell's Canyon to the Boise area. Finding that stretch of river unnavigable for a boat going upriver, he then was asked, some years later, to bring an unprofitable boat, the *Norma,* built in the desert upstream from Hell's Canyon, downriver through the rapids in the heart of the Canyon.

"I'll do it," he said, "or put her where the underwriters will never find her."
And he did.

During the Gold Rush to Alaska in 1900, he took a stern-wheeler from Puget Sound north through the Inside Passage to the Bering Sea and up the Yukon River to Dawson City, a voyage of 2,100 miles. Carrying $100,000 worth of perishable supplies for the Alaska Meat Company on the steamer *Ora,* he broke a twenty-foot-long iron driveshaft in the middle of nowhere several hundred miles up the Yukon River. Seeing a stand of Arctic pine trees a mile or so from the river bank, he took a crew to it, cut down one of the few suitable trees in the area, squared it, framed it with iron taken from the boat's hog chains, and fashioned a main shaft that worked well enough to drive the boat to its destination.

"The company gave me a gold Swiss pocket watch in appreciation," he said as he showed it to friends after his retirement. "You just open the case, push the button, and it chimes."

He was not the only captain to perform incredible feats of daring on the rivers of the region. Despite the fact that in the Long Narrows and the Cascades the current raced at thirty miles an hour, a few skilled pilots were called upon to bring boats downstream through the rapids when the Oregon Steam Navigation Company found them unprofitable on the sector of the river on which they were operating. Invariably, this was done during times of early summer flood, when river flow was at its height, for then the twenty-foot drop at Celilo Falls and the six-foot drop at the Cascades were smoothed out to a tremendous white-water pour. In order to maintain steering-way, the boat called upon her engineer for "Full Speed Ahead," its thirty-mile-an-hour rate added to the velocity of the river bringing its speed up to sixty miles an hour. On two occasions after railroads were built on the Oregon side of the Gorge, the steamer was matched against a passenger train, each time winning by several hundred yards.

Among the legendary and curious events of the period, a streetcar on an icy track slid through an open drawbridge of the Willamette River just as a commuter steamboat passed by, inspiring the newspaper headline: STEAMBOAT COLLIDES WITH STREETCAR. On another occasion, the passengers on a snowbound train caught in a blizzard in the the heart of the Columbia River Gorge were rescued by an iron-hulled boat working as an ice-breaker, chiseling its way up the frozen Columbia to the vicinity of the marooned train, then taking the half-frozen passengers aboard to complete their journey.

For many years in the fertile Palouse Hills country along the lower Snake River, a "Wheat Fleet" of stern-wheelers operated, carrying cargos of sacked grain downriver to Portland, whence it was shipped to a hungry world overseas. During this period, the clamor for a remedy to the choke points on the river system—the portages at Celilo and the Cascades—rose to such a height that the politicians began to listen.

"Every pound of freight going down or coming up the river has to be handled three times," farmers and merchants complained. "Shipping charges sometimes cost more than the commodities are worth."

Calling for an "Open River," the combined interests finally got enough clout that the federal government began to pay attention. Long ago designated as the agency in charge of the rivers and harbors of the nation, the U.S. Army Corps of Engineers devised all sorts of projects to make the rivers of the Pacific Northwest navigable. In 1881, a party directed by Colonel Thomas Symons floated the upper Columbia for a hundred and fifty miles to determine if it were navigable in that sector. Despite their conclusion that it was not, Captain William Polk Gray proved that it was by having a boat designed and built which he took through the worst rapids on the upper river. Of course, he cheated a bit, using a technique called "grasshoppering" by which spar poles were set on each side of the boat, tied by cables to power capstans, then, with the stern-wheel pushing and the spar poles and capstans pulling, the boat literally hopped over the rapids.

In the 1880s, the Corps began a project to increase the rate of flow of the Columbia River at its mouth by forcing it into one rather than several channels, building a seven-mile-long jetty out from the south shore and a four-mile-long jetty out from the north bank. This assured a forty-foot-deep ship channel a hundred miles inland to Portland.

In 1896, a set of locks and a ship canal at the Cascades smoothed out the rapids there so that riverboats and even small ocean-going ships could steam as far upriver as The Dalles. In 1915, a fourteen-mile-long canal and two sets of locks upriver from The Dalles to above Celilo Falls eliminated the portage there. It could now truthfully be said that Lewiston, Idaho, 465 miles inland from the mouth of the Columbia River, had become a seaport.

For twenty years, advocates of a working river were content with the progress they had made. Then commercial interests persuaded the Corps of Engineers to fund a two-year study by Major John Butler called the "308 Report" to suggest what could be done with the Columbia-Snake River system to foster its development during the next fifty years.

Dams for power, irrigation, and navigation were part of the formula. Beginning in 1938 Bonneville and Grand Coulee were built on the Columbia, primarily for power, while in the desert reaches of Idaho, American Falls and Lucky Peak Reservoir on the Boise River were built for irrigation purposes. Then in 1948, when a levee protecting a low-lying area in northwest Portland ruptured, flooding Vanport and drowning twenty-seven people, the developers added a new weapon to their arsenal—flood control.

The dam-building period began in 1949 and ended in 1975. By the time it was done, 161 small, medium, and large dams blocked the rivers of the Pacific Northwest, praised by the progress-promoters, reviled by lovers of wild rivers.

Today, the lower 145 miles of the Columbia runs free as far upriver as Bonneville Dam, as does a 51-mile stretch called the "Hanford Reach" above Pasco, Washington. All the rest of the 1,250 miles of the second largest river in the United States and Canada has been stilled by dams.

On the 1,036-mile-long Snake, the sixth-largest river in the country, 25 miles of its upper sector in Jackson Hole runs free, as does a 93-mile stretch in Hell's Canyon upstream from Lewiston, both preserved after bitter battles between developers and preservationists. The remainder of the once-wild Snake has been stilled by forty-eight dams on the mainstream and its tributaries.

SPREADING THE NEWS
CALIFORNIA'S GOLD MESSENGERS OF 1848

Abraham Hoffman

GOLD MAY BE WHERE you find it, but first you have to know about it. James Marshall found gold at the Coloma sawmill on January 24, 1848, but San Francisco's professional football team is called the Forty-Niners. It took time to alert the people on the other side of the continent about the discovery of gold, and initial reports were often disbelieved and even ridiculed. In the fall of 1848 physical evidence of California's gold was brought east, and President James K. Polk's validation and endorsement of the discovery helped create the epidemic of gold fever that infected thousands of presumably rational people.

The first prospectors to profit from the gold discovery came from within the newly acquired province. As word spread along the Pacific Rim, gold-seekers arrived from northwestern Mexico (especially Sonora), Peru, and Chile, as well as the Hawaiian Islands. The summer of 1848 marked an alleged "golden age" of sorts, with stories that quickly became exaggerations (with a nugget of truth) about miners finding gold merely by turning over a shovelful of earth. Tales of huge nuggets abounded, of gold so plentiful that prospectors left it openly in their tents because it was easier to dig for gold than to steal it.

Two men brought the news of the gold discovery in separate treks across the continent. Edward Fitzgerald Beale seems to appear in history whenever an opportunity arose for adventure or controversy. A midshipman in the U.S. Navy, Beale was detached for land service in California during the U.S.–Mexico War.

He participated in General Stephen W. Kearny's disastrous defeat at the Battle of San Pasqual in December 1846. Beale, along with Kit Carson and an Indian named Andre, managed to get past Andres Pico's Californio lancers and reach Commodore Robert F. Stockton for reinforcements and aid. When fighting ended in California with the Treaty of Cahuenga, Stockton sent Beale and Carson to Washington, D.C., with dispatches. At the war's end in February 1848, Beale, now an acting lieutenant, was back in California.

The other man was Lieutenant Lucién Loeser, a newly promoted Army artillery officer who was preparing to go back east on leave. Loeser and Beale served different commanders in California, Loeser under Colonel Richard B. Mason, the conquered province's military governor, and Beale under Commodore Thomas ap Catesby Jones of the Navy's Pacific Squadron. Jones's abortive takeover of California in 1842 was long forgiven if not forgotten.

Neither Beale nor Loeser was the first person to head east with the news of the gold discovery. As early as July 1848 a letter from Charles White, the alcalde of San Jose, written on March 18, appeared in the St. Joseph *Gazette*. Mormons returning to the Salt Lake area told westward-bound emigrants about it, and from Salt Lake the word went east. Kit Carson, on yet another journey across the continent, arrived in Washington, D.C., on August 2, with letters from Thomas O. Larkin, the Monterey merchant who had served as President Polk's secret agent in California before the war. The letters were reprinted in eastern newspapers, most prominently in the New York *Herald*, but did not yet create any public excitement about gold. At best, gold was one of several minerals mentioned. Eastern newspaper editors treated such correspondence with suspicion and usually attached derogatory comments to them and the exaggerations they were making about California. Still, the stories made an impression. As Hubert Howe Bancroft later observed, "Such cumulative accounts, reechoed throughout the country, could not fail in their effect."

In July 1848, Commodore Jones asked for a volunteer to carry military dispatches and letters to Secretary of State James Buchanan and Secretary of the Navy John Mason. Jones was sending his own dispatches as well as letters from Larkin and Walter Colton, alcalde at Monterey. Colton had learned of the gold discovery on May 29. "Our town was startled out of its quiet dreams to-day, by the announcement that gold had been discovered on the American Fork," he recorded in his diary, noting that some people thought omens were ushering in the event. "The sybils were less skeptical; they said the moon had, for several nights, appeared not more than a cable's length from the earth, that a white raven had been seen playing with an infant; and that an owl had rung the church bells."

At first Larkin himself had not believed the stories coming out of the Sierra foothills, but when he saw the new town of San Francisco rapidly becoming abandoned and huge prices demanded and obtained for shovels and foodstuffs, he knew something significant was in the making. He visited the gold fields and witnessed at first hand prospectors digging out more than $50 worth (in 1848 price values), a princely sum when compared to the dollar or two a day a laborer earned back east. His letter to Secretary of State Buchanan of July 20 reported that some men were making up to $600 a week. "There is an instance of 700$ being taken in four hours," he told Buchanan.

> *Two or three vessels in San Francisco have not a seaman on board. By September I expect we shall with a few exceptions have in this town only the female population and the officers of Government. A few farmers yet remain hurrying in their harvest. The full effect of this state of affairs is not yet felt. How it will end I know not. The future consequence or prospect is not pleasant or moral.*

Ned Beale volunteered to carry the dispatches and letters for Jones. He was also entrusted with "a small amount of gold," as noted by historian Donald Dale Jackson, the amount not specified. Gerald Thompson called it "a small quantity of gold." This would be Beale's second eastward crossing of the continent, but he decided to do it in a rather roundabout way. Beale determined to travel across Mexico and by ship from Vera Cruz to Mobile, Alabama, as the fastest way to get to Washington, D.C. Having traveled east across the North American continent the previous year, he knew the perils and hardships, but he soon found his chosen route as dangerous as the earlier one. He went down on the *Ohio* to La Paz, Baja California, and sailed across the Gulf of California on July 29, to Mazatlan. From there he chartered a ship that brought him to the town of San Blas in the state of Nayarit. He hired a guide and bought a horse and a Mexican sombrero, as well as clothing that would make him fit in more with the population. He took four revolvers and a Bowie knife along for protection.

Beale and his guide found their path infested with outlaws. He held off three bandits at gunpoint in the Sierra Madre Occidental mountains; they had claimed to be local policemen, but Beale took no chances. He escaped another pursuing outlaw gang, and noted the corpses of almost a dozen people who had not been so fortunate. Their breakneck pace brought Beale and his guide to Mexico City in only eight days. Beale reported to Nathan Clifford, the U.S. Minister to Mexico, who gave him more messages for Buchanan. After a brief rest the two men crossed the central plateau region and went up into the Sierra Madre Oriental, where they again had to outrun bandits. On this leg of the journey, they covered 275 miles in two days of hard travel, but they made it to Vera Cruz. Beale then took passage on a U.S. Navy warship, the *Germantown,* to Mobile.

From Mobile, Beale traveled by stagecoach and steamboat, reaching Washington, D.C., on September 14. Four days earlier, the New Orleans *Picayune* had printed a story about his trip. The newspaper described his stopover in Mexico City, quoting him as claiming San Francisco and Monterey were virtually deserted and that miners were making as much as seventy dollars a day with little effort. It was customary for newspapers in those pre-wire service days to reprint interesting stories from other papers, and the *Picayune* account found its way into the St. Louis *Union.* Beale may have somehow leaked his story, but he made no effort to keep the gold he carried a secret from his fellow stagecoach passengers once he was in the United States.

On arriving in Washington on September 14—just 47 days from La Paz—Beale delivered the dispatches to Buchanan and Mason, but he had other messages from Larkin and Colton as well. Soon the Philadelphia *North American* and the New York *Journal of Commerce* were printing Colton's lengthy letters, and the New York *Herald* did the same for Larkin's. Many of the letters to Buchanan also were published. Both men swore they were not exaggerating, but reports of one hundred dollars a day from mining gold, the success of prospectors who had negligible mining skills, and the abundance of gold challenged the credulity of eastern editors. Beale met with Polk on September 18, but Polk had his doubts about the naval officer whom he believed supported Thomas Hart Benton's rival Democratic faction. Doubts about the claims did not stop the reprinting of the Larkin and Colton letters in newspapers from Boston to New Orleans. William Carey Jones, John C. Fremont's brother-in-law, wrote an article about Beale's adventures across Mexico that made Beale a national celebrity, and this story, too, was widely reprinted. Beale did not stay long in the East. He received orders early in October to return to California, and back across the continent he went.

In July, Colonel/Governor Mason made a tour of the gold fields, stopping by Sutter's Fort to enjoy John Sutter's generous hospitality. Encountering prospectors panning for gold, Mason warned them they were trespassing on the newly acquired U.S. public lands, but he prudently said he would not interfere with them. Mason met James Marshall and was shown the spot where Marshall had first found gold. The governor kept his eyes open and took copious notes, bought some gold specimens, and observed the growing number of miners, some of whom were using Indians to do the hard work of digging channels and moving mud. A young lieutenant, William Tecumseh Sherman, who would gain fame during the Civil War, accompanied Mason. In his memoirs, published in 1875, Sherman recalled the tour "as perfectly to-day as though it were yesterday." On the banks of the American River "men were digging, and filling buckets with the finer earth and gravel, which was carried to a machine made like a baby's cradle, open at the foot, and at the head a plate of sheet-iron or zinc, punctured full of holes. On this metallic plate was emptied the earth, and water was then poured on it from buckets, while one man shook the cradle with violent rocking by a handle. On the bottom were nailed cleats of wood. With this rude machine four men could earn from forty to one hundred dollars a day, averaging sixteen dollars, or a gold ounce, per man per day."

Mason could find no legal precedent dealing with miners squatting on land that was now the property of the federal government. He had 660 soldiers to patrol all of California and feared that they might themselves desert for the gold fields. "It was a matter of serious reflection with me how I could secure to the government certain rents or fees for the privilege of procuring this gold," he wrote in his report, "but upon considering the large extent of the country, the character of the people engaged, and the small scattered force at my command, I am resolved not to interfere, but permit all to work freely." Finishing his report on August 17, he chose Lieutenant Lucien Loeser to take the report and 230 ounces of gold (more than fourteen pounds), sealed in a chest designed as a Chinese tea caddy, to Washington, D.C.

Loeser's route was even more roundabout than Beale's race across Mexico. Along with a civilian companion, David Carter, Loeser sailed from Monterey on August 30 on the schooner *Lambayecana,* heading for Payta, Peru. There the two men took a British steamer to Panama, crossed the Isthmus, and took a ship to Jamaica. From there they took yet another ship and arrived in New Orleans on November 23. In the meantime, Mason had decided to send a duplicate copy of his report (minus gold specimens) with another messenger. This unnamed traveler, presumably an Army officer, possibly followed Beale's route across Mexico, arriving in Washington, D.C., on November 22, the same day Loeser reached New Orleans.

While at Payta, either Loeser, Carter, or someone from the *Lambayecana* discarded the August 14 issue of the Monterey *Californian*. An article in the paper told the story of Marshall's discovery of gold at Coloma. Soon newspapers in Payta, Lima, and Callao were printing Spanish translations of the article. By November 30, the first shipload of Peruvian gold-seekers was embarking for California. Chile had heard the news on August 18; the *Polynesian,* a newspaper published in Hawaii, spread the word on June 24. Mexicans began hearing about it in June; by October an overland caravan left from Hermosillo. Smaller groups had already gone north from Mexico. New Zealanders found out about the gold discovery in November, Australians a month later.

As a civilian, David Carter, Loeser's traveling companion, was under no restrictions in describing California, but his interview with a *Picayune* reporter little resembled the increasingly wild descriptions of the easy riches awaiting potential goldseekers. Carter said it was a lot of hard work, the amount of gold found was exaggerated, and many miners had died. However, the *Picayune* also appended an account from the *Californian* that claimed digging for gold did not involve hard work and plenty of it awaited the ambitious prospector.

While Loeser and Carter continued on from New Orleans to Washington, Mason's duplicate copy went to President Polk. The president was in poor health. He was also a lame duck, marking time until his term of office ended in March. He received the duplicate copy of Mason's report on November 22. The colonel's description of the activity in the gold fields impressed Polk. Here was a report that was enthusiastic but tempered with a careful evaluation of the situation in California. Moreover, the very existence of the gold seemed to ratify Polk's decision to go to war with Mexico in the first place. "Under the circumstances," notes historian John W. Caughey, "Polk needed no such prompting to hail it as a patent justification of the war."

Polk had been preparing his final Annual Message to Congress, and he lost no time in including a statement regarding the discovery of gold in California. On December 5 the Annual Message was presented to Congress. No slouch at clever political manipulation, Polk turned history upside down and, using the passive voice, claimed he had known all along what no one else knew about California. "It was known that mines of the precious metals existed to a considerable extent in California at the time of its acquisition," he said. "Recent discoveries render it probable that these mines are more extensive and valuable than was anticipated."

Had a Pulitzer Prize for fiction existed at the time, Polk could have won it hands down for those two sentences. He then went on to give his lame-duck presidential endorsement of the gold discovery:

> The accounts of the abundance of gold are of such an extraordinary character as would scarcely command belief were they not corroborated by the authentic reports of officers in the public service who have visited the mineral district and derived the facts which they detail from personal observation. Reluctant to credit the reports in general circulation as to the quantity of gold, the officer commanding our forces in California [Mason] visited the mineral district in July last for the purpose of obtaining accurate information on the subject. His report to the War Department of the result of his examination and the facts obtained on the spot is herewith laid before Congress. When he visited the country there were about 4,000 persons engaged in collecting gold. There is every reason to believe that the number of persons so employed has been augmented. The explorations already made warrant the belief that the supply is very large and that gold is found at various places in an extensive district of country.
>
> Information received from officers of the Navy [Beale] and other sources, though not so full and minute, confirms the accounts of the commander of our own military force in California. It appears also from these reports that mines of quicksilver are found in the vicinity of the gold region. One of them is now being worked, and is believed to be among the most productive in the world.
>
> The effects produced by the discovery of these rich mineral deposits and the success which has attended the labors of those who have resorted to them have produced a surprising change in the state of affairs in California. Labor commands a most exorbitant price, and all other pursuits but that of searching for the precious metals are abandoned. Nearly the whole of the male population have gone to the gold districts. Ships arriving on the coast are deserted by their crews and their voyages suspended for want of sailors. . . .
>
> This abundance of gold and the all-engaging pursuit of it have already caused in California an unprecedented rise in the price of all the necessaries of life.

Polk proposed establishing a branch of the U.S. mint in California to convert gold into coin as well as "the bullion and specie which our commerce may bring from the whole west coast of Central and South America." He predicted that with California as a source for these Latin American markets, Great

Britain would find the United States a new and powerful economic rival. Trade with China would also benefit from U.S. coins minted in California.

> *The vast importance and commercial advantages of California have hereto-fore remained undeveloped by the Government of the country of which it constituted a part. Now that this fine province is a part of our country, all the States of the Union, some more immediately and directly than others, are deeply interested in the speedy development of its wealth and resources. No section of our country is more interested or will be more benefited than the commercial, navigating, and manufacturing interests of the Eastern States. Our planting and farming interests in every part of the Union will be greatly benefited by it. As our commerce and navigation are enlarged and extended, our exports of agricultural products and of manufactures will be increased, and in the new markets thus opened they can not fail to command remuner-ating and profitable prices.*
>
> *The acquisition of California and New Mexico, the settlement of the Ore-gon boundary, and the annexation of Texas, extending to the Rio Grande, are results which, combined, are of greater consequence and will add more to the strength and wealth of the nation than any which have preceded them since the adoption of the Constitution. . . .*

Two days after Congress received Polk's message, Loeser and Carter arrived in the nation's capital. Samples of gold from the Chinese tea caddy went on display at the War Department library, where newspaper reporters could see the precious metal and forget once and for all their cynicism about the earlier stories. Most of the gold went to the U.S. Mint in Philadelphia where it was assayed and pronounced genuine. The 230 ounces were rated as worth $3,910.10—about $17 an ounce in 1848 values. Some politicians spoke of mak-ing special coins and medals from it.

Polk's Annual Message was published in the newspapers on December 6, and on December 8 Mason's report was published. Polk's validation and en-dorsement of the discovery, and Mason's clear description of the gold fields, had an immediate effect on the stock market. Any lingering doubts were erased by the display of gold at the War Department. Ironically, the stories that earlier had been ridiculed came back to life, reprinted again and again. Though the stories may have exaggerated and distorted the truth, they were now acclaimed as gospel by many of the same newspapers that had pronounced them all a humbug. "However sceptical any man may have been, we defy him to doubt that if the quantity of such specimens as these be as great as has been represented, the value of the gold in Cal. must be greater than has been hitherto discovered in the old or new continent," remarked the *Washington Union,* "and great as may be the emigration to this new El Dorado, the frugal and industrious will be amply repaid for their enterprise and toil."

Gold fever did not spread overnight in the eastern United States. Between August and December 1848, newspaper stories were disbelieved, doubted, considered, accepted, embraced. Polk's endorsement, notes Caughey, "was dramatically substantiated by the arrival of Lieutenant Loeser bearing a tea caddy crammed with 230 ounces, 15 pennyweights, 9 grains of virgin gold . . . for the nation, Leoser's tea caddy touched off the gold mania. . . . It appeared that visible gold was better than words, yea, than many fine words." The fever swept the east, went north to Canada, east across the Atlantic to England and Europe. Parents said good-bye to sons, wives bid farewell to husbands. Those with money bought tickets on clipper ships to go around Cape Horn. Those who lacked funds schemed, borrowed, and begged for the stake that would enable them to go west across the continent. Thousands waited impatiently for the winter season to end and spring to come. With the spring of 1849, gold fever had spawned the Gold Rush.

The men who had written or carried the message lived out their allotted time in various degress of fame and fortune. Polk died on June 15, 1849, less than four months after exiting the White House. Colton wrote *Three Years in California* and died in 1851. Larkin, already a prosperous merchant, served as a delegate to California's Constitutional Convention in October 1849 and died in 1858, age fifty-six. Mason saw his report printed in newspapers all over the world and in thousands of booklets, a document that convinced innumerable people to risk all for the sake of gold. Breveted a brigadier general, Mason left California for Jefferson Barracks, Missouri, where he died of cholera on July 25, 1851, just three years after he had toured the gold fields. Lucien Loeser's subsequent career is unknown, as is that of his companion, David Carter. They played the roles of the Rosencrantz and Guildenstern of 1848, hopefully with a better fate than befell Shakespeare's messengers.

And Edward Fitzgerald Beale? After being promoted to lieutenant, he resigned from the navy in 1851. Between 1847 and 1849 he had crossed the continent from west to east and back again no less than six times. In addition to his trek in 1848, he took California's new constitution to present to Congress the following year. Hired as general superintendent for Indian Affairs for California and Nevada in 1851, he surveyed a possible railroad route while heading west to assume his duties. After resigning this position he became a brigadier general in the California State Militia (thereby confusing later generations of history students who wonder how a naval officer could become a general). In the late 1850s Beale helped create the camel corps and used camels as pack animals in a survey for a wagon road. He bought Fort Tejon, and the area near his property became the location of the first Indian reservation in California, with Beale its superintendent. In 1876 Beale served a year as minister to the Austro-Hungarian Empire. He maintained lifelong friendships with Kit Carson and John C. Fremont. He died at his home in Washington, D.C., in 1893, at age seventy-one, having lived a life that was, as Dan Thrapp put it, "generally respected."

THE SECOND DECLARATION OF INDEPENDENCE

Elmer Kelton

SOME YEARS AGO I read an account of misfortunes suffered by the men who signed the American Declaration of Independence, the price they paid in terms of lost property, lost family members, and long periods spent as fugitives from the British.

Sixty years after that historic signing, fifty-nine men gathered in a rough new town called Washington-on-the-Brazos to draft a similar document declaring Texas to be free from Mexico. The Texas Declaration of Independence was signed March 2, 1836.

I was curious to find out if these men's experiences were similar to those of the American signers of 1776. A big difference existed between the American signers of 1776 and the Texas signers of 1836. The American signers, by and large, were men of rank and property, aristocracy, so to speak. They had a great deal to lose in a material way for sticking their necks out.

Not many Texians—that is the way they referred to themselves in those days—were of this class. The wealthiest of the fifty-nine was said to be Robert Hamilton, fifty-two at the time, an immigrant from Scotland. He had become wealthy in North Carolina and moved to Texas in 1834. After he signed the declaration, his financial background caused him to be sent with George C. Childress to Washington, D.C., to plead the case of the new republic, to seek recognition of Texas and to try to establish commercial relations.

A relatively few others, such as Sterling Clack Robertson, the land empresario, might be considered wealthy. Certainly Robertson had a great deal of material property to lose if the revolution failed. But by and large, most of the signers were not men of much property beyond modest land claims and whatever they might have accumulated in equipment and homes. In fact, fifteen of the fifty-nine had been in Texas less than a year.

Several would pay a price. At least five would get away from the convention in time to make their way back to their military units and participate in the victorious Battle of San Jacinto. Two or three others may have done so, but their record is unclear.

Most of the fifty-nine men never saw each other again. In a few weeks two of them were dead, one killed at San Jacinto, the other accidentally shot on his way there. Before the year 1836 was out, five of the signers were dead.

On average the Texas signers lived a little more than nineteen years after putting their signatures on the document. In actual fact, one was dead in just over a month, but one lived for fifty-nine more years.

Washington-on-the-Brazos, though it would be the capital of Texas for a short time, was not named for Washington, D.C. It was named after Washington, Georgia, the old home of one of Stephen F. Austin's early settlers, Judge Robert M. Williamson, the noted "Three-Legged Willie." He was so named because he was crippled and carried a crutch. The town was surveyed in 1834 at a ferry crossing on the Brazos, not far from modern Bryan-College Station. At that time it was considered some distance from the centers of civilization.

The revolution had finally come to a boil in the fall of 1835. The Texian leaders indulged in a great deal of dissension, bickering, vanity, jealousy, and much jockeying for position. Not until Santa Anna was north of the Rio Grande and disaster was imminent did the Texians temporarily put aside their differences and try for a unified effort. And the smoke had not cleared from the field at San Jacinto before some of the old bickering and backbiting began anew.

Citizens living at Washington-on-the-Brazos guaranteed that the convention would have a place to meet if it went there. Actually they were premature, because they didn't have a suitable meeting hall. Noah T. Byers was in the midst of building a large frame blacksmith shop, though. This is the building in which the delegates gathered. He hadn't put in the windows yet, so the openings were covered with cotton cloth to help keep out the cold March wind. Temperature the day of signing was recorded as thirty-three degrees.

That was one price, the extreme discomfort not only of the trip but of the accommodations. Washington was just a small village and ill prepared to house the men.

It had been an unusually cold, wet winter, and everybody in Texas had suffered from it. The saving feature, from a military standpoint, was that the Mexican troops suffered even more than the Texians because most had come from a Southern climate. They were not prepared for the hard winter they found in Texas. At the battle of the Alamo, and all the way up to San Jacinto, a sizeable portion of the ill-clothed, ill-equipped Mexican army was half dead on its feet from exposure, flu, and pneumonia.

The men who went to Washington-on-the-Brazos paid another price, a pervasive feeling among perhaps a majority that they were on a needless errand when their friends and relatives elsewhere in Texas were dying. Many of the group felt that pulling away from their homes or their military units to sign a piece of paper was an idle gesture, a waste of their time. No doubt some felt guilty about their absence from the scenes of battle.

One in particular had reason later to be glad he was there, though. Jesse B. Badgett had been elected as a delegate from the Alamo. He had come to Texas from Arkansas the year before. He left for the convention just after Santa Anna surrounded the garrison. While he was at Washington, his entire constituency was killed. It is understandable that after he signed the declaration he went back to Arkansas. So far as the record shows, he never returned to Texas.

One of the first moves made after the meeting was called to order in that cold, drafty blacksmith shop was a proposal that the group immediately adjourn back to the war. The motion was voted down.

Sam Houston was there. He argued that the convention did indeed have important work to do. He felt it was important from the international standpoint that the Texas insurgents be given some basis of legality. He argued that a declaration of independence would pave the way for much greater help from the United States. It turned out he was right, although the battle of San Jacinto came before much of that help had time to arrive. A great many men, considerable arms and ammunition, and some money came after independence was a fact won on the battlefield.

It is part of the tradition at Washington that George C. Childress brought a prepared declaration to the meeting with him, that the only thing really needed was ratification. Childress, fresh from Tennessee a few months before, was a nephew of Sterling C. Robertson.

The signing was on Sam Houston's forty-third birthday. Perhaps it was coincidence, but students of Houston's life know that along with his tremendous abilities came an ego the size of a barn. So the choice of March 2 may not have been entirely by happenstance.

All but seven of the signers were American-born. It is no wonder that the

Texas declaration borrowed much from the American declaration of sixty years before.

What of the men who signed it? Who were they?

Eleven came originally from Tennessee and eleven from Virginia. Nine were from North Carolina. Six were from Kentucky, four each from Georgia and South Carolina, three from Pennsylvania, two from New York, one from Mississippi, one from Massachusetts. England, Scotland, Ireland, Canada, and Mexico each produced one signer.

Only two men were native-born Texans, both of Mexican extraction. The reason is plain enough. No Anglos were legally in Texas before the very early 1820s. Therefore, except for the Mexican citizens, there were no legal native sons more than fourteen or fifteen years old at the time the revolution began.

The three youngest men to sign were twenty-four. All three had arrived in Texas just the year before. One, Junius William Mottley of Virginia, paid the supreme price for Texas freedom: He was killed at San Jacinto. In his honor, a county in the Texas Panhandle was named for him.

Ironically, the name was misspelled.

One of the other two, however, lived for fifty-four years more. He was Stephen William Blount, whose company reached San Jacinto the day after the battle, perhaps sparing him from death but possibly giving him a guilt complex the rest of his long life.

The two native Texans were both of San Antonio. José Francisco Ruíz was fifty-three at the time and spoke no English. All the proceedings had to be translated for him. He had been involved in an unsuccessful revolution against Spain in 1813 and was exiled to the United States until Mexico became independent. He served the Mexican government as a military officer until 1832. He was an opponent of General Santa Anna and therefore fell out of political favor.

José Antonio Navarro was forty-one when he signed his name to the declaration. He was a good friend of Stephen F. Austin and became a land empresario himself, settling up land grants after 1824. He was elected in 1834 to serve Texas in the Mexican National Congress, but he opposed Santa Anna and did not choose to let himself be trapped in Mexico City. He pleaded illness and did not go. After signing the declaration, he stayed on as one of twenty-one special committeemen to draft a constitution for the new Texas Republic.

After the war he served as a congressman of the republic but had to resign in 1839 because this time he *was* ill. Against his better judgment he accepted President Mirabeau B. Lamar's appointment as a commissioner on the ill-fated Texan–Santa Fe Expedition in 1841. When the expedition collapsed and its participants were taken to Mexico as prisoners, he was separated from the others. Because of his part in Texas independence he was considered a traitor both to his race and to his country. He was first condemned to die, then commuted to a life sentence. In 1844 he escaped, got on a British vessel bound for Cuba, and finally reached home the following year.

He had paid a stiff price for Texas freedom. He served on the convention that voted in 1845 for annexation of Texas to the United States and helped draft the first state constitution. He served as a state senator. In 1861 he joined the secession movement, and all four of his sons served in the Confederate army. He lived on to 1871, a full thirty-five years after signing the declaration.

One other Spanish-speaking delegate to Washington-on-the-Brazos was not to live such a long life. Lorenzo de Zavala, forty-seven, had been born in Mexico. He was a Texas land empresario before becoming a political refugee from Santa Anna. His home was just across the bayou from the San Jacinto battlefield. Wounded Texian soldiers were taken there for treatment.

After the republic's constitution was drawn up, David G. Burnet was elected president and DeZavala vice president. DeZavala was appointed to accompany the conquered Santa Anna back to Mexico to see that a satisfactory treaty was drawn. The trip was delayed several months, during which time DeZavala became ill. He died in November after having signed the declaration in March.

In those early days of Texas, because of the bitter strife with Mexico, most Mexican citizens of the new republic were not well regarded. DeZavala and Navarro were notable exceptions. Both have counties named for them.

It could be argued that these three men, Ruíz, Navarro, and DeZavala, may have paid the highest price of all the signers. Many on both sides at the time regarded the revolution as a racial war. Santa Anna publicly proclaimed it so. In that respect these men went against their race, their own people, because they hated Santa Anna and the oppressive dictatorship he had established. One can only speculate about the mental and spiritual torment they must have endured over their decision.

One man brought a considerable amount of money with him to Texas and spent it in Texas's behalf. Samuel Price Carson, a former congressman from North Carolina, had fallen on political hard times somewhat like David Crockett. He bought land on the Red River and along the Arkansas border in 1834. He was elected secretary of state of the new republic and was sent to Washington to work for Texas interests. He spent so much of his own money for Texas that in 1837 he had to mortgage a number of his slaves for $10,000. He died a year later, forty years old and in debt, just over two years after having pledged his all for Texas.

Very few of the fifty-nine signers profited greatly in later years. Most appear to have achieved no more than modest financial success, and several suffered poverty.

One luckless signer, John Turner, dropped out of sight. Even the date of his death cannot be pinpointed closer than four years. The only official record of him in later times was when he filed for bankruptcy in Houston in 1844. Four years later, his widow remarried. He helped to found a nation, but he seems not to have shared in any material success.

Despite Texas's reputation as a rich state, the hard fact is that those times were hard, even bitter. Few people were having much luck financially. For most, the wolf was always growling just outside the front door, and the back door, too, if they were affluent enough to have one. Cash money, called "specie," was scarce.

Many had left an easier, more secure life elsewhere to come to Texas and try to build something better for their own later years, or for their children. The Texas they found during and for the decade or so after the revolution was a long way from paradise. But most paid the price, and they endured.

A few of the signers died violent deaths within a few years after the war. George Washington Barnett took his family out of Texas during the so-called Runaway Scrape, when so many fled before Santa Anna's advancing army. But two years later he was killed by Lipan Apache Indians.

Robert M. Coleman was a hard-luck man whose bad luck seemed to throw a shadow across his family. He moved to Texas from Kentucky in 1832 and settled in what became Bastrop County. He was an aide-de-camp to Houston at San Jacinto and later raised and commanded a regiment of rangers. He drowned in the Brazos River at Velasco in July 1837. Two years later his wife and oldest son were killed by Indians near Webberville.

Robert Potter survived the revolution and settled on his veteran's grant on Caddo Lake in Shelby County. He became embroiled in the infamous Regulator-Moderator War which blooded that region for several years. In 1842 he ran into a group of Moderators, who shot and killed him. His body was never recovered from the lake. Eventually President Sam Houston broke up the feud by threatening to bring in an army and declare war on both sides.

At least a few signers were bonafide "characters." One was a Virginian named Martin Parmer, known in his time as "the Ringtailed Panther." He outlived four wives and was living with his fifth when he died at seventy-two.

Samuel Augustus Maverick's name added a new word to the American vocabulary in later years, though the myth which underlies it has virtually no relationship to fact. The popular story is that he owned more cattle than anybody else in Texas. It was said that he did not brand his own cattle, declaring that any unbranded cattle therefore belonged to him. Thus an unbranded animal became known as a maverick. In time the word came to mean anyone or anything that went contrary to general custom.

In truth, Maverick never owned but a relative handful of cattle in his life and was a poor manager even of those. He was a city dweller. He participated in San Antonio's bloody 1840 Council House Fight in which many Indians were killed, fueling Comanche hostility and warfare that continued for more than thirty years.

When Mexican troops under General Woll invaded Texas in 1842 and briefly recaptured San Antonio, Maverick was carried off to prison in Mexico.

Mathew Caldwell was known as "Old Paint" for his patchy black-and-white beard. A scrapper, he was wounded in the Council House Fight. Later the same year he led a militia charge upon a huge force of Comanche Indians who had invaded all the way to the Gulf of Mexico and had sacked and burned the little coastal town of Linnville. Caldwell was quoted as shouting to his troops, "Boys, there are eight hundred or one thousand Indians. We are eighty-seven strong, and I believe we can whip hell out of them. Boys, shall we fight?" The boys said, "Yes," and, unbelievable as it may seem, they routed the Indians at the Battle of Plum Creek.

Like Navarro, Caldwell became a member of the Santa Fe Expedition, was captured and sent to prison in Mexico. He got back to Texas in time to lead two hundred volunteers against General Woll and defeat the Mexican troops at Salado Creek. He got revenge for his imprisonment but died late that same year. At least he did it at home and not in a Mexican prison.

James Collingsworth came to a sad end. A Tennessean, he nominated Sam Houston at the convention for commander-in-chief of the Texas army. As a soldier he was sent to the Brazos bottoms to help refugees escape during the Runaway Scrape. He was back with Houston in time to display conspicuous gallantry at San Jacinto. He became temporary secretary of state under David G. Burnet. He was sent to Washington as a commissioner for Texas but arrived after Congress had adjourned. He went on to Nashville to talk to President Andrew Jackson about the Texas situation. He became a senator, then chief justice of the Texas Supreme Court. In 1838 he ran against the fiery Lamar for president of Texas but somehow became deranged. He committed suicide by jumping into Galveston Bay.

Ironically, Anson Jones, later to be the last president of Texas, wrote that he had realized Collingsworth was going insane, and that he had expected his suicide. Some years later, Jones too would take his own life.

Thomas J. Rusk served a long and distinguished career for Texas. He was sometimes friend, sometimes an opponent of Sam Houston. He declined a chance to become president of Texas but served the state for many years in the U.S. Senate. Ill health and the death of his wife finally brought him more pain than he could endure, and he killed himself at age fifty-three.

The oldest man at the time of the signing was Collin McKinney, seventy, who had settled in 1831 in what was then a disputed area along the Arkansas border. He thought for years that he was living in Arkansas, but it turned out that he had been a Texian all along. He lived to the ripe old age of ninety-five.

Except for the two natives, the oldest signer in terms of time spent in Texas was James Gaines. He was sixty when he went to Washington-on-the-Brazos. Born in Virginia, he went to Texas in 1812 and joined the ill-fated Gutierrez-Magee filibustering expedition. He quit in disgust after seeing Mexicans execute Spanish prisoners. He was alcalde of the district of Sabine as early at 1824.

Haden Edwards, land speculator, accused Gaines of being chiefly responsible for the Fredonian Rebellion of 1826. At that time some rebels in the Nacogdoches area proclaimed the free republic of Fredonia. They were put down by Mexican troops and a militia group headed by Stephen F. Austin.

In 1830 Gaines operated a ferry across the Sabine River. He served three terms as a Congressman in the republic. Adventuresome even into his old age, he took off at age seventy-three for the Gold Rush and died in California in 1856 at eighty.

Though the declaration was about freedom, one delegate lost his freedom at Washington-on-the-Brazos. During the convention, Charles Bellinger Stewart married Julia Sheppard. They had five children during their thirteen-year marriage. He outlived her by thirty-six years. (Texas in those rough early days seems to have been particularly hard on women.)

The last surviving signer was William Carrol Crawford. He had come from North Carolina in 1835 in very bad health. He was thirty-two when he put his signature on the document. Texas turned out to be good for him. He lived another fifty-nine years, dying in 1895 at age ninety-one.

It might be coincidence, or it might be the genes, but Crawford was related to Charles Carroll, the last survivor among the signers of the United States Declaration of Independence.

The men who went to Washington-on-the-Brazos, facing cold and wet March weather, worrying about being overrun by Mexican troops, probably had little thought that what they did there would ever bring them personal fame or fortune. Most had neither at the time, nor did they ever acquire them.

A majority died in modest circumstances. The average Texan today probably couldn't name three of them without looking them up in a reference book.

Fifteen had been in Texas less than a year, and only fourteen of the entire fifty-nine had been there as much as six years.

Some people take the position that what these men did in effect was to steal Texas from Mexico. That is true only if you concede that what the American colonists did was to steal the United States from England. Most of Texas's true "old settlers," like Austin's original Old Three Hundred, were a long time in coming around to the notion of declaring independence. They held out for a long time against what became known as the war party. They asked not for independence but simply for a square deal and decent treatment from Mexico, which had invited them to Texas in the first place.

Not until after the tragic imprisonment of Stephen F. Austin in Mexico and Santa Anna's renunciation of the constitution did they begin to shift around to the independence view. By then they realized Mexico was in the grip of a despot, a cold and merciless dictator whose response to the suffering of his own soldiers was to see to his personal comfort; whose response to criticism was to crush it; whose response to freedom was chains. He had already cut a bloody swath through the northern states of Mexico on his way to put down the rebellion in Texas, so the Texians knew what was in store for them if he prevailed.

Some of the signers paid a hard price, and few ever gained what today would be considered a generous material reward. But because of those Texians, today's Texans are proud and free citizens of the United States.

THE INTREPID FEMALES OF FORTY-NINE

JoAnn Levy

IN 1849, BY CONSERVATIVE estimates, 25,000 people crossed the plains to California. The number arriving that year by sea, from around the Horn and across the Isthmus, exceeded 30,000. This immense migration traveling beneath the canvas of covered wagons and the canvas of sails included many surprisingly adventurous women.

One of them was Mary Jane Megquier who crossed the Isthmus early in 1849, and wrote this of her Chagres River journey: "The birds singing monkeys screeching the Americans laughing and joking the natives grunting as they pushed us along through the rapids was enough to drive one mad with delight."

She cheerfully described the sights, including the church at Gorgona, which was "overrun with domestic animals in time of service. . . . A mule took the liberty to depart this life within its walls while we were there, which was looked upon by the natives of no consequence."

Mrs. Megquier took to travel like a duck to water. On a later trip, after visiting family in Maine, she returned to San Francisco via Nicaragua, without her husband, but in company with two women. She breezily wrote from Nicaragua:

We spent three days very pleasantly although all were nearly starved for the want of wholesome food but you know my stomach is not lined with pink satin the bristles on the pork, the weavels in the rice and worms in the bread did not start me at all, but I grew fat upon it. Emily, Miss Bartlett and myself had a small room with scarce light enough to see the rats and spiders . . .

Lucilla Brown, a more critical traveler, crossed the Isthmus late in 1849, in a company that included "seven females." She intentionally did not write *ladies,* "for all do not deserve the name."

Among those acceptable to her was John Sutter's family. Since they were Swiss, Mrs. Brown could converse little with them, but of the remaining women passengers Mrs. Brown had decided opinions:

There is a Mrs. Brayner, an upholsterer by trade, going on to meet her husband in San Francisco. A Miss Scott, about fifty years old, going independent and alone, to speculate in California—of course, no very agreeable person. Then there is a Mrs. Taylor, whose husband left her some years ago—is said to have a father in California, whither she purports to be bound. She is young and has some pretentions to beauty, and at first commanded sympathy and attention from the gentlemen; but they all left her except the keeper of the hotel at Chagres, a low fellow, who retains her at his lodgings there, and it is to be hoped she will proceed no further.

Women who crossed to California by land also noted the presence of other women. Catherine Haun, whose party took the Lassen route in 1849, wrote that her caravan had "a good many women and children."

Among forty-niners traveling the southern route through present-day New Mexico and Arizona into San Diego was a woman with the wonderful name of Louisiana Strentzel, who met eight families in just one party on this road.

No stranger to gold fever, Mrs. Strentzel wrote from San Diego to her family back home that the latest news from the mines was that "gold is found in 27-pound lumps." She also wrote that her husband hadn't been sick a day since they left, and their two children were red and rosy and outgrowing their clothes. She, herself, she wrote, never enjoyed better health in her life.

Good health was noted by many women on the trails, who enjoyed the invigorating exercise. Others noted the novelty of the landscape, like Harriet Ward, a grandmother: "The scenery through which we are constantly passing is so wild and magnificently grand that it elevates the soul from earth to heaven and causes such an elasticity of mind that I forget I am old."

And Lucena Parsons wrote in her diary: "At the bottom of this valley are some very singular rocks. It appears sublime to me to see these rocks towering one above the other & lifting their majestick heads here in this solitary spot. Oh, beautiful is the hand of nature."

Lucena's journal was not otherwise a happy record. Lucena was a grave counter. Few of her journal entries failed to mention at least one. In all, she counted more than 380 graves while crossing the plains. So commonplace was the face of death by the time her party reached Fort Laramie that she sandwiches mention of it casually between other observations:

> It seems like home again to meet so many on the road. We did not look for it in this wild country. I found the skull of a man by the roadside. I took it on & buried it at the point. There is a blacksmiths shop here for the accommodation of emigrants kept by a French man.

Death was far less a casual matter by the time overlanders reached the dreaded desert. The especial cruelty of the long trek west was that the easy part came first. The rolling grasslands of the prairies, encountered in the springtime when people and stock were fresh, should have come last, not mountains to climb when food, animals, and spirit were exhausted. These mountains, the rugged Sierra Nevada, formed the final obstacle to California's golden promises. They took their toll in wagons smashed and abandoned. There were accidents. But, unless trapped by snow, emigrants had little fear of failing to cross the Sierra. Not so, the hot, dry forty-mile gauntlet of desert lying between the Humboldt River and the Carson or Truckee rivers flowing from the eastern Sierra.

By the time overlanders approached this final desert, they and their animals had plodded and slogged and climbed and descended nearly two thousand miles. In a meadow near the Humboldt River's sink, the travel-weary emigrants cut grass for their worn and thin mules and oxen, dried as much as they could carry, and hurried on. There was no forage on the desert's final forty miles.

Few passages of women's diaries and letters are more poignant than those recording this desert crossing. Sallie Hester's 1849 diary entry is eloquent testimony to the hardship:

> Stopped and cut grass for the cattle and supplied ourselves with water for the desert. Had a trying time crossing. Several of our cattle gave out, and we left one. Our journey through the desert was from Monday, three o'clock in the afternoon, until Thursday morning at sunrise, September 6. The weary journey last night, the mooing of the cattle for water, their exhausted condition, with the cry of "Another ox down," the stopping of the train to unyoke the poor dying brute, to let him follow at will or stop by the wayside and die,

and the weary, weary tramp of men and beasts, worn out with heat and fam-
ished for water, will never be erased from my memory. Just at dawn, in the
distance, we had a glimpse of the Truckee River, and with it the feeling:
Saved at last!

Another 49er family, Josiah and Sarah Royce, with their two-year-old
daughter Mary, crossed the Carson River in October. To avoid the heat, they
traveled the desert at night. In the dark, they missed the fork to the meadows
and its precious grass. Far upon the desert, they realized the mistake. Sarah's
recollection of that moment never faded:

So there was nothing to be done but turn back and try to find the mead-
ows. Turn back! What a chill the words sent through one. Turn back, on a
journey like that; in which every mile had been gained by most earnest labor,
growing more and more intense, until, of late, it had seemed that the cer-
tainty of advance *with every step was all that made the next step possible.*
And now, for miles, we were to go *back. In all that long journey no steps ever*
seemed so heavy, so hard to take, as those with which I turned my back to the
sun that afternoon of October 4, 1849.

Most overland emigrants on the California Trail kept to the tried and true
Carson and Truckee routes, but every rumor of a faster, easier way found an
ear anxious to believe. At the Humboldt especially, with the dreaded desert
ahead and the high mountains beyond, even the most conservative travelers
considered a convincingly proposed alternative. In 1849, thousands succumbed
to the temptation. Either through argument or the example of the wagon
ahead, much of the tail end of that year's migration turned north from the
Humboldt for Peter Lassen's ranch. They succeeded only in exchanging one
desert for another, while *adding* 200 desperate and dangerous miles to their
journey—traveling north nearly to the Oregon border.

Catherine Haun's party took that road. She remembered well the hardships:

The alkali dust of this territory was suffocating, irritating our throats and
clouds of it often blinded us. The mirages tantalized us; the water was unfit
to drink or use in any way; animals often perished or were so overcome by
heat and exhaustion that they had to be abandoned, or in case of human
hunger, the poor jaded creatures were killed and eaten. . . . One of our dogs
was so emaciated and exhausted that we were obliged to leave him on this
desert and it was said that the train following us used him for food.

No one can measure the fear and suffering endured by these people on the Lassen route, or by those on the desert crossings to the Truckee and Carson rivers, or on the southern trail into San Diego. But the fear and suffering of emigrants on another route into California could not have been surpassed.

In October 1849, from a camp south of Salt Lake City, more than three hundred people followed Jefferson Hunt, a guide familiar with the Old Spanish Trail to Los Angeles. A pack train overtook them, and in it was a man with a map showing a cutoff from this trail. The tantalizing prospect of short-cut immediately danced in the minds of impatient emigrants. The temptation was too much for a Methodist minister named John Brier, who fired others with his zeal for the cutoff. Although Jefferson Hunt refused to take it, on November 4, 1849, approximately twenty-seven wagons did. Among them were four families, including the Briers. Their path took them into a vast and desolate desert, a hellhole they would name Death Valley.

Thirty-four men, mostly young and mostly from Illinois, calling themselves Jayhawkers, entered the desert valley. Three of them died there. The Reverend Mr. Brier, his wife Juliet, and their three young sons followed the Jayhawkers in a desperate search for a way out. When one young man suggested to Juliet that she and her children remain behind and let them send back for her, she adamantly refused:

> *I knew what was in his mind. "No," I said, "I have never been a hindrance, I have never kept the company waiting, neither have my children, and every step I take will be toward California." Give up! I knew what that meant: a shallow grave in the sand.*

Juliet Brier earned the Jayhawkers' great respect and affection, one recalling that in walking nearly a hundred miles through sand and sharp-edged rocks that she frequently carried one of her children on her back, another in her arms, and held the third by the hand. At Jayhawker reunions she was spoken of as a heroine for caring for the sick among them. Her own recollection was modest:

> *Did I nurse the sick? Ah, there was little of that to do. I always did what I could for the poor fellows, but that wasn't much. When one grew sick he just lay down, weary like, and his life went out. It was nature giving up. Poor souls!*

Care for her own family consumed most of Juliet's strength. In one forty-eight-hour stretch without water, her oldest boy Kirk suffered terribly:

The child would murmur occasionally, "Oh, father, where's the water?"
His pitiful, delirious wails were worse than the killing thirst. It was terrible.
I seem to see it all over again. I staggered and struggled wearily behind with
the other two boys and the oxen. The little fellows bore up bravely and hardly
complained, though they could barely talk, so dry and swollen were their lips
and tongue. John would try to cheer up his brother Kirk by telling him of the
wonderful water we would find and all the good things we could get to eat.
Every step I expected to sink down and die.

The Brier family, with much suffering, reached safety on February 12, 1850.
The other three families lost in Death Valley also survived. The Wade family
celebrated deliverance on February 10. The Bennett and Arcan families, heroically
rescued by two selfless young men, escaped the valley of death on March 7 . . .
four months and three days after their fateful decision to take the cutoff.

The Brier family made a home in Marysville, the Wades in Alviso, the Ben-
netts at Moss Landing, and the Arcans in Santa Cruz. Captivated by the beautiful redwoods there, Abigail Arcan announced to her husband: "You can go to
the mines if you want to. I have seen all the godforsaken country I am going to
see, and I'm going to stay right here as long as I live."

And she did. Her first necessity, of course, like all women new to California, was a home. California offered few comforts, however, and almost nothing
homelike.

Forty-niner Anne Booth came around the Horn in a ship she continued to
live aboard for more than a month in San Francisco's Bay, and wrote, ". . . it is
true, there are many disadvantages and privations attending life in California;
but these I came prepared to encounter, and by no means expected to find the
comforts and refinements of home. . . ."

In mining camps, many 49er women continued to live in the wagons that
brought them, which Mrs. John Berry found "very disagreeable."

The rains set in early in November, and continued with little interruption
until the latter part of March and here were we poor souls living almost out
of doors. Sometimes of a morning I would come out of the wagon and find
the . . . shed under which I cooked blown over & my utensils lying in all di-
rections, fire out & it pouring down as tho' the clouds had burst. Sometimes I
would scold and fret, other times endure it in mute agony . . .

And how she yearned for a comfortable bed:

Oh! you who lounge on your divans & sofas, sleep on your fine, luxurious beds . . . know nothing of the life of a California emigrant. Here are we sitting on a pine block . . . sleeping in beds with either a quilt or a blanket as substitute for sheets (I can tell you it is very aristocratic to have a bed at all) . . .

In towns, of course, were hotels—if one stretched the definition. The celebrated St. Francis Hotel of San Francisco opened in 1849 and was so high class even then that it boasted sheets on its beds. No other hotel did. A reminiscence of a lady guest from those early days confirms that her bed there was "delightful." Two "soft hair mattresses" and "a pile of snowy blankets" hastened her slumbers, which were soon interrupted:

I was suddenly awakened by voices, as I thought, in my room; but which I soon discovered came from two gentlemen, one on each side of me, who were talking to each other from their own rooms through mine; which, as the walls were only of canvas and paper, they could easily do. This was rather a startling discovery, and I at once began to cough, to give them notice of my interposition, lest I should become an unwilling auditor of matters not intended for my ear. The conversation ceased, but before I was able to compose myself to sleep again . . . a nasal serenade commenced, which, sometimes a duet and sometimes a solo, frightened sleep from my eyes . . .

A 49er woman living in Santa Cruz knew about thin walls, too. She was Eliza Farnham, a widow who had come round the Horn with two children and a woman friend to claim property left by Eliza's late husband. She described the "casa" she inherited on her Santa Cruz ranch, as, "Not a cheerful specimen, even of California habitations—being made of slabs, were originally placed upright, but which have departed sadly from the perpendicular in every direction. . . ."

Mrs. Farnham focused her initial housekeeping wants on simply getting a stove installed. During the three-day period that Eliza called the "siege of the stove," a hired man failed at the task, as did her friend Miss Sampson. Then Eliza tackled it: "On the third day, it was agreed that stoves could not have been used in the time of Job, or all his other afflictions would have been unnecessary."

Not afraid of labor, Mrs. Farnham set herself the task of building a new house. "My first participation in the labor of its erection was the tenanting of the joists and studding for the lower story, a work in which I succeeded so well, that during its progress I laughed, when I paused for a few moments to rest, at the idea of promising to pay a man $14 or $16 per day for doing what I found my own hands so dexterous in."

Eliza Farnham, who conquered a stove, built a house, and put her Santa Cruz land to growing potatoes, quickly recognized that women in California would have to work.

And indeed 49er women did work. Some even mined. A newspaper editor saw a woman at Angel's Creek dipping and pouring water into the gold washer her husband rocked. The editor reported that she wore short boots, white duck pantaloons, a red flannel shirt, with a black leather belt and a Panama hat.

Louise Clappe tried her hand at digging gold, too:

> I have become a mineress; that is, if the having washed a pan of dirt with my own hands, and procured therefrom three dollars and twenty-five cents in gold dust . . . will entitle me to the name. I can truly say, with the black-smith's apprentice at the close of his first day's work at the anvil, "I am sorry I learned the trade;" for I wet my feet, tore my dress, spoilt a pair of new gloves, nearly froze my fingers, got an awful headache, took cold and lost a valuable breastpin, in this my labor of love.

An easier and more profitable avenue to gold, for most women, was the selling of familiar domestic skills, like Abby Mansur's neighbor at Horseshoe Bar: "She makes from 15 to 20 dollars a week washing . . . has all she wants to do so you can see that women stand as good chance as men."

Mary Jane Caples made pies. "My venture was a success. I sold fruit pies for one dollar and a quarter a piece, and mince pies for one dollar and fifty cents. I sometimes made and sold a hundred in a day, and not even a stove to bake them in, but had two small dutch ovens."

One woman boasted; "I have made about $18,000 worth of pies—about one third of this has been clear profit. One year I dragged my own wood off the mountain and chopped it, and I have never had so much as a child to take a step for me in this country. $11,000 I baked in one little iron skillet, a consider-able portion by a campfire, without the shelter of a tree from the broiling sun."

Another woman wrote, from San Francisco:

> A smart woman can do very well in this country—true, there are not many comforts and one must work all the time and work hard, but there is plenty to do and good pay. If I was in Boston now and know what I now know of California I would come out here—if I had to hire the money to

bring me out. It is the only country I ever was in where a woman received anything like a just compensation for work.

Running a boardinghouse was the commonest money-maker for women. One woman earned $189 a week after only three weeks of keeping boarders in the mines. She shared with her boarders accommodations decidedly minimal, as she wrote her children back East:

We have one small room about 14 feet square, and a little back room we use for a storeroom about as large as a piece of chalk. Then we have an open chamber . . . divided off by a cloth. The gentlemen occupy one end, Mrs. H and daughter, your father and myself, the other. We have a curtain hung between our beds but we do not take pains to draw it, as it is of no use to be particular here.

Luzena Wilson set herself up in the boardinghouse business, too. Despite its rustic beginnings, she had grand plans for her Nevada City enterprise, which she elevated with the title "hotel":

I bought two boards from a precious pile belonging to a man who was building the second wooden house in town. With my own hands I chopped stakes, drove them into the ground, and set up my table. I bought provisions at a neighboring store, and when my husband came back at night he found 20 miners eating at my table. Each man as he rose put a dollar in my hand and said I might count him a permanent customer. I called my hotel "El Dorado."

But running a boardinghouse was hard work, as Mary Jane Megquier attested from San Francisco:

I should like to give you an account of my work if I could do it justice. I get up and make the coffee, then I make the biscuit, then I fry the potatoes and broil 3 pounds of steak, and as much liver, while the hired woman is sweeping and setting the table. At 8 the bell rings and they are eating until nine. I do not sit until they are nearly all done . . . after breakfast I bake 6 loaves of bread (not very big) then 4 pies or a pudding, then we have lamb, for which we have paid $9 a quarter, beef, pork, baked turnips, beets, potatoes, radishes, salad, and that everlasting soup, every day, dine at 2, for tea we have hash, cold meat, bread and butter, sauce and some kind of cake and I *have cooked every mouthful that has been eaten excepting one day when we were on a steamboat excursion. I make 6 beds every day and do the washing and ironing and you must think I am very busy and when I dance all night I am obliged to trot all day and if I had not the constitution of 6 horses I should have been dead long ago but I am going to give up in the fall, as I am sick and tired of work.*

In full agreement was Mary Ballou, who kept a boardinghouse in the mines. Her complaints included the additional inconvenience of unwelcome animals.

Anything can walk into the kitchen and then from the kitchen into the dining room so you see the hogs and mules can walk in any time, day or night, if they choose to do so. Sometimes I am up all times a night scaring the hogs and mules out of the house. I made a blueberry pudding today for dinner. Sometimes I am making soups and cranberry tarts and baking chicken that cost $4 a head and cooking eggs at $3 a dozen. Sometimes boiling cabbage and turnips and frying fritters and broiling steak and cooking codfish and potatoes. Sometimes I am taking care of babies and nursing at the rate of $50 a week but I would not advise any Lady to come out here and suffer the toil and fatigue that I have suffered for the sake of a little gold.

One woman determined to get her gold the old-fashioned way, by marrying it. She placed what must have been the first personals ad in a California newspaper, under the head:

A HUSBAND WANTED

By a lady who can wash, cook, scour, sew, milk, spin, weave, hoe (can't plow), cut wood, make fires, feed the pigs, raise chickens, rock the cradle, (gold rocker, I thank you, Sir!), saw a plank, drive nails, etc. These are a few of the solid branches; now for the ornamental "long time ago" she went as far as syntax, read Murray's Geography and through two rules in Pike's Grammar. Could find 6 states on the atlas. Could read, and you can see that she can write. Can—no, could—paint roses, butterflies, ships, etc. Could once dance; can ride a horse, donkey or oxen . . . Oh, I hear you ask, could she scold? No, she can't you_____for-nothing _____!

Now for her terms. Her age is none of your business. She is neither handsome nor a fright, yet an old man need not apply, nor any who have not a little more education than she has, and a great deal more gold, for there must be $20,000 settled on her before she will bind herself to perform all the above. Address to Dorothy Scraggs, with real name. P.O. Marysville.

Of course there were all kinds of ways women could earn a "little gold," and they did. Catherine Sinclair managed a theatre. A French woman barbered. Julia Shannon took photographs. Sophia Eastman was a nurse. Mrs. Pelton taught school. Mrs. Phelps sold milk. Mary Ann Dunleavy operated a 10-pin bowling alley. Enos Christman witnessed the performance of a lady bullfighter. Franklin Buck met a Spanish ("genuine Castillian") woman mulepacker. Charlotte Parkhurst drove a stage for Wells Fargo. Mrs. Raye acted in the theatre. Mrs. Rowe performed in a circus, riding a trick pony named Adonis.

And some women danced, some sang, some played musical instruments, some dealt cards, some poured drinks. What readily comes to mind with the subject of gold rush women are these saloon girls and parlor house madams. And who were these so-called soiled doves? They were Chilean, Mexican, Chinese, French, English, Irish, and American. No stereotype encompasses them all, for they and their experiences were as diverse as the population. A few were phenomenally successful, most merely survived. Despite popular nineteenth-century assumption that women were driven into prostitution by seduction and abandonment, most pursued the profession for economic reasons.

Among the first, believed to have arrived in San Francisco in 1849, was a Chinese woman named Ah Toy. She was a "daughter of joy," the Chinese expression for prostitute, but she was more than that. She was an extraordinary woman. First, she was independent of any man, Chinese or Caucasian, remarkable for an Asian woman. Second, she spoke English, also most unusual for a Chinese woman. Third, she was assertive and intelligent, for she quickly learned to use the American judicial system, regularly taking her grievances to court.

Obviously, she was adventurous, determined, hardworking, bright, independent, aggressive—the very qualities of a successful 49er. She shared those qualities with thousands of pioneering women who demonstrated the courage and determination required by the unique circumstances of gold rush California.

And yet when most people think about 49ers, they think of them as men. And yet, *women*—women with gold fever like Louisiana Strentzel, suffering overlanders like Sarah Royce and Juliet Brier and Catherine Haun, the boardinghouse keepers like Mary Ballou and Luzena Wilson and Mary Jane Megquier, potato growers like Eliza Farnham, the pie makers, the washerwomen, the seamstresses, prostitutes, actresses, circus riders, nurses, teachers, wives, mothers, sisters, and daughters—*women* were 49ers, too.

THE JAYHAWKING OF SALINA

Judy Magnuson Lilly

AT DAWN ON SEPTEMBER 17, 1862, Horace L. Jones, hotel owner and manager of the Kansas Stage Company station in Salina, Kansas, checked the feedbags in the corral near the center of town. He expected a mail stage later that morning. Gunsmith Carl Tressin was up and writing a letter in his small hardware store. On plank shelves were his stock of tin and iron goods as well as the hunting rifles, shotguns, and pistols he intended to spend the day repairing. On their claims outside of town, settlers rose from their grass-filled bed ticks to tend their livestock before turning to other work of the morning. In a cabin by Walnut Creek, Jane Coburn prepared the body of her small son for burial. She already knew the day would not be an ordinary one. Everyone else in the valley would realize this soon enough.

Situated along a bend in the Smoky Hill River, one hundred eighty-five miles from Leavenworth, the settlement of Salina, Kansas had sprung to life in 1858, three years before Kansas's birth on January 29, 1861. At first, only a small trading post comprised the business district, but soon the need for other services arose. A flour and gristmill opened, as well as a blacksmith shop, livery stables, wagon shop, two hotels, and a gunsmith and tin shop. Fate cheated the frontier village out of boomtown activities during the great rush to the Pike's Peak gold fields in 1859 because the Smoky Hill trail, which ran through Salina, proved less desirable than the Platte River road to the north or the Santa

Fe–Arkansas River route to the south. Although the Smoky Hill trail was shorter than the other two, farther west of Salina, travelers found a scarcity of water, wild game, campfire wood, and grass for grazing during certain seasons of the year. They risked not only the threat of Indians and white marauders, but also the possibility of becoming lost when the Smoky Hill ended and a well-defined trail disappeared.

By 1860 Salina's population was still too insignificant for the census takers to enumerate, and with the start of the Civil War a year later, it shrank even more when a number of Salina men left their homes and claims in the hands of family members to join the fighting. With the nation and state of Kansas consumed with either war or gold mining, the village remained in its primitive condition as a frontier location during the four-year Civil War. Its role on the western edge of settlement was to provide a jumping-off place for hunters, military troops, freighters, and the trickle of prospectors to and from the gold fields. This community, rooted in the grassy Smoky Hill River valley, became a buffer between the relatively settled eastern third of the state and the uncharted region west to the Rocky Mountains.

It was this vulnerable position, plus a false sense of security, that allowed the town and its environs to fall victim to fifteen armed guerillas on this mid-September morning. The band rode out of the northeast before most folks in town—a mix of fifty or sixty American and European-born settlers—had rubbed sleep from their eyes.

Guerrilla warfare along the Kansas-Missouri border from 1855 to 1865 employed the tactics of covert surveillance of an area and surprise, retaliatory raids. Guerillas sought to dominate quickly and completely without putting themselves at great risk. On this morning the rough-looking bunch herded a few stolen ponies through the dusty streets, brandishing their weapons and threatening to burn the town if the settlers put up a fight. They professed to be raiding for the Confederate cause, but to the community of Union supporters they appeared to be no more than common horse thieves.

The townspeople realized later the gang had camped for days along the Saline River to the north. Riding into town a few at a time, the men had traded with local merchants and given their business to the blacksmith and gunsmith, paying their bills with gold dust. But no one in the valley had been suspicious. Jayhawking commonly occurred along the Kansas-Missouri border, where both Union troops and Confederate bands were known to confiscate anything from washing off a clothesline to horses from the barn. But frontier settlers in Kansas thought they were immune to such activities. Even danger from the plains Indians to the west had not materialized. As one man put it, "Wolf had been cried so often when no wolf was near, that we had begun to believe that the animal did not exist."

On the morning of the raid, the guerillas rode directly to the stage station and hotel that sat along the Smoky Hill River on Iron Avenue, one of the town's two main streets. Securing the loose ponies they had herded, they took several large stage mules from the barn and quickly spread through town, raiding the two or three stores for guns, ammunition, food, tobacco, and other supplies they needed. They rounded up horses and mules, pounded on doors and gathered the Salina men together in the middle of the street where Horace L. Jones, the stage manager, and another man were already under guard.

A young man named Albert Brown, who in two weeks would celebrate his eighteenth birthday, had just arrived in town when he saw horsemen thundering along the road from the Schippel brothers' Saline River ferry northeast of Salina. Brown supposed the riders to be soldiers from Fort Riley but soon saw his mistake. He and two other men tried to organize a resistance, but the raiders had planned their attack well. Tough characters, dressed in buckskins, descended upon them with revolvers drawn. The three Salina men were ordered to leave their guns and consider themselves prisoners, "which we finally concluded was best to do," Brown recalled in a 1879 newspaper account. "Before going, however, I placed a Colts five-shooter in my coat pocket so that I was not afraid of being shot without some chance of returning the compliment."

Prussian immigrant Carl Wilhelm Tressin had been in Salina only a few months, having found the town to be an ideal location for "a hard working man without means." On this fall early morning he was astonished to see six men enter his store, pointing six cocked revolvers at him. When the leader asked how many guns and weapons he had in the store, Tressin told them to take whatever they wanted. The thieves bagged about $300 worth of weapons, including a double rifle worth $75.

The women in town were left undisturbed in their homes, being threatened with the death of their men if they made any trouble. When Agnes Mead, whose husband James L. Mead would later figure in the growth of Wichita, Kansas, was told to hand over all the guns in their hotel quarters, she reached for two rifles standing by the door, a muzzle-loading musket and an old Indian relic with a barrel full of sand that her husband had found on the prairie. She convinced the intruders there were no others, even though the good hunting rifles were in the kitchen.

Christina Phillips Campbell, who ran a trading post with her husband, Alexander, was fixing breakfast when the excitement erupted. Alexander Campbell ran out to investigate. Shortly, two coarse-looking men came into her house, one holding a large revolver in each hand while the other went after the plunder. "They didn't have to hunt long," she recalled, "for there were four guns right in sight, one Sharps rifle, two muskets and one shot gun."

When she asked what they were going to do with the men, she was told to keep quiet and no harm would come to anyone. Once the robbers had left, Christina took action. "I ran to the back door of the store and went to work gathering all the small kegs of powder, lead, and caps. I hid them in barrels of wheat that were stored in the back of the store. I had just returned to the house when two of them marched my husband up to open the store door for them. I do not know all they got, but whatever they wanted they took, except the ammunition which was hid in the wheat."

Although the thieves gathered all the mules and horses they could find during their ride into town, they did not completely sweep the countryside. One settler later wrote to family in Illinois: "I suppose that by this time you have heard of the raid that was made on Salina by the jawhackers [sic] about a month ago and no doubt [are] wondering if our horses was taken along with the rest. For some reason or other they did not pay us a visit at all and I am very glad they did not for they would have found us unable to make any resistance never dreaming of such a thing happening away out here."

Like Alexander Campbell, nearly every man in town rushed out of their homes at the first sounds of galloping horses. When one fellow looked out the window that morning and noticed the activity down by the river, he told his hunting partner he'd see what was afoot. On the way he saw two women "making signs which I did not understand." Failing to heed their warnings, he continued to the center of town and upon rounding the corner was greeted by "a great big greasy fellow [who] pushed a six-shooter into my ribs and said, 'You are wanted down yonder.'"

Despite the potential for violence in this early morning raid, the incident, which lasted no more than thirty minutes, seemed to carry its lighter moments. While the Salina men were corralled in the middle of the street, someone brought out a half bushel of apples that were passed around for the guards and prisoners alike to enjoy. A certain amount of joking between prisoners and guards went on, particularly over the comical confusion experienced by those who blundered into the robbery in progress. One man had emerged from his cabin that morning while the band was in route to town and witnessed a stranger roping one of his two ponies that grazed on the prairie. When his other horse eluded the thief's lariat, the owner caught and saddled it and took after the offending party, only to lose it, too. Albert Brown, among those in the street, recalled, "Although we sympathized with [the man who lost both horses], we could not help suppressing a smile at his ludicrous look."

Another unsuspecting victim who just happened on the scene was a buffalo hunter and scout named Ed Johnston. He had stayed the night before at the home of Irish settlers, Jane and Joseph Coburn, south of town. The Coburns' three-year-old son had been seriously ill with diphtheria. When Johnston awoke that morning, he found the little boy had died during the night, and the boy's mother implored Johnston to ride to town and make preparations for the funeral.

"I started at daylight to get friends to help Mrs. Coburn and to Salina to get the boy's coffin," Johnston later recalled. "I got to Salina about sun up and saw about ten or fifteen people gathered at the door of Jones' place. A man came to me before I dismounted, put a revolver to my head and told me to dismount and join the others. Well, I had run into a trap."

As soon as the raiders had secured the spoils—as much ammunition, arms, tobacco, and supplies as they could carry—they thundered off, traveling south-west with their herd of horses and mules. According to James R. Mead, in his book, *Hunting and Trading, 1859–1875*, the captain stayed behind his band of men to apologize to the Salina citizens for what they had had to do. He advised everyone to "get even with somebody else" for the trouble they'd been caused. Then he bid the dazed townspeople good day and rode from town.

What happened after the dust had cleared that day?

Everyone's first thought was to send a runner to Fort Riley, fifty miles away, to notify authorities. Borrowing an overlooked mule that belonged to the storekeeper, settler Bob Bishop set off on a journey that took him five hours. Meanwhile, the men in and around Salina either rushed about organizing a posse to follow the raiders or turned their attention to mundane matters. James R. Meade later wrote of the incident in a letter to his family in Iowa, acknowl-edging that when the excitement died down, he did a job of surveying that af-ternoon. Another local claimholder had managed to keep possession of his horse, and the next morning he "put in the blue stem wheat on the sod and [in the] afternoon . . . worked at the same."

Ed Johnston, the emissary for Jane Coburn whose little boy had died, ad-mitted, "I had the time of my life to decide whether I would stay and help Mr. Coburn." The lure of a mounted chase after the outlaws won out when John-ston decided "on promise of settlers to go to their [Coburns's] assistance I joined the settlers in pursuing the robbers."

The first of the settlers to start after the guerilla band were Tom Anderson and his friend, Robert Muir, who were on their way by late that same afternoon. Their intention, Muir wrote in a letter, was to go around to a road ranch thirty-five miles west of Salina and rally the eight or ten hunters who lived in the vicinity into surprising the horse thieves. "We put our horses through as fast as they could go but it was no use. They were doing the same. You may have an idea of how fast they went when I tell you that they took the mules out of the stage over fifty miles west of Salina two hours before sundown."

Back in Salina another party of men searched the county for mounts and weapons, while they waited for reinforcements. According to Albert Brown, fifteen soldiers did come to the town's aid. Confirming this fact is an entry in the diary of early settler, Reverend A. A. Morrison: "Friday, September 19, 1862. Some fifteen or twenty of the citizens and some twelve or fifteen of the soldiers from Fort Riley started out after the robbers."

Anderson and Muir, riding alone and a little ahead of the large posse, followed the marauders' tracks southwest along what locals called the Fort Riley–Fort Larned road. Established two years earlier, the crude road took military troops and supply trains from Fort Leavenworth to Fort Riley and on to New Mexico by way of Fort Larned on the Santa Fe Trail. The Kansas Stage Company had recently received the contract to carry mail between the military posts and had set up mail stations and stage stops along the way. The trail of the guerrillas led the pursuers to the first of two road ranches visited by the outlaws. It belonged to the brothers, Irve and Henry Faris, at Clear Creek Crossing in present-day Ellsworth County.

Road ranches, isolated eating and trading establishments, were spawned in the 1850s and 1860s by the rush for gold to the part of western Kansas that became Colorado. While some were well equipped with a blacksmith shop and even a saloon, many, like the two along the guerillas' escape route, were corrals and simple sod or log dwellings that provided eating and sleeping accommodations for stage passengers and others.

The raiders found little to steal at the Faris ranch. Henry Faris and a neighbor were out hunting with their ponies and arms. The thieves succeeded in making Irv Faris a temporary prisoner while they sacked the house and then moved on, leaving Faris unharmed. The next stop, four miles west, was the ranch of Daniel Page, a college student and teacher before he came west, and his partner, Joseph Lehman, reported to be an experienced plainsman. In addition to killing buffalo and wolves for a living, the men owned a trading and mail station along the stage route at the Smoky Hill Crossing where travelers forded the river. This location would become the site of Fort Ellsworth (later the name changed to Fort Harker) near modern-day Kanopolis, Kansas.

Daniel Page and a neighbor, P. M. "Smoky Hill" Thompson, were returning to the ranch with a load of prairie hay when the band arrived. Page had a revolver in his belt, but the ruffians got the drop on him. Then they turned their guns on Thompson and demanded his arms. From atop a load of hay, Thompson replied in his usual cavalier manner that he could only offer them a pitchfork. The leader of the band took his pleasantry well enough and declared they had "no way to utilize" the fork. However, they did relieve the two men of a pony, a double-barreled shotgun, and mules belonging to the stage company.

As the Salina men trailed the band, they discovered that once past the Smoky Hill River, the guerillas had continued to follow the stage route with their ever-growing herd of mules and horses and chanced upon the eastbound stage near the head of Oxide Creek, which emptied into the Smoky Hill from the south. Aboard the stage were William Griffenstein, often called "Dutch Bill," who later served as mayor of Wichita, and possibly several more travelers. All were made to leave the stage while the thieves seized the mules, cut open the mail bags and scattered their contents about the prairie. When the Jayhawkers tried to take the stage driver's prized whip, he begged them to leave it. In the end they relented and gave the whip back to him before they sped away. The driver, James Hall, and the passengers were left to walk fifteen miles to the Page and Lehman ranch.

Anderson and Muir from Salina found the stranded passengers at the ranch. After feeding their horses, they took the stage driver back to the abandoned stagecoach, hitched it to their horses and brought it back to the ranch. Tom Anderson confirmed in a recounting of the raid years later that when they arrived at the Page and Lehman ranch, they found the large posse from Salina there with a team and provisions. He does not mention that any soldiers accompanied the Salina men. An explanation for this omission might be found in Albert Brown's account. He recalled that the large Salina group arrived at Smoky Hill Crossing (the Page and Lehman ranch) "about sundown and shortly after our arrival we were informed by the sergeant in command that he could go no farther, as he had orders to that effect." Apparently the soldiers turned back at this point, but the settlers prepared to push on and were joined by Anderson, Muir, and four or five hunters.

Anderson recalled, "[S]o after resting our horses we started early the following morning. When we came to the sand hills at the head of Cow Creek we found the guerillas had camped and concluded that we were probably twenty-four hours behind them."

While several in the party insisted that pursuit was useless, the majority of the men voted to continue. They followed the robbers' trail to the mouth of

Walnut Creek on the Arkansas River and found that the group had divided into two parties, one going up Walnut Creek, the other crossing the Arkansas. The posse made camp and argued over what should be done. Finally, Anderson recalled, "Joe Lemon (Lehman) volunteered to follow the Santa Fe Trail and ascertain whether the two parties came together again, we agreeing to await his return. Our hopes were that the guerillas might camp somewhere a day or two, to rest and graze their stock. But in that we were disappointed."

While they waited for their scout's return, Bob Bishop, the man who had ridden the mule to Fort Riley, arrived in the camp with word that the commander of the Post refused to provide the citizens any assistance. "So with this discouraging news," Anderson remembered, "and realizing how poorly equipped we were for an encounter with the robbers, a large number signified their determination to give up the chase and returned home, to which all finally agreed."

Tom Anderson's recollection that no soldiers came from Fort Riley contradicts Albert Brown's statement and A. A. Morrison's diary that soldiers accompanied citizens as far as the Smoky Hill Crossing. Another curious contradiction was made by Bob Bishop's brother who in an account of the raid in the *Edwards Atlas of Saline County 1884,* wrote the following: "A party of soldiers came up and with a number of citizens went in pursuit of the raiders." Later, he would say that he knew the statement was incorrect, and the publishers had made the error, a seemingly unlikely explanation. The issue of whether or not soldiers from Fort Riley joined in a portion of the chase remains a mystery.

Regardless, the following morning, without waiting for their scout, the Salina men broke camp and rode all day for the Smoky Hill ranch. Joseph Lehman was apparently on their heels for he arrived during the night, reporting that he found no evidence that the two bands of guerillas had ever come together. Tom Anderson summed up the frustrations of the party of farmers and hunters who had lost the tools of their trade during the whole affair: "The next morning we returned to Salina. Thus ended a fruitless search."

And what happened in the hours and days following the guerrilla raid on Salina? Tom Anderson claimed that nothing was heard of the party of raiders again. Nor was any of the property recovered. However, James R. Mead wrote in a letter from Salina on September 28, 1862, that he had got two ponies back and was out only one mare and one rifle. Mead also wrote years later that he learned the robbers had crossed into Texas eventually and "joined their brethren in the war."

As to the help from the settlement for the Coburn family Reverend A. A. Morrison's diary entry of Thursday, September 18, reports, "Went up to Coburns' to attend to the burying of his little boy."

While the stolen property was vital to the settlers' livelihood—guns and ammunition for hunting, horses and mules to transport hides, pelts, tallow, and other goods to the Leavenworth market and for making improvements to their claims—the Salina raid lacked the grimness and tragedy of William Quantrill's attack on Lawrence, Kansas, that would occur less than a year later on August 21, 1863. On this day, more than one hundred and fifty men and boys were murdered, while much of the town of Lawrence was destroyed. In the raid on Salina the townspeople had their lives and homes threatened, but no deaths resulted and no buildings were burned. Intent on enlarging their cache of arms and supply of horses and mules, the raiders took only what they could carry on horseback, making no effort to hunt for cash or valuables. Still, the fear experienced by settlers and townspeople was not lessened by the nonviolent outcome. What happened during those early dawn moments had folks reminiscing for years afterward. The jayhawking of Salina was the closest thing to a Civil War confrontation the young settlement would experience.

MAUD—KIDNAPPED BY PANCHO VILLA

Douglas V. Meed

IT ALL SEEMED SO very romantic, Maud Wright remembered. She was standing by the stove tending a boiling pot of beans and frying two large steaks for her husband Ed and his hired hand, Frank Hayden. While supper cooked she sang a little song, half in English, half in Spanish, to her two-year-old son Johnnie, who was gurgling and laughing in his playpen.

It was a cool March evening and as the sun slid beneath the mountains and the light faded, the valley was bathed in a golden glow. Maud finally felt secure and happy even though the revolution in Mexico, raging now for almost six years, had ripped apart most of Chihuahua. Now there was a large garrison of federal troops loyal to President Carranza stationed at Pearson, only a few miles away. Pancho Villa, his power broken, was on the run and she thought the bad times were finally over.

She gazed out of the window watching their cattle and a dozen horses grazing nearby. She also looked fondly at the sawmill Ed had built practically singlehanded. They had done much in six years and she was proud of the strength and energy she had poured into their efforts. If things remained calm perhaps her parents could rejoin them in their little Mexican Eden. She chuckled at the thought. How quickly things changed.

Back in 1910, twenty-one-year-old Maud Hawk and her family were logging in Oklahoma and she was working alongside her father and brothers swinging an axe, hauling on a cross-cut saw and driving a mule team with equal skill. The vibrant young woman soon caught the attention of a cowboy who promptly paid court and soon professed his love. But her father, who did not want to lose a good hand and who had no use for cowboys, would have none of her romance.

After dire threats, the suitor was run off and Father Hawk moved the family to New Mexico. Undaunted, the young man, Edward Wright, vowed he would return and claim his beloved. He used his savings to buy a ranch in the Mexican province of Chihuahua where there was a fairly large American settlement, many of whom were Mormons.

Trailing an extra horse, he left the ranch and headed north to search for Maud who he had heard was living somewhere near the mining camps in southwest New Mexico. Ed rode up the dusty road to Polomas and crossed into the United States at the sleepy border town of Columbus, New Mexico.

From there he rode across the arid flatlands to Deming, turned west and made a long dry ride to Lordsburg. On the way he inquired for news of the Hawk family at every small settlement and ranch along the road.

He must have learned from someone that the Hawks were located near the mining town of Silver City. With that information he turned north to the high country. The area still had a few remaining, if disappointed, gold and silver seekers prospecting near mined out claims on Bear Creek. From them, Ed got hot coffee and more rumors about the Hawks.

With growing hope, he trekked into Silver City and to his great joy found people who knew Maud's family and gave him directions to their nearby home.

Riding high into the cool, clean air of the mountains, Ed traveled northeast for seven miles until he reached the small settlement of Pinos Altos. Altogether, he had ridden more than 150 miles.

Nestled among the towering ponderosa pines, Ed saw a small frame house with a thin spiral of smoke rising from a stone chimney. Outside was a slim young lady, whose eyes turned toward the approaching rider. Straining their eyes both Ed and Maud came to the same joyful recognition.

Ed spurred his horses into a gallop as Maud ran toward him. Reining in, Ed leaped out of the saddle and pulled the running Maud into his arms. Finally, ther were together again.

When her father still opposed their friendship, the two secretly met one night and declared their undying love. Ed's two fine horses were saddled and under a moonlit sky the two lovers mounted and rode south. At El Paso, Texas, they found a willing clergyman and became man and wife. They crossed the

Rio Grande and rode south through the desert and mountain country until they reached a grassy valley and their ranch.

They were hard workers and the ranch prospered. Ed built the sawmill for added income and hired Frank to help out. A few months later Maud wrote her parents and effected a reconciliation. Her father, who was now convinced that Ed was more than a cowboy drifter, gave the couple his blessing.

Although the Mexican Revolution had broken out in 1910, the Wright Ranch was far from the fighting. The family's luck, however, began to run out in August 1912. It was then that "Red Flaggers," troops loyal to the counter-revolutionary General Pascual Orozco, rode up to their corral. With perfunctory grunts, they stripped saddles and blankets off their worn-down, lathered horses and hitched them up on fresh Wright mounts and then galloped off without so much as a thank you.

"They were not real soldiers. They were a bunch of thieves," Maud said later, but in the chaos resulting from two years of fighting, an exchange of worn-out horses for quality mounts was not the worst that could befall a small rancher. In the weeks that followed things got worse. Pancho Villa's ragged troops, who were fighting the "Red Flaggers," rode up to the ranch house and at gunpoint ransacked their home, seized food, blankets, and anything of value. They butchered and ate a few head of cattle, and confiscated, in the name of the Revolution, all the horses. By 1913, homesteaders in the area became fearful for their lives and the Wrights, along with 1,300 other Americans, abandoned their farms and ranches and returned to the United States.

Ed found work at ranches and sawmills in Texas and New Mexico. In the spring of 1914 a son, Johnnie, was born. In the fall of that year, in spite of the danger, Ed and Maud decided to return to the ranch. Soon Frank rejoined them.

Events moved swiftly in Mexico. Orozco's forces were smashed and he was later killed by a posse of Texas ranchers. The leader of the Revolution, Francisco Madero, was murdered. Pancho Villa rose up in revolt against his successor, a half-drunken general named Huerta. Villa, allied with the new leader of the Revolution, Venustiano Carranza, defeated Huerta and drove him out of the country. Villa soon revolted and his Grand Army of the North was broken in a series of battles with federal troops. It had been a hectic time, but the Wrights had survived and prospered. Things quieted down when a large garrison of Federal troops moved into Pearson.

It all seemed peaceful the evening of March 1, 1916, when Maud heard hoofbeats drumming along their ranch road. It must be Ed and Frank returning from Pearson with supplies, she thought. She went to the front door to wave hello when she saw them. There were fifty or more Villistas riding hard toward the ranch house. They were easily recognized by their large floppy sombreros and the crossed gunbelts buckled across their chests. Sadly, at the same time, Ed and Frank rode up leading two pack mules loaded with provisions.

The Villistas confronted them, and at gunpoint seized the bridles of their horses and led them around a bend in the road. The Villista leader ordered his men to seize all livestock and to ransack the ranchhouse for anything useful. This done, he snatched two-year-old Johnnie from his mother's arms handled the child to Senora Marino, the Wrights' maid and took Maud prisoner.

Forced to mount one of their worn-out mules, Maud rode off with the men leaving behind her wrecked ranchhouse, her abandoned baby, and her dreams of a peaceful life. Ed and Frank were nowhere to be seen.

The outlaw band rode all night. Shortly after dawn they reached Cave Valley some thirty miles from the ranch. As they topped a rise and rode into the valley, Maud saw a massive camp. There were, she estimated, more than 3,000 men and their horses. Most of the soldiers were huddled around campfires boiling coffee and frying beans. What she saw was the remnants of Villa's once proud army, whose 50,000 men had once been the most powerful military force on the North American continent. Now, his command was smashed, and Villa was scheming for a way to regain his power in northern Mexico.

Politics, however, were not Maud's concern. Cold, hungry and deeply afraid, she brightened momentarily when she sighted Ed and Frank. They were both mounted on the same horse, their hands tied behind their backs. Spurring her mount, she rode to them and spoke quickly. She told Ed about Johnnie being given to Senora Marino and agreed, if either of them got free, they would find the child, take him to the United States, and bid Mexico farewell forever. Then three horsemen rode up and led Ed and Frank along a trail behind a hill, and the men soon vanished.

Maud was ordered to dismount and squat on the ground by a campfire. She noticed that the usual swarm of "Soldaderas," camp followers who cooked, nursed, loved, and sometimes fought alongside their men, were strangely absent. Also missing were pack animals, bed rolls, and artillery. She assumed this was the remnants of an army stripped for raiding.

Pancho Villa, astride a giant white stallion, trotted up to her campfire, refused to speak to her, but assigned two men to guard her. He told the men that if any man touched her that he would have him shot. Then he rode off.

Maud, fluent in Spanish, listened in growing fear when the men around her laughingly discussed how they planned to kill all the gringos and burn and loot Columbus, New Mexico. Her fears came close to panic when the Villistas who had led off Ed and Frank returned alone. She thought that, surely, the two men had been killed.

Suddenly a squalling bugle call echoed across the valley and the army was on the march. They rode until mid-afternoon when they met up with other troops driving a herd of thirty cattle. The army halted, the cattle were shot, and fires started. The carcasses were chopped into large chunks with machetes and then impaled on sticks or ramrods and held over the fires. Within minutes the bugle blew and the Villistas bit into the meat, burnt black on the outside and bleeding raw on the inside. What wasn't gulped immediately was tied onto their saddles and munched at leisure.

At first Maud, so afraid for her husband and baby, was unable to eat, but within a few days she tore into burnt cowflesh like any *soldadera*.

They marched northwest by devious routes through the mountains hoping to shake off any pursuit by federal troops. They butchered anything their out-riders brought in, scrawny cows, old horses, mules, and even burros. It was not a gourmand's delight but it kept Maud alive. They were on the move day and night. They stripped the ranches in the area, and if there were Americans about, they killed the cowboys. Many slept in their saddles and some slipped from their mounts and hit the rocky ground with a bone-shattering thud. During brief stops Villa came by Maud's campfire to chat with his men.

Maud realized that most of these men were not the tough, experienced, and disciplined fighters of Villa's old division of the north. Many were impressionable youngsters fresh from the farm or rancho. She listened as their chief told them they would become rich from looting Columbus. "And the poor devils believed him," she later recounted.

Villa's motives for attacking Columbus have always been murky. Some historians maintain that a merchant there cheated him on a gun-running deal and he wanted revenge; others say he hoped to capture fresh horses and weapons from the nearby army post to resupply his battered forces. Another theory has it that he hoped the U.S. Army would retaliate by invading Mexico (they did) and he would rally the people against the invader and again become a hero (he didn't). The truth will never be known.

Overhearing officers talk with spies who rode into camp regularly, Maud learned that Villa was expecting a large shipment of guns and ammunition to arrive in Columbus within a few days. When it arrived, the officers said, they would strike.

After a few days, still in shock and grief over the fate of her husband and son, Maud summoned up the nerve to speak to Villa. She asked him why he didn't just shoot her and get it over with. Villa laughed and told her that if she made it through this march and was still alive when they reached Columbus, he would let her go. As he rode off, Maud realized he didn't believe she would survive their trek though the mountains of Chihuahua.

After nearly a week of marching, sometimes for ten hours without stopping even for water, they emerged onto the plains near the New Mexico border. There they attacked the American-owned Palomas Cattle Company. She watched as they captured an American cowboy and shot him off his horse. When he fell to the ground one of the mounted raiders reached down, grabbed his hair and dragged him while others whooping and hollering shot him half a dozen times. They butchered several hundred head of cattle, ate them, and moved on.

At one time, they did not eat or drink for more than thirty-six hours, and several of the men collapsed and died from hunger, cold, and exposure. After nine days they camped a few miles south of Columbus near the little village of Palomas. There Villa decided that, because of a shortage of ammunition, only four hundred handpicked men would take part in the raid.

One of the officers offered Maud a rifle, telling her she would be required to ride into Columbus and shoot her countrymen. Maud later recounted, "Instead of taking it, I had to open my big mouth and tell him if I ever got my hands on a gun he was the first person I would shoot, and I really meant it." She believed, she said, "I could have gotten two or three of them before they got me. I thought about it a lot."

After midnight on March 9, Villa, Maud, and the selected men converged in a draw about half a mile from Columbus. The four hundred residents there were huddled among mostly adobe dwellings and a few frame houses. There were two hotels, several general purpose stores, and a railroad depot, which lay astride tracks that stretched eastward to El Paso and westward to Douglas, Arizona.

Although the borderlands were always dangerous, the villagers felt safe while the soldiers of the United States Army's Thirteenth Cavalry Regiment were camped near their homes.

The Villistas, however, were waiting silently until they saw signal lights on a hill just west of town. Then about four o'clock in the morning, while Columbus bathed in the yellowish glow of a full moon, Villa gave the word to attack.

Screaming "Viva Villa" and "Muerte a los gringos," the men galloped into the town shooting and burning. Soon Columbus was engulfed in flame. Americans, men and women, some with small children in their arms, half-clad and dazed, stumbled into the streets to be shot down by the raiders as their homes burned.

Susan Moore, the wife of a Columbus store owner, recalled, "About 4:30 in the morning I was awakened by some shots. . . . That is a machine gun," she told her husband. The two dressed quickly. A few minutes later the couple heard glass shatter and saw a raider with, "the butt of his gun smashing in the west bedroom window." Then the front door burst open and a dozen Villistas poured into their home.

As John Moore stepped between the invaders and his wife, Susan said, "The leader raised his gun and shot and the others raised their sabers and began shooting and stabbing him."

One of the men, Susan said, "with his gun pointed at my head demanded 'gold and money' but I told him I had none." Then he spied Susan's wedding band, grabbed her and tried to wrestle off the ring. Afraid the tight ring would not come off and the raider would cut off her finger, she twisted it off and handed it to him. As he admired his new trophy, Susan stared helplessly at the prone body of her beloved husband laying in a pool of spreading blood. Shocked, she knew he was dying. One of the raiders stripped off John's wedding ring, another dangled John's pocket watch while a third, with a grin, began to strip off his clothes.

While the raiders were distracted, Susan spun around, dashed into the kitchen and out the back door. She ran as fast as she could. Suddenly, bullets whistled past her ears and then there was a sharp blow striking her right leg. She knew she had been hit.

Susan staggered fifty yards and fell. She pulled herself up and, hopping on one leg and dragging the other, she reached a barbed wire fence. Heaving herself over the barbs, she crawled behind mesquite bushes and lay there bleeding and covered with mud. She thought that surely her time had come. She tore her petticoat, bound her leg, and groaning, fell unconscious.

While Susan lay wounded, the soldiers of the American Thirteenth Cavalry Regiment stationed near the town roused into action. Within minutes they brought a machine gun into action, and that coupled with accurate rifle fire began cutting down the raiders in large numbers.

Seeing a light burning in the Thirteenth Regiment's cookhouse, half a dozen raiders barged in. Undismayed, one the the cooks, cursing, drenched the invaders with boiling army coffee. Another burly cook, swinging a rolling pin, smashed the skull of another Villista. The rest of the raiders beat a hasty retreat from the hornet's nest of outraged cavalry cooks.

Villa watched the carnage from a nearby hill and, realizing the raid was turning into a disaster as his men began fleeing the town, spurred his horse and turned south. In the confusion Maud rode up to him and asked if he was going to keep his promise to her. Villa nodded and pointed her north.

The freed Maud set out toward the flaming town and spurred her tired mule into a trot. Although bullets were flying past her head, she was free at last. As she reached Columbus her mule, frightened by the shooting, bucked and tried to bolt. Using all her strength to curb the crazed animal, Maud dismounted and led him toward the fighting. Avoiding the sprawled bodies of dead and dying raiders she heard a faint voice calling. It was one of the men who had been assigned to guard her. He was lying on the ground with blood streaming from a lethal head wound. In the light from a burning building she recognized him as the man who had continually taunted her. Every morning he had greeted her with vicious threats.

Maud stared at the sword lying by the man's side. Her first thought was to plunge it through his heart. It would be, she later confessed a waste of time. The man was dying. Lying alongside him was his dead horse, with an ornate silver-mounted saddle. She pulled it off the dead beast and placed it over the worn saddle on her mule. She left the man to die alone in the dark.

Maud marched on. As the shooting died and dawn began to break, she sighted a windmill. Without water for more than twenty-four hours, she and the mule both half ran and half trotted toward the stock pond. As the morning haze cleared, she saw the ranch house and the corral. After woman and mount had gulped greedily from the pond, she locked the mule in the corral and walked toward the ranchhouse. In the faint light she saw a man's body sprawled dead on the porch. Then she heard groaning.

Following the sound out into the desert, she spotted Mrs. Susan Moore lying in a pool of blood. Maud dragged the woman to the ranchhouse, found some cloth, cleaned off the dirt and blood, and stuffed a towel into the wound hereby choking off the bleeding.

Shortly after sunup, American soldiers burst into the house with guns drawn. Seeing the two women, they quickly carried Mrs. Moore to the makeshift hospital at the army camp and escorted Maud to the American commanding officer, Colonel Herbert J. Slocum. He turned her over to his wife, who cleaned her swollen face, hands and feet, and put her into a hot tub.

It had been nine days of hell, but it was over. But what of her husband and son? On the afternoon of March 10, Mrs. Slocum accompanied Maud on the train to El Paso. As they arrived at the station, Maud was surrounded by a score of reporters who wired her story to newspapers all over the country. Mexican President Carranza promptly sent troops to find Johnnie. They soon found the two-year-old safe in the hands of Senora Molina. Sadly the bodies of Ed and Frank were located. They had been shot to death.

President Carranza ordered a special train to bring Johnnie to El Paso and arranged to have photographs taken of the reunited mother and child to demonstrate his benevolence. It was joy mixed with grief when Maud held Johnnie in her arms and posed for the photographs.

Villa's raid killed ten civilians and eight soldiers; six soldiers and two civilians were wounded. His men burned most of Columbus to the ground. They not only got very little booty, but more than one hundred of his raiders were killed by the U.S. Cavalry. In less than a week, American Brigadier General John J. Pershing led an American army into Mexico. They did not catch Villa but during a year of pursuit they scattered his troops and broke his power in Mexico forever.

Later Maud and Johnnie rejoined her parents at Safford, Arizona. In later years Maud married a New Mexican farmer. They had seven children, two sons and five daughters. She lived ninety-two years and died in 1980. She never returned to Mexico.

FAST GUNS AND DEAD MEN:
THE STORY OF JOHN WESLEY HARDIN

Leon Claire Metz

THE NAME JOHN WESLEY Hardin sounds friendly enough, perhaps because he was named for John Wesley, the founder of Methodism. Hardin's father was a Methodist preacher, and John himself first saw daylight on May 26, 1853, in a modest home along the Red River in Bonham, Texas. He became one of ten children. All except he and his brother Joseph turned out well. Of course, Joe Hardin became an attorney. A mob later lynched Joe at Comanche, Texas, although not likely because he was an lawyer.

John Hardin began his career early, in school stabbing another young student although not seriously. Five years later, in October 1868, during an outdoor party, John took to wrestling Madge, a black man, the match no doubt originating in fun. When the black boy bested him, John had trouble accepting that. The two met again days later, John on horseback, the black youth walking. John claimed the black man grabbed his horse's reins, so what was Hardin to do except shoot him five times. The black man became victim number one, and John Wesley Hardin became a wanted man.

With the federal army now seeking him, Hardin fled to Trinity County, Texas, where at Hickory Creek Crossing in December he ambushed three Union soldiers (two with a shotgun) crossing the steam. Nearby farmers buried them in the creek bed.

John then rode over to Navarro County south of Corsicana where he worked as a schoolteacher. One female student later testified that "John Wesley Hardin prayed before class every morning."

After three months Hardin gave up teaching to work as a cowboy in the same county. There he shot a federal soldier who apparently recognized him as a wanted man. With his man-killing count now at five, Hardin in January 1870 rode into Towash, Texas, where in December he killed Benjamin Bradley during a drunken brawl.

John explained that killing to his father, James Gibson Hardin, and the father, knowing his son to be a good boy, cautioned him to be more careful. John said he would, but less than two weeks later on January 20, Hardin and a circus roustabout tangled at Brenham, Texas. Hardin put a bullet in him.

From Brenham, Hardin drifted over to Kosse in southwestern Limestone County where he happened upon a young lady who said she had trouble sleeping alone. John agreed to help resolve this problem, but they had no sooner gotten comfortable than her husband or boyfriend broke into the room. With the cuckold man threatening and swearing angrily, Hardin tried to buy him off with a handful of change. The man grabbed for the money, but in his haste he scattered dimes and pennies all over the floor. As the boyfriend fumbled around on hands and knees recovering loose change, upon rising he found himself staring straight into the face of an unsmiling youth holding a six-shooter that exploded. Hardin had now racked up number eight.

Back in Brenham, a tall gambler named Phil Coe dubbed Hardin as "Young Seven Up," a reference to a popular card game in which one needed seven cards to win. Not long afterwards, Hardin met William Preston Longley, a dangerous Texas gunman and manslayer. The two men became rivals in terms of killing people, although Longley would eventually be legally hanged. Hardin didn't weep.

Hardin now drifted toward home, his parents living at Mount Calm in Hill County, Texas. For a while he taught school and helped preach on Sunday, but by January 1871, he again said good-bye to the quiet life. He drifted to Lakeview, Texas, where lawmen charged him with one count of horse theft, and four counts of murder. However, while being transferred to Waco for trial, Hardin killed his guard, Private Jim Smally, and escaped.

Within two weeks officers again snared John Wesley Hardin, his captors being identified by Hardin only as Smith, Jones, and Davis. While these names could have been factual, the possibility of three men traveling together with such common monikers defies good sense. Hardin probably couldn't remember the correct names, so his memoirs mentioned only phony ones. At any rate, as the officers and Hardin camped for the night, Hardin loosened his bonds, killed two men with their own shotgun and the other with a revolver. A seventeen-year-old boy now had twelve dead men sprawled on his back trail.

In early March 1871, John Wesley Hardin fleeing his hectic past, joined a cattle drive heading north along the Chisholm Trail from Texas toward Abilene, Kansas. It proved quite adventurous, with Hardin's first killings being two Oklahoma Indians whom the youth said had attacked him. (His memoirs later mentioned that he hoped to meet a few Indians on the war path.)

After fording the Little Arkansas River, in the confusion two different herds merged, one with Hardin as an outrider, the other being a trail herd driven north by Mexican vaqueros. Tempers from both outfits ran short, and when the smoke cleared, six vaqueros lay dead. Hardin had slain five of them, the youth now having killed twelve men, the last five or so within a few days of his eighteenth birthday.

Hardin now became the talk of the trail, Fred Duderstadt, a well-known stockman from DeWitt County, Texas, mentioning in his journal that "cowboys stopped by the Hardin night camps just to get a glimpse of the famed Kid gunman. . . ."

From this moment on, John Wesley Hardin would be forevermore known in many circles as "Little Arkansas," or just "Arkansas," the reference being not to his height, since he was average in that respect, but to his shooting skills on the banks of the Little Arkansas River.

When Hardin reached Abilene, Kansas, he was paid off and thereafter hit the saloons and brothels. Meanwhile, the city fathers on April 15, 1881, had appointed William Butler Hickock, better known as Wild Bill Hickok, as the town marshal. He was almost thirty-four and had been on the job six weeks when John Wesley reached town.

The two men quickly made themselves known to each other, Hardin's memoirs indicating that they got along well. Hickok of course had rules against carrying firearms, and Hardin openly toted two of them. But that "lawlessness" didn't initially seem to bother Hickok.

Still, both men drank too much, and both had short fuses, and one day with both apparently in their cups, Hickok ordered Hardin to either remove his guns or be arrested. Hardin removed them from holsters, handed them butts forward toward the marshal, then spun them around and backed Hickok down.

The question therefore is, "Did it happen? Or did Hardin just claim it happened?" Most historians do not believe the story, and no other account exists except for Hardin's memoirs. This writer believes it did happen although admittedly Hardin's memoirs were frequently untruthful, or at least distorted. However, this was the kind of stunt Hardin would lay awake at night and dream about. To Hardin he was the best meeting the best. Such an act was not meant to threaten Hickok, it was meant to impress him. It was classic Hardin.

As for Hickok, he had nothing to prove anyway. He knew what was happening, and why it was happening, and he probably just shook his head and walked away.

Oddly, just a few hours later, as Hardin and a one-armed friend named Paine sat in a restaurant, a group of rowdy customers began cursing Texans. Hardin rose and said, "I'm a Texan."

One of the fellows jumped up, both drew but Hardin drew first. He wounded the man in the arm, and as he lurched forward, Hardin shot him in the head. Hardin then dashed outside, vaulted on his horse and rode to his cow camp a few miles distant. Apparently no one followed.

On August 6, with the cattle season closing down in Abilene, Hardin, his cousin, Gip Clements, and a cattleman friend, staggered into the American Hotel late at night and stumbled up the rickety stairs to their rooms. Hardin and Clements shared the same bed in the same room, whereas the cattleman had a room alongside.

Hardin later wrote that a sneak thief slipped into his room, and Hardin shot him. Then because Hardin feared Hickok would not understand the killing of a thief, John Wesley left immediately for Texas.

But there was no sneak thief, although a story did immediately start that Hardin had killed a man for snoring. The newspapers mentioned only that the cattleman victim had been sitting up in bed reading when a bullet tore out his heart. Here's what likely happened.

Within an hour after going to their rooms, the cattleman's raucous snoring shook the paper thin walls. Hardin and Clements yelled a few times for him to roll over, and he probably did. But then he started snoring again, and that brought more yells. So the cattleman then decided to sit up in bed and read, thinking that might keep him awake. Of course, he fell asleep and started snoring once more. Next door, Hardin, not knowing the man was sitting up, decided he would "really" wake him, so he sent a bullet through the wall. When only silence echoed from the other side, Hardin, probably realizing he had fired too low, dressed in a hurry and started back to Texas.

BACK IN GONZALES COUNTY on October 6, 1871, John Wesley Hardin resumed his practice of wearing guns, only to be stopped by black policeman Green Paramore who put a revolver in Hardin's face and told him such practices were illegal. Hardin stuck the weapons out, butts forward, then spun one gun in his hand. It exploded, and Paramore went down, instantly dead. A column in the *San Antonio Express* said "It is probable that no desperado [meaning Hardin] who ever drew the breath of life has killed so many men. Some fifteen or twenty have fallen before the smoking muzzle of his revolver, and these are not a drop in the bucket to the number who have vicariously died by his hand. . . ."

Meanwhile, a posse rode down from Austin to avenge Paramore. Hardin allegedly killed three. The only known account is in Hardin's memoirs.

A year later on February 2, 1872, the eighteen-year-old John Wesley Hardin married the fourteen-year-old Jane Bowen, an articulate young lady who throughout her brief lifetime maintained a pugnacious defense of her husband. The couple initially lived upstairs in her father's house, and they would have three children. Still, Wes was something of an absentee husband and father. With the law constantly after him, he would spend more time sleeping on the ground than in his wife's bed.

After a brief honeymoon, Hardin drifted down to Trinity County where he engaged Phil Sublett in tenpins (bowling). As usual, an argument ensued over who won, so Hardin reached for his pocket gun—the first known instance of Hardin being a three-gun man—and jammed it in Sublett's ear. Bystanders broke it up, so the two men met shortly afterwards in the street where Hardin shot Sublett with a six-shooter, and Sublett shot him with a shotgun. Both staggered away, Hardin being the more seriously wounded. Shortly afterwards, he surrendered to Sheriff Richard Reagan, and recovered in jail. On September 22, Reagan transferred him to an Austin jail, and from there he went to Gonzales County to face several murder indictments. However, on November 19, someone slipped him a saw. . . . and John Wesley Hardin was quickly running loose again.

During this period of the early 1870s, in and around Gonzales and numerous surrounding counties, the Sutton-Taylor Feud flared. Although both families were Texas cattlemen, each had separate loyalties. The Taylors—of which Hardin aligned himself—were unrepentant Confederates; the Suttons tended to cooperate with—or at least accept—Union occupation forces.

With Texas still under Reconstruction, a Unionist named Jack Helm assumed authority in east-central Texas. He would bring incorrigible Texans (Confederate supporters: outlaws, cattle thieves, rowdies) to justice.

Meanwhile, Hardin rode free, pausing long enough in Cuero, Texas, to shoot a man for taking his hands out of his pockets when John told him not to. Then on the 15th of May, 1873, he likely participated in the shooting deaths of Jake Christman and Jim Cox.

Shortly afterwards he rode into Albuquerque, Texas, in western Gonzales

County, and with a shotgun sent Jack Helm to the Promised Land. This was Hardin's most sensational killing yet, and Helm's death—celebrated and approved by much of the state—propelled Hardin onto front pages all over Texas.

With the East Texas Sutton-Taylor Feud now underway, Hardin and Taylor partisans laid siege to Captain Joe Tumlinson's ranch, Tumlinson being a former state policeman. With roughly two hundred men involved altogether, the siege lasted for two days and one night. The struggle ended with a peace treaty, and Tumlinson—out of all the fighters—eventually died in bed of old age.

This left only Billy Sutton, a well-to-do cattleman, still living and he dispatched most of his cattle along the trail toward Kansas, announcing that he would take ship across the Gulf, leaving from Indianola, and meet everybody in the Kansas destination. But that was not to be. On March 4, 1874, two of Hardin's relatives and closest comrades, James and William Taylor shot Sutton and his foreman, Gabe Slaughter, dead on the wharf. The Sutton-Taylor Feud had ended.

In the meantime, John Wesley Hardin had been collecting quite a sizable cattle herd of his own, none of it purchased. He owed much of the credit to his attorney brother Joe, for Joe had buried the cattle origins deep in a maze of sophisticated paperwork. During the week of May 21, Wes Hardin rode over to Brown County to take possession of some of these cattle, then returned to Comanche to be around during the birth of Joe's son. Well, Hardin celebrated a little heavy that evening, and came stumbling out of a saloon only to encounter Brown County deputy sheriff Charles Webb. Exactly what happened next is controversial, but the two men engaged in surly banter only a minute or so, and then the bullets started to fly.

When the smoke cleared, Webb was dead and Hardin was running. He bundled up his wife and children, and fled to Florida.

Back in Comanche County, John Wesley Hardin's brother Joe went to jail charged with theft of cattle, the attorney's dishonest paperwork finally catching up with him. Then on Friday, June 5, 1874, a mob entered the jail late at night, overpowered the guards, removed Joe and two Dixon boys, all three considered part of the Wes Hardin Gang, led them two miles from the community, and lynched them from an oak tree.

On June 21, a mob of thirty-five masked men broke into the DeWitt County jail, dragged out three additional members of the "Hardin gang," and lynched them near the cemetery.

As for Hardin himself, the State moved slowly, but on January 20, 1875, it offered a "reward of $4,000 for the apprehension and delivery of the body of the notorious murderer, John Wesley Hardin. . . ." This reward made Wes Hardin the most wanted man ever in the state of Texas. And Hardin realized now that with such a sum riding on his head, the Texas Rangers would follow him across the ice cap. So he rounded up his family and fled to Florida, where he went by the *alias* of John Swain.

In Florida an irony arose that with Hardin on the run, his family paid the price. They did without, hid, lied in his behalf while he, a fugitive from justice, imprisoned them in circle of grief while he caroused in the Florida saloons and wagering houses.

But the Florida escapade ended on August 23, 1877. Texas Ranger John Barclay Armstrong, plus a Florida sheriff and his deputy, climbed aboard a Pensacola train carrying John Wesley Hardin home. They caught the gunman sitting alongside the aisle smoking his pipe. After clubbing him into submission, they put him in chains, and started him on his way to Austin, Texas.

Upon arrival at the Austin jail, the Rangers carried Hardin over their head through a huge throng of well-wishers. On September 18, Comanche Sheriff F. E. Wilson and several deputies arrived to escort Hardin to trial. Furthermore, the governor assigned thirty rangers from Company E to accompany them, one of these being Sergeant James Gillett. The sergeant referred to Hardin as "the most desperate criminal in Texas." Heavily shackled and handcuffed, Hardin stumbled along between Gillett and ranger Henry Thomas, the officers describing Hardin as "walking very slowly between us."

The *Daily Democratic Statesman* wrote, "A very large crowd of people gathered to see this knight of the six-shooter as he passed from the jail to the carriage." Some twenty or more rangers then rode before and behind the carriage along the road to Lampasas, a newspaper reporting that "more people rushed to see him than if he had been a rhinoceros. . . ."

Hardin's two-day trial for the murder of Brown County deputy sheriff Charles Webb started on Friday, September 28, Wes being represented by five lawyers. The trial lasted several days, although testimony was not preserved. The state introduced eight to ten witnesses, the defense two, although none were identified. After deliberating nearly three hours, the jury returned a verdict of murder in the second degree, and assessed Hardin's punishment as twenty-five years of hard labor in the Texas state penitentiary.

In prison Hardin resisted adjusting. In his mind he had never killed anyone who did not deserve it, so why was he given such an awful sentence? He made several escape attempts, and was brutally beaten. Then as the months and years slowly passed, he claimed a disabling illness, perhaps real, perhaps imagined, this as much as anything being a way of avoiding hard labor.

He could send a letter once a week, scratching it out, leaving margins at top, bottom and sides, front and back. Then he would fill in the margins, his tiny scrawl being almost impossible to read.

He joined the prison debating team, writing his wife that he and another man had debated whether or not women should have the right to vote. Hardin took the stance that women did not have the rights, and he won the debate.

He wrote his son John Wesley Hardin, Jr., on July 3, 1887, saying, "Truth is a rare and precious gem. . . . Let me today urge upon you the great necessity of observing and adhering to truth and justice. These will make you the most noble, the most generous, the most manly, the bravest boy in your neighborhood, just as your father would have you be, and by the grace of God you can be."

Hardin commenced the study of law, and on January 1, 1889, wrote the lawmakers of Texas, offering five specific prison reforms regarding homicides. He suggested a softening of jail conditions as well as a reduction in length of imprisonment. Then on January 1, 1893, he wrote Governor James Stephen Hogg, saying, "my highest hope, object, aim and ambition is to yet lead a life of usefulness & peace in the path of rectitude and righteousness."

On October 29, 1893, he petitioned Governor Hogg again, his long rambling letter pointing out perceived errors in his trial. Now that he had explained his unjust confinement to the chief executive, he closed by writing, "If you think so, please be kind enough to grant me a pardon."

John Wesley Hardin walked out of prison a free man on February 7, 1894, his wife Jane having died probably of consumption nearly two years earlier. In Gonzales County he took the Bar examination, and on July 21, the District Court of Gonzales licensed Hardin to practice in any of the Texas district and lower courts.

Little is known about Hardin's brief east Texas law practice. One Gonzales newspaper, *La Opinion Del Pueblo,* thanked Hardin for his successful legal efforts on behalf of the Mexican-American community. The newspaper said Hardin represented six Mexicans who on October 6 protected themselves and their families, and then went to jail. In court Hardin defended the group "with such eloquence and spirit" that the judge released three men and bonded the others out.

Hardin then moved to Junction, Texas, to practice law. There he met the attractive Carolyn "Callie" Lewis. She was fifteen and acted every bit of it; Hardin was forty-one and feeling every day of it. They married in London, Texas, on January 9, 1895, and within a week had separated. She went back to her parents; he moved to Pecos, Texas, in March filling attempted murder charges against George A. "Bud" Frazer, a former Texas Ranger. Frazer had allegedly attempted to kill James Miller, a shirt-tail relative of Hardin's who would himself go on to become a hired gunman known as "Killin'" Jim Miller. On March 5, Miller obtained a change of venue to El Paso, Texas.

The Frazer trial concluded in El Paso in mid April with a hung jury. So while Miller returned to Pecos, Hardin stayed in El Paso, hanging out his law shingle on the second floor of the Wells Fargo building downtown. He also started thinking about writing his autobiography.

On May 1, Hardin entered the Acme Saloon, lost steadily, and insisting he had been cheated, he scooped up the pot and walked off. No one interfered. On the following night he walked into the Gem Saloon, and grew weary of losing. So he stuck a .41 caliber Colt in dealer Phil Baker's face, snapping, "Since you are trying to be so cute, just give me back the ninety-five dollars I lost." Hardin stuck the bills in his pocket, holstered the Colt, and strolled out humming, *Annie Laurie*. He later told the *El Paso Morning Times* that he took the money "in order to acquit myself manly and bravely."

A few days later a judge found him guilty of "unlawfully carrying a pistol." The court fined him $25.

Meanwhile, in November 1894, a Grand Jury in Eddy County, New Mexico, indicted Martin Mrose for a number of violations, acts causing the southern New Mexico Livestock Protective Association to offer a $1,000 award for his arrest. Martin promptly fled to Juarez, Mexico, directly across the Rio Grande from El Paso, Texas. He took Beulah Mrose with him, she being his mistress/wife.

After being jailed in Juarez, Mrose retained Hardin as his attorney, paying him $250. However, when Hardin became more interested in Beulah than in her husband, the client/attorney relationship deteriorated. In fact, with Beulah now having possession of much of Martin's ill-gotten gains, Hardin began spending it. On June 18, 1895, Hardin took Mrs. Beulah Mrose as "a full partner in my manuscript and business matters."

With his newly acquired funds, Hardin purchased a half interest in El Paso's Wigwam Saloon. It was supposed to have become "Hardin's Wigwam Saloon," but John kept drinking up and gambling away the profits. He quickly lost his business interest.

On June 29, 1895, Martin Mrose attempted to slip into El Paso from Juarez after dark and speak with his wife. But word leaked out, no doubt from a jealous Hardin, and four lawmen met Martin at the bridge and shot him dead with shotgun and rifle fire. At Concordia Cemetery, only Beulah and her attorney, John Wesley Hardin, showed up as mourners.

Nevertheless, the relationship between Beulah and Hardin quickly deteriorated although they did finish the manuscript, a book entitled *The Life of John Wesley Hardin as Written by Himself*. It is still in print today with the University of Oklahoma Press.

But during a brief Hardin's absence, a drunken Beulah flirted with police officer John Selman, Jr., and he jailed her for carrying a revolver. An enraged Hardin, upon returning the next afternoon, had Beulah on her knees in their furnished rooms, threatening to make her write a note saying she was committing suicide. As screaming and yelling echoed up and down the corridors, landlady Annie Williams sent for the police.

Young John Selman subsequently arrested Hardin for disturbing the police, and Hardin posted a $100 peace bond.

Days later Beulah pressed charges against Hardin, city officers arresting Hardin after finding him in the Acme Saloon having a few drinks to clear his head.

A Justice of the Peace fined Hardin $5, but Hardin did not have the money. So the judge reduced the fine to $2.50. Hardin didn't have that either, but agreed to return and pay it later. As for Beulah, she left town, she and Hardin never seeing each other again.

Following Beulah's departure, Hardin made drunken, imprudent statements about having hired officers to kill Martin Mrose. Jeff Milton, one of those officers, grabbed Hardin by the ear and marched him to the newspaper office where on August 10, Hardin published a humiliating public apology.

John Wesley Hardin had now hit the bottom of the barrel, both literally and figuratively. He had nowhere to go, and no money to go on. He had no family, no funds, and no friends unless one counted the multitude of toddies who followed him about. It was time for him to go, and he probably knew it.

On August 18, John Wesley Hardin and Constable John Selman met in the street, and quarreled. Hardin claimed to be unarmed, but said, "I'll get a gun, and make you shit like a wolf all around the block."

On the following night, August 19, 1895, at about 10 P.M. Hardin walked into the Acme Saloon on San Antonio Street, bellied up to the bar, took a drink, rolled the dice, turned to the bartender and softly said, "Brown, you have four sixes to beat."

At that instant Constable John Selman stepped up behind, fired four quick shots, and Hardin was history. He was buried in El Paso's Concordia Cemetery, three graves south of Martin Mrose. Today his grave is one of El Paso's best-known tourist attractions.

John Selman went on trial for murder in April 1896, was released by virtue of a hung jury. While out awaiting retrial, U.S. Deputy Marshal George Scarborough shot him to death in an El Paso alley on Easter Sunday, 1896. Selman is also buried in Concordia Cemetery.

George Scarborough was acquitted of murder, resigned his commission, became a cattle/railroad detective, was wounded by outlaws in southern Arizona, and died on the operating table at Deming, New Mexico, on April 5, 1900. He died four years later to the day after John Selman died on the operating table in El Paso.

John Selman, Jr. took a fifteen-year-old girl to Juarez allegedly to marry, was jailed, escaped, lost his El Paso police job, and thereafter became a wanderer. He died of a heart attack at Belton, Texas, at the age of sixty-seven.

As for Beulah Mrose, she became a street derelict and was found dead in Sacramento.

BILL CODY GETS BUFFALOED

Rod Miller

EMBARRASSED AND DISARMED, WILLIAM F. Cody and Lew Simpson rode back to camp at the mercy of their captors.

Cody, himself, explained:

> [W]e had to drive our cattle about a mile and a half to a creek to water them. . . . On our way back to camp we suddenly observed a party of twenty horsemen rapidly approaching us. . . . When they had come up to us, one of the party, evidently the leader, rode out in front and said:
>
> "How are you Mr. Simpson?"
>
> "You've got the best of me, sir," said Simpson, who did not know him.
>
> "Well, I rather think I have," coolly replied the stranger.
>
> [T]hese men, much to our surprise had got the drop on us . . . so quietly and quickly that it was accomplished before we knew it.
>
> "I'll trouble you for your six shooters, gentlemen," said the leader.
>
> "I'll give 'em to you in a way you don't want," replied Simpson.
>
> The next moment three guns were leveled at Simpson. "If you make a move you're a dead man," said the leader.

Throughout the exchange, Cody sat silent—stunned, perhaps, and scared—in his saddle.

Not the typical picture one draws of Buffalo Bill, the legendary Pony Express rider, soldier, scout, Indian fighter, buffalo hunter.

Then again, he was eleven years old at the time.

It happened in 1857, and Cody's role was a minor one in a small act on the stage of the Utah War—which has, itself, largely faded into obscurity. At the time, however, Washington, D.C., Utah Territory, and the entire United States were consumed by a frustrated government's foray against intransigent Mormons.

The story had its beginnings in upstate New York in the early 1820s with the boy Joseph Smith's heavenly visitations and continued with the formal organization of the Church of Jesus Christ of Latter-day Saints—commonly known then and now as the Mormons—in 1830. Hounded out of New York, Smith and his followers were later forced out of Ohio, then Missouri, settling in Illinois where the Prophet Joseph was murdered by a mob in 1844.

Many believed that would be the end of his church. But one of Smith's underlings, Brigham Young, assumed leadership of the sect and, when forced out of Illinois, led an exodus of Biblical proportions beginning in 1846 to the Great Basin, in what was then Mexico, where Mormon settlement began in 1847. A religious society was established, founded on principles considered un-American. Its tenets included communal economics, plural marriage, and a theocratic government in which the line between church and state was hazy, if not invisible.

In 1848, with the end of the Mexican War and the Treaty of Guadalupe Hidalgo, the largely independent Mormon Kingdom of God came under United States jurisdiction. Attempts to establish a Territorial government independent of church influence were unsuccessful, thanks to inept officials sent by the federal government and a lack of interest on the part of the Mormons in cooperating with a nation that had refused assistance when they were under attack during their residence in the States.

The situation came to a head in 1857 when the federal government declared the Mormons in rebellion and sent a large contingent of the United States Army to whip them into submission. Brigham Young, then Governor of Utah Territory, had no official notice of the expedition. Upon hearing of the Army's approach, he declared martial law, activated the militia, and said that he would "treat them [the Army] . . . the same as if they were an avowed mob."

A *Deseret News* editorial further testifies to Mormon attitudes:

It is most readily obvious to all that the administration of our Government is becoming rotten even to loathing, when anonymous liars and a whoring, lying, venomous late associate justice [a reference to federal appointee W. W. Drummond—but that's another story] can incite the expenditure of millions of public treasure in an unjust, outrageously wicked and illegal movement against a peaceful and known zealously loyal people inhabiting a region they had reclaimed and which no other ever had desired. . . . [C]ease your ungodly crusade against an innocent people, and return to the old landmarks of meteing even-handed justice to all.

Colonel Albert Sidney Johnston, field commander of the marching Army, was no less vitriolic. This, from a dispatch to his superiors:

> The communication of Brigham Young . . . and the act of the Legislative assembly at the last session show a matured and settled design on the part of the sect of Mormons to hold & occupy this territory independent of and irrespective of the authority of the United States. They have with premeditation placed themselves in rebellion against the Union and entertain the insane design of establishing a form of government thoroughly repugnant to our institutions—occupying as they do an attitude of rebellion and open defiance, connected with numerous overt acts of treason. . . . I have ordered that wherever they are met in arms that they be treated as enemies.

An army of some three thousand soldiers in the field requires vast amounts of goods for sustenance. When that army is on the march across barren plains and mountains hundreds of miles from sources of supply and populated by often-hostile Indian tribes, transporting those goods is a complex and hazardous undertaking.

Which brings us back to Buffalo Bill. His sister explains his involvement:

> [Russell,] Majors & Waddell contracted to transport stores and beef cattle to the army massing against the Mormons in the fall of 1857. . . . Will was assigned duty as "extra" under Lew Simpson, an experienced wagon-master, and was subject to his orders only. There was the double danger of Mormons and Indians, so the pay was good. Forty dollars a month in gold looked like a large sum to an eleven-year-old.

Simpson's train consisted of twenty-five Murphy wagons, each loaded with three tons of freight and pulled by several yokes of oxen. Thirty-one men made up the crew. According to Bill Cody, "All were heavily armed with Colt's pistols and Mississippi yagers, and every one always had his weapons handy so as to be prepared for any emergency." Except Mormon raiders, it seems.

Along with others in the caravan, Simpson's train followed the well-worn path northwest from Leavenworth through Kansas, entering Nebraska near the Big Sandy and meeting the Platte River near Fort Kearney. Cody's account notes the familiar landmarks and way stations along the westering trail—Court House Rock, Chimney Rock, Scott's Bluff, Fort Laramie, Red Buttes, Independence Rock, and Devil's Gate. The only incident of note in the early going was a buffalo stampede through the train along the Platte River, resulting in broken wagons, tangled teams, and scattered stock.

Cody's encounter with the Mormons occurred near the Green River at a place known since as Simpson's Hollow. He picks up the narrative:

> Simpson saw that he was taken at a great disadvantage, and thinking it not advisable to risk the lives of the party by any rash act on his part, he said, "I see now that you have the best of me, but who are you, anyhow?"
>
> "I am Joe Smith," was the reply.

In this, Cody's recollection is obviously mistaken, "Joe" Smith having been dead and in his grave in Illinois for some thirteen years by this time.

The leader of the Mormon cavalry was Lot Smith. His band, along with others led by the likes of the notorious Porter Rockwell, were ranging through the area harassing soldiers and herds and supply trains. Brigham Young sent out the militia groups with instructions to drive off stock, destroy supplies, burn forage, and do everything possible—short of killing—to make life miserable for the approaching army and to prevent their entry into the Salt Lake Valley.

Simpson's train was the third attacked by Lot Smith and his raiders. Smith, with his twenty followers, had the night before ridden to the edge of the light cast by campfires and asked for the captain of two other trains—a man named Dawson. Smith's account reports:

> I told him I had a little business with him. He inquired the nature of it, and I replied by requesting him to get all of his men and their private property as quickly as possible out of the wagons for I meant to put a little fire to them. He exclaimed: "For God's sake, don't burn the trains." I said it was for His sake that I was going to burn them.

And he did.

While he found some of Dawson's antics under pressure "laughable," Lot

Smith claimed Lew Simpson "was the bravest man I met during the campaign." Smith failed to mention young William F. Cody—unaware as he was of the legendary status in store someday for the lad.

When Cody and company arrived back at camp, all the men were disarmed and under guard, and Simpson admitted they were at a disadvantage without their guns. The fiery Smith claimed the Mormons needed no advantage, and asked what would happen if he returned the arms.

"I'll fight you!" Simpson said.

"[W]e know something about that too," Lot Smith replied, "take up your arms!"

The freighters refused, however, exclaiming, "Not by a damn sight! We came out here to whack bulls, not fight."

According to Smith's account, Lew Simpson said that if he had been there earlier, before the men were disarmed, and they had refused to fight, he would have killed every one of them.

Lot Smith offered Simpson a wagon loaded with provisions so "his crowd of cowardly teamsters" wouldn't starve on the plains. Simpson demanded two, got them, then begged Smith not to burn the train while he was in sight, as "it would ruin his reputation as a wagon master." Smith, though, said he lacked the time to be ceremonious and set the wagons afire.

Cody said they made a spectacular sight, "a very hot, fierce fire" with dense clouds of smoke. "Some of the wagons were loaded with ammunition, and it was not long before loud explosions followed in rapid succession."

According to military records, the three Russell, Majors & Waddell trains torched by the Mormon militia the night of October 4, 1857, resulted in the destruction or ruin of nearly a ton and a half of ham, 92,700 pounds of bacon, 162,900 pounds of flour, 68,832 rations of desiccated vegetables, and similarly large quantities of beans, coffee, sugar, tea, vinegar, and other goods.

A hyperbolic magazine account of the burnings, published in San Francisco in 1890, reported a deadly end for the freighters:

> Taking their arms and equipments and giving them but little provisions, the Mormons forced the men to recross the wilderness to Leavenworth, Kansas, one thousand miles distant, with no means of procuring food or defending themselves against the Indians but their pocket knives. Of the two hundred and thirty men that composed the party, only eight ever reached the border settlements, the remainder having fallen by the knife of the savage, or died from starvation.

The truth of the matter is considerably less dramatic. The four hundred or so men from the supply trains, in fact, pushed on to a site near Fort Bridger where they spent the winter with the troops. The abandoned fort itself consisted of nothing but ashes and ruined stone walls, having been burned by the Mormons, who claimed title to it. Cold, they were, and hungry, but far from starvation. Cody said the larders did become depleted toward spring and that they survived on one-quarter rations and ate "dreadfully emaciated" mules and oxen. "But for the timely arrival of a westward-bound train loaded with provisions for Johnston's army some of our party must certainly have fallen victims to deadly hunger," he wrote.

Throughout the winter, negotiations between Mormon leaders and federal representatives defused the situation and all-out war was avoided. The troops entered Utah Territory peacefully and established Camp Floyd some forty miles southwest of Salt Lake City. It remained, the largest concentration of troops in the nation at the time, until the outbreak of Civil War when the officers and men either left the service to fight for the South (as did the commander, Albert Sidney Johnston, shortly after reassignment) or marched eastward to fight for the Union.

Camp Floyd (renamed Camp Crittenden for Kentucky Senator J. J. Crittenden, since Secretary of War John B. Floyd, for whom it was originally named, had turned against the Union) was dismantled and everything but arms and ammunition has auctioned off piece by piece at bargain basement prices. So the end of the "Utah War" saw Brigham Young and the Mormons once again get the best of the Feds, fattening their coffers considerably at government expense.

Meanwhile, Cody and the bull whackers were long gone, having hit the trail eastward immediately following the winter of 1857–58 at Fort Bridger. The uncompensated loss of wagons and supplies on the expedition eventually led to the bankruptcy of Russell, Majors & Waddell.

"[A]s soon as we could travel," Cody's account reads, "the civil employees of the government, with the teamsters and freighters, started for the Missouri River . . ."

So, having been "buffaloed" by Lot Smith and his Mormon militia raiders, the boy William F. Cody rode off into the sunrise where he would grow up to become the man of Western lore and legend, Buffalo Bill.

THE FOURTH COMPANY

Candy Moulton

SARAH MOULTON STOOD ON the rolling deck of the *Thornton* clutching daughter Lottie's glove-covered fingers in one hand and holding her extended belly with the other. Husband Thomas stood beside her holding Sophia, who was two. She knew the other children, Sarah, Mary Ann, William, Joseph, and James Heber were getting settled on the ship. With other converts to the Church of Jesus Christ of Latter-day Saints, they had journeyed from their home in Irchester, Northampton, England, to board this wooden vessel that even now had sailed from the dock at Liverpool and was headed into the Irish Sea.

Making this trip possible was the Perpetual Emigration Fund (P.E.F.) of the Mormon Church and the careful hoarding of shillings and pounds tucked away in a fruit jar Sarah kept hidden from her family for years. When the opportunity presented itself to travel to America, and across that marvelous land to Great Salt Lake City where Brigham Young had settled his Saints in 1847, Sarah told Thomas the family must make the trip. He hesitated, believing it too costly even with the P.E.F. assistance, until she showed him her fruit jar of money.

But before they could depart, Sarah's sister contracted smallpox and died. She passed the disease to some of her young nieces and nephews, including Lottie. Though the children had recovered, with a pox mark still clearly visible on the four-year-old's hand, Thomas again felt his hopes dashed. He knew she would not pass the health inspection required to board the ship, and they couldn't leave her behind. But Sarah showed her determination that her family was destined to make the journey as she sewed gloves for the youngest daughters. When the Moultons trooped before the ship's health inspectors, luck—Sarah would believe it to be divine providence—was with them. Lottie was not asked to remove her gloves.

Packing for a large family is never easy and certainly the chore wasn't pleasant for Sarah; she had taken only essential items, but after the fateful health inspection while still at the dock and before boarding the ship, she found herself sorting through the family's possessions to reduce the baggage. There wasn't room for everything on the crowded ship. Having jettisoned some of their goods, the concerns and work of preparing for a journey that would take more than half a year were finally behind Sarah. Standing on the ship's deck with Lottie's pox-marked hand firmly clasped in her own, she realized that they were really and truly on their way to America. Once the sails filled, and when the family members had reached and settled into the area they would occupy in the ship on the trans-Atlantic crossing, Sarah relaxed.

Three days later, on May 6, 1856, she gave birth to her seventh child; the eldest daughter, also called Sarah, had been the offspring of Thomas and his first wife, Esther, who had died. Christened Charles Alma, the baby was one of three born to the English, Scottish, and Scandanavian people who made up the party of immigrants led by James Grey Willie. Willie had been designated as captain of the travelers under the strict Mormon organization that replicated a military company. They were part of a pioneering experiment that would go terribly wrong before they reached Deseret, the state known now as Utah. For them it was Zion, a place to join fellow believers in the gospel of the Latter-day Saints that had been given to Joseph Smith decades earlier.

WHILE LIVING IN PALMYRA, New York, Joseph Smith had been visited by Moroni, whom he thought to be an angel of the Lord. Believing himself to be a new prophet, Smith founded the Church of Jesus Christ of Latter-day Saints, or Mormon Church, on April 6, 1830. Just six months later he announced that he had received a Revelation: "And ye are called to bring to pass the gathering . . . (and) they shall be gathered in unto one place upon the face of this land."

Joseph Smith accepted the Revelation as direction from the Lord and promised the gathering place "would be called Zion."

Smith relocated the church from its birthplace in New York first to Ohio then to Missouri, and finally to Nauvoo, Illinois. Hostility and outright attacks on the Mormon people precipitated the moves. In Illinois on June 27, 1844, a mob killed Smith and his brother Hyrum. Subsequently Brigham Young, who had been President of the Quorum of the Twelve Apostles, took over for Smith. When the persecution grew too strong in the winter of 1846, Young gathered the Saints and led them west yet again. This time they went to the Missouri River, where they established a camp on the west side of the wide channel during the winter of 1846–47. That camp became known as Winter Quarters and was the primary staging point for all Mormon migrations after that time.

In the spring of 1847, Young took his Pioneer Party, consisting of 144 men and boys, three women, and two children across the land known as The Great American Desert. He sought a place of refuge for his followers, a place where they would no longer be persecuted as they had been in the years since the founding of the church. He sought Zion.

Though ill with what was most likely Rocky Mountain Spotted Fever caused from the bite of a tick as the Pioneer Party crossed South Pass in present-day Wyoming, Brigham Young designated the Great Salt Lake Valley, on the western side of the Wasatch Mountain Range, as The Place. It became Zion, and the location to which all Mormons in those early days of the infant church wanted to travel.

Smith had started the church practice of proselytizing, sending out missionaries to meet with—and convert—Indians in the West shortly after the church founding. In 1837, the missionaries left America and headed to England, where within eight months, they baptized some 2,000 converts. The baptismal figure rose to more than 7,000 people by 1840, and the following year the family of Thomas Moulton joined the Mormon fold.

Sarah's friend, Mrs. John Tingey, urged her to attend Mormon meetings led by John Tingey, an early convert in England who served as a Mormon Church branch president in Irchester. Sarah did not go to the meetings, but one day Mrs. Tingey brought to the Moulton home a religious tract, "The Voice of Warning" by Parley P. Pratt, one of the church leaders in America, a member of the Quorum of the Twelve Apostles, who had also spent time on missionary work in England. Sarah didn't discard the paper, but left it lying on the table along with Thomas's supper. That night he ate his meal and read the words of Parley Pratt. Subsequently, on December 29, 1841, Thomas and wife Sarah, along with their two eldest children Sarah and Mary Ann, joined the Mormon Church. The elder Sarah immediately began saving money for the day when they could make their way to Zion.

Thousands of Mormons journeyed to Deseret from 1847 until 1856. The first parties went overland from Nauvoo, Illinois, to Winter Quarters to Great Salt Lake City. Before venturing west, the Mormons saw many of their leaders killed or falsely imprisoned. Heading west they didn't want to run the risk of further conflict with the people so they forged their trail across what became Nebraska north of the Platte River; travelers headed to Oregon and after 1849 to California, generally used a route that was south of the Platte.

By 1852 the earliest converts in England made their way to Zion, traveling by ship across the Atlantic to the mouth of the Mississippi River, then taking steamboats up the river to departure points at Winter Quarters and other sites along the Missouri including the town of Wyoming, Nebraska. There they joined wagon trains to cross the prairies and plains. In some cases young Mormon men filled wagons with grain and other supplies in Deseret then drove them east across the trail, stockpiling some supplies at way stations the Mormons had established along the route and selling the remainder when they reached the Missouri River towns. Then they exchanged their cargo for incoming converts, whom they took back to Deseret.

The Down and Back Trains, as they became known, were active for years. Because of them, many young men routinely followed the Mormon route, so they were familiar with every landmark and obstacle on the road. The program was funded in part by the P.E.F., which had been established with $5,000 in 1849. The goal was to pay for the transportation costs for the European converts to help them reach Zion. Once there, they would repay what had been expended in their behalf, so the fund would continue into perpetuity.

"The few thousands we send out by our agent at this time is like a grain of mustard seed in the earth; we send it forth into the world and among the Saints, a good soil, and we expect it will grow and flourish, and spread abroad in a few years so that it will cover England, cast its shadow in Europe and in the process of time compass the whole earth," the Fund's Letter of Instruction noted.

The first use of the P.E.F. came in helping Mormons still living along the Missouri River in their move to Zion, but in 1852 its primary purpose switched to assisting foreign converts. The first 251 people brought from England in 1852 were in a party that became known as the "Poor Company." The real migration began in 1853 when 2,312 people made their way from England to Zion under provision of the P.E.F.; they were followed by 3,167 travelers in 1854, with one-third of them receiving P.E.F. assistance.

By 1854 Church leaders recognized that the missionaries had been successful in Ireland, Scotland, Denmark, and Sweden as well as in England, so they decided to "work now and enlarge this Fund," according to the *Deseret News* of October 19, 1854. While those who could were asked to contribute to the fund, people who wanted to emigrate were urged to the purpose of "saving every penny and bending every effort toward the goal of emigration," reported the *Millennial Star,* a Mormon publication produced in Liverpool.

And Sarah Moulton faithfully did just that, dropping into her fruit jar a penny or sometimes more whenever she had money she could spare. As the coins multiplied, so did the family. Joining Thomas's eldest daughter, Sarah, whose birth mother died while she was a toddler, and Sarah and Thomas's eldest daughter Mary Ann, four years younger than Sarah, were William, Joseph, James Heber, Charlotte (Lottie), and Sophia, born in October 1853.

The call to emigrate to America touched the hearts of converts in England and on the continent so that the numbers grew to 4,225 people making their way to Zion in 1855, with 1,161 of them using resources of the P.E.F. However, by then it became evident that the fund was running out of money and could not continue transporting immigrants as it had been doing.

Thus was born the experiment that became the defining icon of the Mormon migration, known not for its success, but rather for the pure and total disaster that occurred in the fall of 1856 on the high plains of what became Wyoming. And the Moultons were right in the middle of it all, sustained by Sarah's faith and little else.

It began a year earlier in September 1855, when Brigham Young wrote to the president of the European Mission as reported in the December 22, 1855, edition of the *Millennial Star*: "I have been thinking how we should operate another year. We cannot afford to purchase wagons and teams as in times past. I am consequently thrown back upon my old plan—to make hand-carts, and let the emigration foot it, and draw upon them [the handcarts] the necessary supplies, having a cow or two for every ten. They can come just as quick, if not quicker, and much cheaper—can start earlier and escape the prevailing sickness which annually lays so many of our brethren in the dust. A great majority of them walk now, even with the teams which are provided."

Young laid out the plan in precise detail: "They will need only 90 days' rations from the time of their leaving the Missouri River, and as the settlements extend up the Platte, not that much. The carts can be made without a particle of iron, with wheels hooped, made strong and light, and one, or if the family be large, two of them will bring all that they will need upon the plains."

The Church President continued, "I think the emigration had better come the northern route from New York, or Philadelphia, or Boston, direct to Iowa City. . . . Their passage [by train] through to Iowa City will not cost more than

8 or 9 dollars, and they will only have to be supplied with money for provisions and a few cows, which should be of the very best quality. . . . Of course you will perceive the necessity of dispensing with all wooden chests, extra freight, luggage, etc. They should only bring a change of clothing."

Though he recommended rations for ninety days, Young believed the travelers with their carts could make the journey in seventy days moving from twenty to thirty miles each day "with all ease, and no danger of giving out, but will continue to get stronger and stronger; the little ones and sick, if there are any, can be carried on the carts, but there will be none sick in a little time after they get started. There will have to be some few tents."

So Young wrote to Missionary President Franklin D. Richards in Liverpool, England: "In your elections of the Saints who shall be aided by the Fund, those who have proven themselves by long continuance in the Church shall be helped first, whether they can raise any means of their own or not; . . . if they have not a sixpence in the world." He warned Richards about allowing new converts to be included in the emigration because their "chief aim and intention may be to get to America." In other words, he wanted to be sure the faithful and dedicated Mormons had the first opportunity to travel the ocean to America with help of the P.E.F., not simply people who sought better opportunity.

Richards himself noted that the possibility of using handcarts to cross the plains instead of wagons pulled by ox teams "has been under consideration for several years. The plan is novel, and, when we allow our imaginations to wander into the future and paint the scenes that will transpire on the prairies next summer, they partake largely of the romantic. The plan is the device of inspiration, and the Lord will own and bless it."

If only the handcarts had completed the journey during the summer of 1856, then the experiment would have been a complete success. It was true that handcart company pioneers could get started earlier each morning; they had no oxen to yoke and hitch to wagons. With fewer possessions they had Spartan camps that could be easily set up and quickly dismantled. Young knew the people could walk the route; since 1849 he'd seen men and women carrying backpacks and little else traveling the western roads on their way to California's gold fields. If those seeking wealth could walk more than 2,000 miles from the Missouri to the American Fork, certainly people following their faith could trek the 1,400 miles from Iowa City and Winter Quarters to Zion.

The handcart treks began in early 1856 when Cap'n Edmund Ellsworth and 274 members of the First Company crossed the Atlantic on the *Enoch Train* and *S. Curling,* which sailed from Liverpool on March 23 and April 19, respectively. Following them was Daniel D. McArthur's Second Company that included 497 people who were packed onto the *S. Curling* along with the 320 members of the Third Company, Welsh immigrants led by Cap'n Edward Bunker.

For the travelers the Atlantic crossing was relatively uneventful. The *Enoch Train* passengers were divided into five wards with a captain over each ward who answered to three Church elders. Every morning and evening a bugle blast called them to prayer, and they held regular meetings. On April 30 they reached Boston, having recorded four births and two deaths at sea. They boarded a train headed toward New York City, then continued by rail to Iowa. The Second and Third Companies had similar routines prior to their ships' arrival in Boston, though company leaders recorded two births and six infant deaths on the trans-Atlantic crossing. Once in America, they, too, continued their journey by rail to Iowa City. After they had reached Iowa all three parties reorganized their supplies, filled their handcarts, and began the walk to Zion. The first two parties left Iowa City two days apart (June 9 and June 11, 1856), often traveled together, and both reached Great Salt Lake City on September 26.

Most people in the Third Company were Welsh and after their rail trip from New York to St. Louis, some of it made in cars designed to haul livestock, they boarded a steamboat for the next leg of the trip to Iowa City. There they found that the handcarts weren't ready. So they helped complete them. On June 28, the Third Company started its handcart trip across the plains. They arrived in Great Salt Lake City on October 2.

If that had been the end of the handcart travel for the year, this story would end here, and end in the success Brigham Young had envisioned and on the note that Franklin Richards had made that "the Lord will own and bless it."

But the *Thornton* with its cargo of around 764 Saints, including Sarah Moulton and her family, had left Liverpool on May 3 and the *Horizon*, carrying additional members of the Fifth Company led by Edward Martin did not sail until May 25.

Members of the Fourth Company made it to Iowa City with adequate time to make their walk across the plains, but when they got to that point they found no handcarts at all; the members of the First, Second and Third Companies had taken every available cart and used all of the cured wood needed to build carts.

Undaunted, the Fourth Company men began building carts, using green wood; women made the tents that would provide shelter as they traveled. On July 15 Captain Willie led his party of around five hundred people with 120 handcarts, 5 wagons, 24 oxen, and 45 head of beef cattle and cows from Iowa City. The Fifth Company under direction of Captain Edward Martin followed just two days later, their 146 carts also made from green materials. And two Mormon wagon trains, one with 33 wagons guided by Captain W. B. Hodgett, and the other of 50 wagons led by Captain John A. Hunt, also began the trek in late July following the two handcart companies.

Captain Willie had restricted baggage to seventeen pounds per person, and when the *Thornton* docked in New York, Sarah had jettisoned more of the family's belongings. Now as she loaded the two handcarts, even more goods found their way into the discard pile.

For Sarah and the rest of the Moultons, the journey started easily enough as they pulled their two handcarts across the plains from Iowa City toward Winter Quarters. Waving grasses, flowers, and wild fruit covered the land. There were plenty of fish in the streams. They could obtain honey from settlers as they passed and they had milk from the cows they trailed. She and Thomas pulled a covered cart, in it rode Sophia and baby Charles, who was cradled on a pillow, plus Lottie whenever the cart was going downhill. Lottie had to walk the rest of the time as did Heber, who had turned eight in early July. At times Sarah tied a rope around Heber's waist so he could not stray far from her side, Lottie never wandered so she needed no tether. The older children pulled and pushed the open cart.

Organized in military fashion, the Willie Company was divided into five groups of 100 people in each with a sub-captain in charge. There were about a hundred Scots and another one hundred Scandinavians in the company; the remaining travelers were English. Each 100 people had five round tents to share and twenty handcarts. The wagons that were part of the company hauled the tents and provisions. As part of the organization, men were given certain responsibilities, and Thomas Moulton became the camp butcher.

It required twenty-eight days to pull the handcarts the 277 miles from Iowa City to Winter Quarters. Willie reached that site, and the town of Florence, Nebraska, that had grown up around it, on August 11. Already the green wood that had been used in making the carts was failing. As J. H. Latey wrote in the *Millennial Star,* "The companies stay here longer than they otherwise would in consequence of their carts being unfit for their journey across the Plains; some requiring new axles, and the whole of them having to have a piece of iron screwed on to prevent the wheel from wearing away the wood."

The delay cost precious travel days, and not until August 18 did Willie again lead his people onto the trail. But the decision to go so late in the year, knowing they still had more than 1,100 miles to travel, had been bitterly fought and made.

John Chislett was one of the sub-captains who traveled with the Fourth

Company, keeping an official record of the Willie Company's travel. He wrote, "The elders seemed to be divided in their judgment as to the practicability of our reaching Utah in safety at so late a season of the year, and the idea was entertained for a day or two of making our winter quarters on the Elkhorn, Wood River, or some eligible location in Nebraska; but it did not meet with general approval. A monster meeting was called to consult the people about it."

Four men with the party had been to Great Salt Lake City and other elders were in Florence to help with the emigration. Only one of those people who knew the trail and the potential weather conditions they faced urged Willie's Company to remain where they were for the winter. "The emigrants (sic) were entirely ignorant of the country and climate—simple, honest, eager to go to 'Zion' at once," Chislett wrote. "Under these circumstances it was natural that they should leave their destination in the hands of the elders." Levi Savage told them they "could not cross the mountains with a mixed company of aged people, women, and little children, so late in the season without much suffering, sickness, and death." Despite his pleas that they make a winter camp and continue to Zion the following year, the decision was made: Willie's Company would go on.

So the immigrants loaded their repaired carts and set out from Winter Quarters on August 18. In spite of discarding more personal possessions, the carts were more heavily laden than they had been on the four-week crossing from Iowa City. Each cart had on it an additional ninety-eight pound sack of flour. "Our flour ration was increased to a pound per day; fresh beef was issued occasionally, and each 'hundred' had three or four milch cows," Chislett wrote.

The weight from the extra flour broke axles on the already weakened carts slowing the pace of travel as people had to stop regularly to make repairs. Instead of eating the bacon, the travelers used it to grease axles on the carts. It only took about twenty days to consume the extra flour, after which the carts were not so heavy, and the party could move more quickly. But there had been other problems. A buffalo stampede at Wood River swept up some of the company's oxen, so then the milk cows and beef cattle had to be used as draw animals.

Weeks into their journey, Franklin Richards, who was traveling with a party of missionaries on his return from England to Zion, overtook the Willie Company. The missionaries used carriages and light wagons pulled by mules and horses. Recognizing the potential for real disaster, the missionaries proceeded on toward the west, promising to arrange for supplies at Fort Laramie and to send relief from Great Salt Lake City.

———

SARAH MOULTON SPIED THE military barracks and other buildings at Fort Laramie in late September. Already frost coated the tents in the morning when she arose. There were few supplies for the party at the fort. Willie took stock of the situation, quickly realizing that if they traveled at the same speed they had been moving, and if they ate the same rations, the people he led would run out of flour when they were still some 350 miles from their destination. So he ordered the flour ration cut from one pound to three-quarters of a pound per day, and implored the people to travel faster.

Again, the Saints lightened their loads, throwing aside clothing, bedding, and personal items. They even discarded the buffalo robes left for them at Fort Laramie by the missionary party. When Thomas pitched out the family teapot lid, in his effort to make travel easier, Sarah retrieved it; she had already given up so much on this crossing. But the tedious walking, the shortage of food, and the increasingly harsh weather conditions started taking a toll. Company leaders cut rations again as the Saints struggled through freezing streams, and into snowstorms.

Willie and his people made it to the final crossing of the North Platte River, and struck across the desolate high plains region, struggling over Avenue of Rocks and on to Horse Creek. They passed Independence Rock having neither the time nor the desire to carve their names in that granite outcrop as so many other travelers before them had done. Following the Sweetwater, they crossed and recrossed the freezing stream. By then the winter snows had started and many days they struck out heading straight into the blinding, icy blast. The children began chewing on strips of rawhide pulled from the cart wheels or the boots of people who died. They stripped and ate bark from willow trees as they walked west trying to ease the hunger in their bellies.

Some of them began to die. "Every death weakened our forces," John Chislett wrote. "In my hundred I could not raise enough men to pitch a tent when we camped." That fact struck the Moultons as well. Thomas had his duties as camp butcher and years later Lottie remembered, "One night the wind was blowing very hard and my mother and brothers were trying to pitch a tent. As fast as she would get it up, the wind would blow it over again. My father threw his knife and stuck it in the ground and said, 'If there is not men enough in this camp to put up my wife's tent, I won't kill another beef.' Right now there were plenty of men to pitch her tent."

Willie's party ate the last of their flour on October 19 and forced themselves to shelter in a willow patch at the Three Crossings of the Sweetwater. During the night a foot and a half of snow covered their camp, scattering the remaining draft animals. In the morning five people did not awake, but the ground was so hard-frozen, that they couldn't dig a grave so they buried the deceased in a snowbank and struggled on. "When any in my hundred died I had to inter them," Chislett wrote, adding, "I always offered up a heartfelt prayer to that God who beheld our sufferings, and begged him to avert destruction from us and send us help."

Along the Sweetwater about two miles below Rocky Ridge they ran into the face of the storm as winter burst upon them in full force. Chislett wrote, "We were overtaken by a snowstorm which the shrill wind blew furiously about us. The snow fell several inches deep as we travelled along, but we dared not stop, for we had a sixteen-mile journey to make that day, and short of it we could not get wood and water."

FRANKLIN RICHARDS REACHED GREAT Salt Lake City on October 4, not long after Willie's party left Fort Laramie, and days before the Martin Company got to that post. The Hunt and Hodgett wagon trains were even farther back on the trail. In a meeting with Brigham Young, Richards explained the situation: there were around a thousand people still out on the plains without adequate food, shelter, or clothing. He had purchased buffalo robes for the Willie Company to get when they reached Fort Laramie, but knew it wasn't enough, there had been little food to buy.

Richard's arrival coincided with the beginning of the semi-annual Mormon Church Conference, a gathering that always drew hundreds of people to Great Salt Lake City. Upon hearing the news, Young decided what his Conference message would be: "[M]any of our brethren and sisters are on the plains with handcarts, and probably many are now seven hundred miles from this place, and they must be brought here, we must send assistance to them."

After giving further instructions, Young added, "I shall call upon the Bishops this day. I shall not wait until tomorrow, nor until the next day for 60 good mule teams and 12 or 15 wagons, I do not want to send oxen I want good horses and mules. They are in this Territory, and we must have them. Also 12 tons of flour and 40 good teamsters, besides those that drive the teams. . . . To take charge of the teams that are now managed by men, women and children who know nothing about driving them. Second, 60 or 65 good spans of mules, or horses, with harness, whipple trees, neckyokes, stretchers, lead, chains, &c. And thirdly, 24 thousand pounds of flour, which we have on hand."

Noting that faith, religion, and the "profession of religion" would not save the people, Young added, *"Go and bring in those people now on the plains."*

Young in his October 5 speech, said he wanted the rescue mission to begin the next day. "I want the sisters to have the privilege of fetching in blankets, skirts, stockings, shoes, etc., for the men, women, and children that are in those handcart companies [plus] . . . hoods, winter bonnets, stockings, skirts, garments, and almost any description of clothing." This came from the man, who in outlining the handcart plan just a year earlier had suggested people needed to "only bring a change of clothing."

The first rescuers struck the trail within hours of Brigham Young's call to action. By the end of October more than 250 teams were on the road with aid. The advance relief train led by George D. Grant, with William H. Kimball and Robert T. Burton assisting, camped at Big Mountain, just east of Great Salt Lake City the first night of their rescue mission. They made the 113 miles to Fort Bridger by October 12, just five days after Young's plea. On October 15, they reached the Green River, another fifty-three miles back along the trail. With no sign of the Willie Company, or those behind him, the rescuers sent out scouts who could travel more quickly than the relief wagons.

As the Moultons and other members of Willie's party huddled in their snowy misery beside the Sweetwater River on October 19, the advance rescue scouts, Joseph A. Young and Stephen Taylor, reached camp from the west with word that supplies were on the way. "More welcome messenger never came from the courts of glory than these two young men were to us," Chislett wrote. Riding with Young and Taylor were Cyrus Wheelock and Abel Garr. The four did not remain with Willie's party, but they continued east searching for Edward Martin's Company.

Soon after those advance scouts found the Willie Company camp, the first rescue wagons reached it. "Shouts of joy rent the air; strong men wept till (sic) tears ran freely down their furrowed and sun-burnt cheeks. . . . Restraint was set aside in the general rejoicing, and as the brethren entered our camp, the sisters fell upon them and deluged them with kisses." Nineteen-year-old Sarah Moulton wrapped her arms around John Bennett Hawkins, one of the rescuers.

The rescuers found wood and built a fire, then some of them prepared food for the starving Willie Party while others handed out warm bedding and socks. But the celebration was short-lived; nine people died that night. The food and fire helped, as did the warm bedding, but the Saints could not stay where they were any longer. Rescuers told the weary travelers they had to keep moving since there were so many others even farther back on the trail, no doubt suffering from the same cold, lack of food, and exposure.

So with the help of their rescuers, the Moulton family rose up along with their companions and they began the climb up the hills away from the river. On the second day of their resumed march under the direction of William Kimball, they faced the shelf rock of the incline known as Rocky Ridge. It was bitterly cold, steep, slick, and miserable. They slipped and slid on the snowy, icy ground and many frosted their hands, feet, and faces. Heber trailed along, pulled by the rope around his waist, until a woman in the company took his right hand and helped him up the hill. The warmth and protection her hand offered saved his right hand, but the left one, exposed to the freezing temperatures was severely frostbitten and later he lost those fingers. Charlotte wore the gloves her mother had made to cover the pox mark on her hand.

Finally at the end of that horrible, hard day, the Fourth Company set camp at Willow Creek, a place somewhat sheltered by a rock bluff. They were on the brink of crossing South Pass, and had already seen the first of the relief parties, but the rescue was too late and another fifteen people died in the night. Thirteen of them were buried October 24 in a common grave while the other two were placed in a separate grave.

The next day, on October 25, the company reached South Pass itself, and they could see Oregon Buttes to the west. Even more important, they found flour and plenty of wood on hand for their needs. Daily after that as they trudged west, the Saints met relief wagons. For many the long walk ended at Fort Bridger on November 2, 1856, when they arrived to find fifty teams sent from Great Salt Lake to haul them the remainder of the way. Some Saints continued to walk defiantly; they eventually dragged their battered carts into the city in late November.

The Moultons gladly abandoned their handcarts at Fort Bridger and accepted the offer of a ride. At the foot of Little Mountain in Emigration Canyon, they met Samuel Cussley, a relative they had never met. Years later Lottie recalled, "Father and Mother did not know that they had relatives anywhere in Utah. When the relief trains came to meet us one of the men said, 'Is there a Thomas Moulton in this company?' and to their surprise it was my mother's brother-in-law by the name of Cussley. He had, oh, so many of the good things that children like, pie, cake, etc., but there was nothing looked so good as the good bread and butter."

Finally, about noon on November 9, 1856, the wagons filled with starving immigrants stopped in front of the old tithing office in Salt Lake City.

Sarah Moulton stood beside the wagon, holding baby Charles in her arms, with Lottie by her side. The blessing she had received in England before beginning the trip came true. Though some seventy people traveling with them and another 150 people in Edward Martin's Company had died on the crossing, none of the Moultons perished.

Less than a month later, on December 5, 1856, daughter Sarah married John Bennett Hawkins.

THE IDAHO GOLD DUST MURDERS

Pat Decker Nipper

GOLD WAS BOTH A reason for growth and a cause for concern in Idaho Territory. Capt. E. D. Pierce discovered it in 1860 as a prospector for the army. He had visited the various gold fields in California, Oregon, and Canada, trying unsuccessfully to find enough of the precious ore to help the Union cause in the Civil War. When he heard about Nez Perce Indian's claims that they had seen "stones sparkling" on their reservation in north-central Idaho, he tried to get permission to enter the reservation but failed. Convinced that there was gold to be found, he and his group of prospectors decided to enter the reservation illegally, using a roundabout route through the mountains. While in the mountains, they pitched camp next to a stream that contained a few gold nuggets. Word spread quickly, and by 1861, so many mining hopefuls had come to the territory that the population had grown from two hundred to over seven thousand.

About the same time, gold was discovered in the Boise Basin and within a year, thirty thousand people were living and working in the region. As a result of the gold strikes, mining became Idaho's first industry. On the down side, both of these gold strikes attracted some unsavory types.

One of the primary problems with the gold rush was lawlessness. Tent cities sprang up so quickly that no structured form of control had time to develop. The primary form of law enforcement, therefore, was maintained by vigilante committees. They acted as judge, jury, and executioners, hanging most of the perceived perpetrators where they found them. Formal trials were seldom held, but the threat of vigilantism did offer some deterrent to crime.

One bunch of vigilantes became so zealous that in 1862, in the mining town of Bannack, they even hanged a judge, a coroner, and a sheriff whom they had elected. The sheriff, Henry Plummer, was rumored to be a former desperado, and many of the robberies and murders along the trails were attributed to him and his "gang of outlaws." Though there was no evidence to support the rumors, the vigilantes carried out their own form of justice and hanged all three men.

Many of the area's leading citizens were involved in vigilantism, while others were major critics of their actions. One nineteenth-century writer, Nathaniel Langford, favored the vigilantes and labeled them "glorious empire builders." He did admit, however, that "many of these [vigilantes] were worse men than those they executed." Several other critics considered the vigilantes nothing more than outlaws themselves.

Among those trying to support justice under the laws of the United States was Hill Beachey, a leading citizen of Lewiston, then capital of Idaho Territory, and owner of the Luna House, Lewiston's first hotel. Little did he know that he would eventually be called upon to stand before a group of vigilantes and face them down, at great risk to himself.

Beachey's hotel was a multi-purpose building, containing the stagecoach office as well as the town jail, located on the second floor. Beachey's closest friend was Lloyd Magruder and both were highly respected by the populace in general. In fact, Magruder had accepted the Democratic nomination to run as Idaho Territory's representative in Congress. Unfortunately, he never lived to hold that office or even to run for election.

Magruder was a merchant and trader, born of Scottish immigrants. His entrepreneurial spirit had brought him and his family to Idaho Territory from California. When he saw an opportunity to make a living traveling by mule train to the gold fields on the eastern border of the territory, he took up the challenge. His mule train was loaded with everything the miners needed—wagon wheels, shovels, food, gold pans, scissors—anything useful and hard to get in the primitive areas of the mines. He exchanged his goods for gold, the current medium of exchange. On his trips both to and from the gold fields, he hired a number of guards, usually men who were headed to the mines anyway. He knew that his merchandise, and later the gold, would be tempting targets for the many unscrupulous characters who always flocked to a new gold discovery. By August 1863, he had made a number of successful trips to and from the gold mining areas and perhaps had grown too complacent about safety.

On his final and fatal trip, Magruder left Lewiston with sixty mules, loaded with his usual stock of merchandise for the miners in Bannack and Virginia City. He took along a number of armed guards that he had hired in Lewiston, men he had determined were honest and hard workers. Because of his Scottish heritage, he believed in getting his money's worth from his help.

The pack train followed the old Nez Perce Indian trail between the forks of the Clearwater River and over the Bitterroot Mountains. This trail was the quickest route to the eastern side of the mountain range, but it was steep and treacherous. The Nez Perce Indians had followed this trail to the buffalo grounds in what is now Montana, instead of the easier, more northern Lolo Trail. Here, on the southern route, they had less chance of meeting their sworn enemies, the aggressive Blackfeet. Also, the trail had been something of a tribal secret for generations. They had told Lewis and Clark about the Lolo Trail, but they didn't mention this southerly trail, other than to say that high, difficult mountains blocked the passage.

When Magruder and his convoy made it past the mountains, they turned southward to the Bannack mines. However, after they arrived in Bannack, which was still part of Idaho Territory at the time, they discovered that most of the miners had moved on to the newer and reportedly richer strikes at Alder Gulch, around Virginia City, now in the state of Montana.

Virginia City was originally named Verona, Idaho Territory, a misspelling of Varina, the wife of Jefferson Davis, President of the Confederate States of America. This indicates that Virginia City was a rebel town in Union territory during the Civil War. Much of the war here was not fought with rifles, but rather with a rope, as in vigilantism.

Because the gold produced in Virginia City was sought after by both sides of the war, the Confederate population disrupted attempts of the Union Republicans to administer the Territory and rule the town. Whatever conflicts existed between Northern and Southern sympathizers, Magruder was fairly oblivious to it. He set up his temporary store in several large and sturdy tents on the outskirts of town, tethering his mules behind the store.

While doing business in Virginia City, Magruder met and hired an out-of-work teamster named William Page. Maybe he felt sorry for the man, since he was getting up in years and didn't seem too bright. Nevertheless, Page helped Magruder distribute his goods in Virginia City, acting as supply clerk and general "gofer." Magruder also hired two men he recognized from Lewiston, James Romaine, and David Renton, to guard his merchandise. They looked big enough to keep any rowdy miners in line if they came around intending to steal any of the goods. They even slept in the store occasionally at night.

After several weeks of frantic trading, Magruder had accumulated a tidy sum of gold dust. With his business finished, he decided it was time to return to his home in Lewiston. Besides, it was already October and he knew that winter came early to the mountains. Snow would soon close the trails and he wanted to be home well before that happened.

When they were getting ready to leave for Lewiston, Romaine and Renton convinced Magruder to hire their friend D. C. Lower, another Lewiston man who had taken up residence in Virginia City, to join the crew. Magruder agreed but felt he still needed more men to get his gold and his mules back home safely. He hired two brothers as guards—Horace and Robert Chalmers—and another teamster named William Phillips to work with the mule string. Though most of the mules would not be carrying much in the way of a load, they were reliable mules and he didn't want to lose them.

On his way through Bannack, Magruder stopped long enough to write a letter to his wife, saying he would be leaving the area in twelve days. This was just another bit of caution, since he actually planned to be on the trail within the week. He thought that any robbers who saw the letter would miss him by a number of days.

After the pack train started away from Bannack, they met miner Charles Allen on the way at the Beaverhead River. Allen wanted to join the convoy, so Magruder agreed. He now had nine men to go with him. He was happy with this size group, thinking this many men could hold off any thieves they might meet on the trail.

For three days and nights the group traveled uneventfully, taking turns standing watch during the nights. The trail was in good shape. A brief rain storm a week earlier had dampened the dust, but the trail had dried sufficiently so it was no longer muddy. The pack train was making good time.

On the fourth day, as they traveled the trail, Lower rode up to Page and told him to drop back so he could talk to him. Page did as he was told and Renton and Romaine explained their plan to steal the gold. They intended to kill Magruder, Phillips, Allen, and the Chalmers brothers, and all Page had to do was keep his mouth shut. They would do everything that needed to be done. Just knowing the plan frightened Page nearly out of what few wits he had. He was afraid that he himself would be killed if he told Magruder of the heinous plans, so he did nothing.

On the fifth night, the group made camp in a narrow, isolated spot on the trail high in the Bitterroots. Frost was already beginning to form since the mountain was well over a mile high. A steep cliff loomed above the camp on one side, with a sheer abyss dropping off on the other. It was not a perfect camping spot by any means, but the group was exhausted from the heavy climb. As they made camp, Lower whispered to Page that this was where they planned to do the deed. All Page had to do was to sleep next to Phillips and keep an eye on him. If he woke up and tried to stop the killings in any way, Page was to stab him to death. Page agreed, being too frightened to protest. Apparently the other three men had decided they needed Page to wrangle the animals.

After supper, they put their plan into action. Lower said he wanted to build a fire and took an axe with him to chop wood. He followed Magruder, who went ahead to look after the animals. Magruder was a trusting and loyal man and he assumed the people he had hired were the same. This trusting nature was his undoing.

Page was so tired and cold that he curled up in his bed roll to keep warm. Despite his unease, he fell asleep and slept until midnight, when he heard Renton and Lower coming back to camp. In his confusion, he thought it was his turn to take the watch, but instead they told him to continue lying in bed while they went to get axes. After that, they proceeded to kill the Chalmers brothers. Page could hear the blows as he cowered in his bed roll.

He heard somebody shoot Allen, and then Romaine hit Phillips on the head with the axe two or three times. Finally Renton told Page it was all over. He didn't need to be frightened anymore. They told him he could just relax, tend the animals, and share the gold with them.

After the killings, the men stripped their victims and wrapped their bodies in blankets, tying them closed with the picket ropes from the extra mules. They threw the bodies over the rim of the canyon and built a large fire to burn every item that might identify the victims. While they were destroying every indication of the crime, Romaine gave Page moccasins to wear around the camp with the rest of them, to make it looked like Indians had committed the crime in case anybody discovered it. Chances were that a heavy snowfall would cover all the evidence before anybody even knew that Magruder had been killed.

They put everything that had not burned—belt buckles, buttons, rings—into a cloth bag and hid it under a log. Because Romaine had blood on his pants, he burned them and wore a pair of Allen's instead. They kept the victims' revolvers, but disposed of the shotguns and rifles, which would just draw unwanted attention as they made their escape out of Idaho.

They sent Page up the hill to the spot that Magruder had been killed and told him to extinguish the fire Lower had started there, which he did. When he returned, he found the three killers counting up the gold, which they reckoned to be eleven or twelve thousand dollars worth, not as much as they had hoped. (Later, as the story of the murder grew, so did the amount of gold—up to as much as $30,000.)

The men discovered that a lot of the animals had strayed off, so they just left them. They put packs on two mules, which they considered enough for their own needs, and set off down the trail. Some of the mules that had previously strayed now began to follow them, so the three killers shot most of them, keeping a total of eight.

Meanwhile in Lewiston, Beachey was worried about his friend Magruder's most recent trip to the gold fields. Something had bothered him about this trip from the start. He had been so worried, in fact, that he dreamed of Magruder's murder shortly after he and his mules had left town. In his dream, he saw Magruder go to a camp fire at night to light his pipe. He then saw a dark figure slip up behind him with an axe. He seemed to hear the axe thud into Magruder's skull and woke up, knowing that his friend had been killed.

There was no way to communicate with Magruder so Beachey tried to put the dream out of his mind, thinking it was all foolishness. However, by mid-October when Magruder still had not returned from his trip, Beachey was sure something terrible had happened to him.

When he saw four strangers stop at the stagecoach counter in the Luna House to buy tickets to Walla Walla, he became suspicious. The men were fidgety, shifty, nervous. He knew they weren't staying in his hotel, which was unusual in itself. Most people who planned to take the stage stayed at the Luna House so they could get an early start the next morning. The men were, in fact, staying at the less notable Hotel DeFrance under assumed names. They had known that Beachey was Magruder's friend and that he might somehow recognize them.

After watching them closely, Beachey decided they were behaving in a guilty manner. He remembered seeing some of them in town before Magruder's recent trip. Judge John Berry was sitting with him in the Luna House lobby that night and Beachey pointed the men out. As soon as they left, he asked the judge for permission to arrest them immediately. The judge refused, saying there was nothing to connect them to a crime. Mere suspicions were not enough; Beachey needed proof.

Determined to find proof, Beachey went directly to the stables behind the Luna House and asked if any new mounts had been stabled there. The man in charge, Chester Coburn, said that no, he was not stabling any new horses. He and some friends were planning to ride the stage the next day, however. They were taking the same coach as the questionable four. Beachey could do nothing except warn him and his friends to be on the lookout for trouble. He said he had a bad feeling about those men. He sensed that they were somehow responsible for Magruder's delayed return. Coburn said they would remain watchful. Meanwhile, he suggested that Beachey search other stables around town to see if somebody else might be boarding the horses. Beachey conducted a late-night search, but he had no luck finding the horses before the stage left the next day.

Beachey was still troubled, so he sent his friend Mose Druilard to Orofino to find another friend, an army captain named A. P. Ankeny. Druilard was to ask him and a man named Schull if they had heard any word from Magruder. Meanwhile, he found a hosteler a short distance outside of Lewiston who had agreed to care for the horses, saddles, and mules for four men until spring. When he looked at the stock, Beachey recognized Magruder's horse and saddle. He knew he had found the answer to his concerns. Here was proof that Magruder wasn't coming back, and that the four men who had just taken the stage had either stolen the stock and probably the gold, or had been the murderers he had seen in his dream.

Beachey went to Sheriff James Fisk, who swore out warrants for the arrest of the four men. Beachey and his friend Thomas Pike set out after the stage. When they arrived at Walla Walla, they discovered that they had missed the stage, which was on its way to the Dalles on the Columbia River. They rode as fast as they could to the Dalles, but again they arrived too late; the stage had gone on to Portland. They continued on to Portland, knowing that from there, the men could board a steamship for San Francisco.

While they were in Portland, Captain Ankeny caught up with them. He had no news about Magruder, but was ready to help pursue the four men, capture them, and bring them back for trial. He suggested he rent a tugboat and try to catch the steamer. He would then convince it to turn around and return to Portland. If this plan failed, he would return to Portland anyway and they would all ride south together to California. When they reached Yreka in northern California, they could telegraph San Francisco and ask the San Francisco police to meet the steamer at the dock and apprehend the men.

Ankeny's tugboat plan did fail. His tug reached the mouth of the harbor after the steamer had already passed. The boat returned to Portland, and he and Beachey set out for California while Pike returned to Lewiston. Beachey and Ankeny took the stage to Yreka and when they arrived, Beachey telegraphed the San Francisco police to be on the lookout for the four men. He gave complete descriptions of them, then took the stage on to San Francisco by himself.

The San Francisco police received the message too late to meet the ship carrying the fugitives. However, Beachey's descriptions were so accurate that they managed to find and arrest the men anyway. By the time Beachey arrived, the four—Page, Romaine, Renton, and Lower—were behind bars.

Not only had the San Francisco police captured the men, but they had even recovered some of the gold dust through the San Francisco mint. This gold was later turned over to Magruder's widow and family, as it rightfully belonged to them.

After Beachey got the extradition papers signed in San Francisco, Captain Lee of the Bay City Police accompanied him on the move back to Lewiston by steamer. They kept the criminals in handcuffs for the entire voyage up the Pacific coast and across Washington Territory on the Columbia River.

When they reached Walla Walla, a U.S. Army escort joined the party and they continued up the river to Lewiston, where they were met by a large group of vigilantes. Beachey had to talk them out of an immediate hanging. He had promised the authorities in California, that these four would receive a fair trial. Otherwise, extradition papers would not have been signed. Reluctantly, the vigilantes backed off and Beachey took his prisoners on to Lewiston.

Beachey turned the men over to Sheriff Fisk as soon as he arrived. The sheriff placed three of the men, Renton, Lower, and Romaine, in one room of the jail in the Luna House. Then he located Page in a cell by himself. It did not take long for Beachey and the sheriff to decide that Page was a weak man. He was the one who would tell them what happened to Magruder, as soon as the killers were behind bars and couldn't harm him.

One version of what happened next was that the sheriff walked Page past a room in the hotel where four nooses were hanging. In another version, an angry mob assembled outside Page's window, threatening to lynch them all. Whichever version prevailed, Page finally agreed to inform on the others and turn state's evidence in exchange for his own release.

By the end of the three week trial, on January 23, 1864, after hearing Page's testimony, the jury declared the other three "guilty of the crime of murder in the first degree, as charged in the indictment, and the punishment therefor shall be death." Page, the judge decreed, was free to go.

On Friday, March 4, Renton, Lower, and Romaine were hanged in a little ravine southeast of town. A large crowd turned out to see justice done in a legal and lawful manner. It was the first lawful hanging in Idaho Territory.

Although William Page was given his freedom, as promised, he did not keep it for long. He was killed by a man named Albert Ilgo within the year during a saloon brawl. Because Page had been so despised for allowing the murders to take place, everybody was glad to see the end of him. They never even prosecuted Ilgo.

FROM THE HEART OF CHAOS:
FINDING ZITKALA-ŠA

Nancy M. Peterson

ON APRIL 27, 1938, heavy curtains furled apart to reveal the opening scene of the New York Light Opera Guild's annual American opera. The sophisticated audience sniffed, straightened, and whispered to their neighbors as a sharp, clean scent drifted out among them. It was pungent, invigorating, crisp as mountain air. The aroma evoked a land of simple savages and a time that seemed as far-removed from 52nd and Broadway as Shangri-la.

Yet the scent from a green branch of burning sage spoke of home to balding, spectacled, fifty-one-year-old William F. Hanson, who had composed the opera. And it would have been poignantly familiar to the conflicted woman who had helped him write it. But Gertrude Simmons Bonnin had not lived to see this Broadway premier of their collaborative work, *The Sun Dance*. Hanson had driven down to Washington, D.C., for her funeral just three months before. It was the final irony in the life of the woman who called herself Zitkala-Ša.

SIXTY YEARS EARLIER, EDUCATOR Captain Richard H. Pratt was certain he had the solution to the Indian problem: "Kill the Indian and save the man!" If government schools annihilated every trace of tribal culture in a child, Pratt declared, they could create students able and eager to step into American society. He had no plan for those such as half-blood Yankton Sioux Gertrude Simmons, who found it impossible to complete the journey—and impossible to return home.

The Quakers who ran White's Manual Labor Institute in Wabash, Indiana, genuinely believed Captain Pratt's method was best for Indian children. In 1884, they visited the Yankton village to recruit students, promising wonders such as a ride on the iron horse, and a beautiful country where one could pick red apples from trees. Seduced by the glowing promises and her eagerness to learn, Gertrude prayed that the Great Spirit would make her mother say "yes."

Her mother, hesitant, reluctant, finally yielded to Gertrude's pleas to go east to boarding school. Taté Iyóhiwin had wed three white men, and Gertrude was the result of the third brief, unhappy union. Gertrude's father, a man named Felker, took no part in their lives. Taté Iyóhiwin refused to burden the girl with his name and reverted to the surname of her second husband, Simmons, but she had always warned Gertrude against the whites' ruthless double-dealing.

She often told her how white power had pushed the free-roaming Yanktons onto a small triangle of land hard against the Missouri's east bank in what was now southeastern South Dakota. They had forced a march to the reservation that had cost the lives of Taté Iyóhiwin's first child and her brother. White power had eliminated the buffalo and left the Yanktons dependent on substandard government rations barely adequate to sustain life. She had made sure Gertrude knew these hard stories, as well as the Yankton legends the girl so enjoyed. Smaller than others her age, Gertrude was a bright, spirited child, with an excellent memory for the fireside tales that both entertained and taught tribal values. The woman feared the white teachers' methods, distrusted their intent. Yet she saw no other hope for her daughter's future, or the future of her people. The children must learn to talk for them, be their bridge to understanding. The missionaries took eight-year-old Gertrude away to Indiana.

At school Gertrude and her classmates endured a traumatic submersion in an alien world. She was immediately stripped—as one would skin an animal—of everything familiar: long braids, clothing, language, religion, dignity and especially understanding. She had rebelled whenever possible—they had to drag her from under a bed and tie her to a chair to cut her hair—but almost in spite of herself she'd learned English quickly. The harsh world of glaring lights, clanging bells, clattering shoes, and military discipline also held the magic of books. Her thirsty mind had soaked up knowledge from the white man's papers. It was three years before she again saw her mother.

Back with the mother she had wept for, on the prairie she had so longed to see, Gertrude felt lost and alone. The prairie seemed empty now; she had needs her mother's lodge could no longer fill. Gertrude threw away her hard shoes and tight muslin dresses and for four years tried to feel at home. "I seemed to hang in the heart of chaos," she wrote later, ". . . neither a wild Indian nor a tame one." By the time she was fifteen, Gertrude was openly miserable. She talked of returning east to school.

Her mother could not understand. What did she want? What could more years of school accomplish? They had always been so close. Why couldn't she be happy at home? The un-chinked logs of the crude cabin that had replaced their warm tipi held only one book, an Indian Bible. She offered it to the girl, hoping to soothe her. To Gertrude, it was only a symbol of their barren life, pitifully inadequate. Her rejection sent Taté Iyóhiwin out into the frigid wind that scoured the Dakota hilltops. A moment later, hearing her mother's piteous wails of frustration and grief, Gertrude knew she was the cause. She shrank away from this latest wash of guilt, but she could not suppress her craving to learn. In turmoil, against her mother's wishes, Gertrude returned to White's Institute in February 1891.

She pushed thoughts of home away, determined to excel in the white world. Perhaps this was the best way to help her people. Before she graduated four years later, Gertrude had developed talents as a singer, violinist, pianist, and orator. Her graduation speech promoting women's suffrage so impressed a Quaker in the audience that the woman offered to pay Gertrude's tuition to attend Earlham College in Richmond, Indiana. Gertrude sought her mother's approval; again, it was denied. She enrolled without it.

She developed exceptional skills in oratory, winning the right as a freshman to represent Earlham in the 1896 Indiana State Oratorical Contest. The only woman competitor, she gave a fiery defense of Indian people's character and actions. Yet, she acknowledged, their future lay in "seeking the treasures of knowledge and wisdom" white society offered. As they waited the judges' decision, a competitor's supporters unfurled a banner ridiculing Earlham because it was represented by a "squaw." Gertrude gritted her teeth and stared defiantly at the white crowd. She felt vindicated when she won second prize, but her glory had a bitter taste. She knew that her mother, hurt and angry, would scorn her accomplishment.

A lingering illness ended Gertrude's college studies. Unwilling to return home, she accepted a teaching post at the U.S. Indian Industrial School at Carlisle, Pennsylvania, where Captain Pratt presided. Pratt liked Indians and respected their abilities. He was certain Indian children could learn as well as any immigrant group, once separated from their families and totally immersed in white culture. One simply had to erase the Indian identity. His thriving campus seemed to prove the point. In 1899, he sent Gertrude west to recruit more students.

At home, she found shocking poverty. In the dozen years since the passage of the Dawes Severalty Act of 1887, which ended tribal land ownership and assigned Indians individual plots, large amounts of reservation land had been surrendered to white settlers. Gertrude's mother had written her of increasing white encroachment. Whites were cruel hypocrites, Taté Iyóhiwin said, offering holy papers with one hand and debilitating firewater in the other. One evening, seated outside with Gertrude as darkness revealed settlers' lights one after another, Taté Iyóhiwin sprang up, thrust her closed fist at the nearest and shot out her fingers as if they could smite the white intruders with her bitter curse. Gertrude could almost feel the force of her mother's hatred pass from her accusatory fingers to the settlers' lodge.

Despite her mother's bitterness, with great ambivalence, Gertrude enlisted students for Carlisle. Education seemed their only hope. Education had opened the world for her. Eastern society had embraced her. She was now twenty-one, and acclaimed by eastern papers as a "charmingly artistic and graceful" violinist. She was also a pianist and in demand as a speaker. A column in the April 1900, issue of *Harper's Bazaar* lauded her "beauty and many talents . . . a rare command of English and much artistic feeling." She was attaining success in the white culture.

Still, she knew Pratt never considered that the culture his students left behind had its own value. When she returned to Carlisle, her anger grew at whites who toured the school with satisfied smiles, never questioning "whether real life or long-lasting death lies beneath this semblance of civilization." Increasingly furious and hurt by injustices she witnessed, she sat in her room like a petrified woman, wishing in her pain she could turn to "unfeeling stone."

Finding release in music, she resigned from teaching and enrolled in the New England Conservatory of Music in Boston. She found studies in voice and piano absorbing but, apart from the natural world, she traded her faith in the Great Spirit for the white man's papers, which gave her little comfort. And she grew ever more aware of disdainful, deceitful treatment by many whites who claimed to be the Indian's friend. She decided the wrenching experience of boarding school assimilation was cruel and wrong. She poured out her pain and fury by writing about her life, knowing thousands of other Indian children had suffered the same agony.

She had endured so much to learn, yet those back home acted hurt—even betrayed. Education had so alienated her from her family that a resentful relative challenged Gertrude's use of the Simmons name. Gertrude felt driven to create an identity that was Indian, yet hers alone. When the *Atlantic Monthly* published her stories in early 1900, she signed them Zitkala-Ša, Lakota for Red Bird.

In these stories and others, she demonstrated her love and respect for her people's rich culture, her traumatic conversion to white men's ways, and the terrible price she and others paid when they denied their heritage. Her writing skill and honesty were praised by critics. But her former teachers were outraged that she expressed no gratitude to those who had taught her. She had betrayed them, used the skills they had given her to tell the world only of the painful times. She wrote of trudging "in the day's harness, heavy-footed, like a dumb sick brute." Of testing "the chains which tightly bound my individuality like a mummy for burial." There was no mention of the good times, of kind people who had taught and assisted her. She dared to champion the culture they had done their best to make her forget. Captain Pratt and the Carlisle newspaper, which had several times published her work, denounced her new writings.

Driven to preserve what she could of her culture, and determined to demonstrate its value, she translated and compiled folk tales from the Yanktons' oral tradition into a children's book. Siouan storytellers were many, each with his or her own individual style, and they customarily tailored each version of a tale to that evening's particular audience. Creating one standard version, understandable to any audience, was a formidable task. Her people distrusted the white man's written word with good reason. One word, forever frozen on a page, could embody no nuances of meaning like that carried in a storyteller's tone of voice, posture, or expression. It lacked face-to-face explanation that could prevent misunderstanding. What's more, one standard version might be missing some tidbit, some nugget of meaning known to some storytellers but not all. The truth lay in the whole body of the tradition.

Translating the tale into English was an additional challenge, necessary, Zitkala-Ša noted archly in her preface, "since America in the last few centuries has acquired a second tongue." She used her second tongue with skill and imagination to detail the adventures of Iktomi, the trickster; the badger and the bear, and other folk tales she thought children would enjoy. *Old Indian Legends* was published in 1901. Her publisher was soon urging a second volume.

That year, her third in Boston, she came to love and almost married Carlos Montezuma, a Yavapai physician who practiced in Chicago. But he could not sustain a successful practice on the reservation and she felt she must return there, to reconcile with her mother and collect stories for her second book of folk tales. Terribly torn between different lifestyles, she broke her engagement and returned west to clerk on the Standing Rock Reservation. There she met

Raymond Bonnin, a Yankton who shared her love for and devotion to tribal tradition. She married Bonnin in 1902 and spent the next thirteen years working on the Uintah Reservation in eastern Utah.

These years produced a beloved son, Ohiyo, in 1903, some satisfaction in helping the Utes, and much frustration. Here, she was Mrs. Raymond Bonnin, wife, mother, and assistant to her husband. She missed music and books— people who could talk of both—and especially time to write more of her own stories. Zitkala-Ša's dreams lay dormant.

Then in 1912, William Hanson, a high school music teacher from nearby Vernal, Utah, proposed a project that reawakened Gertrude's creative energies. Hanson had long worked to preserve Ute culture. Now he asked Gertrude's help on an ambitious project: to write and produce an opera based on Indian culture. Gertrude immediately urged the theme of the Plains Indians' Sun Dance. The religious ceremony, essentially Sioux in origin, had been banned by the government since 1883 as a "heathen rite."

Always eager to champion Indian culture—ever ready to fight government repression—Gertrude spent weeks working closely with Hanson. Insisting on historical and spiritual accuracy she interpreted the legends for Hanson, played tribal chants on her violin, and edited his lyrics. The support of Gertrude and Raymond Bonnin gave Hanson access to music seldom heard by white men. The Bonnins gained the essential cooperation of elders to allow the simulation of sacred ceremonies and the use of authentic costumes.

The Sun Dance, performed by a mix of Utes, Vernal residents, and the high school chorus, earned excellent reviews when it opened in Vernal in February 1913. Praised as "an artistic triumph" "musically . . . magnificent" and affording "absolute satisfaction," it was performed twenty-four times to enthusiastic Utah audiences. When favorable notices appeared in the national press as well, it was a time of celebration for the coauthors.

With this validation of her creative abilities and feeling renewed optimism about the future, Gertrude joined the new Society of American Indians (SAI). The SAI, unlike other Indian rights groups, allowed only Indians as voting members. It was devoted to reforming laws affecting Indians, preserving their history and culture, working for citizenship and better education, and promoting self-help and cooperation among the tribes. With new-found energy, she organized local SAI meetings, established a community center to provide hot meals, and organized sewing clinics. In 1916, she expressed her feeling of rebirth as an Indian in a poem published in SAI's *American Indian Magazine.* She titled it "The Indian's Awakening," and in it she described her painful severance from her people and their culture and her joyful reconnection. For the first time in fifteen years, she signed her name Zitkala-Ša.

That October she was elected secretary of the national group, and in April 1917, the Bonnins left Utah for Washington, D.C. While Raymond studied law and then served in the army, Zitkala-Ša lectured widely and lobbied Congress for Indian causes. Aware of what white audiences expected when they met an Indian, she appeared in a fringed, beaded, buckskin dress, her long, heavy braids reaching below her hips. Although congressional committees knew her as Mrs. Raymond, or Gertrude Bonnin, she testified in traditional dress to emphasize her authenticity. If she felt the need, she said she was a full-blooded Yankton, and even more impressive, a granddaughter of the famous Sitting Bull. She knew that would get their attention and was cynically confident none of them had the slightest idea that a full-blooded Yankton could not be a Hunkpapa's granddaughter.

Outspoken and ambitious, she openly sought SAI leadership posts previously filled by men. She was the first female board member and attended the SAI conventions. Traditionally, only men spoke, but Gertrude took the podium and advised the predominately male audience to be proud of their Indian blood, to be ready to walk new trails, and next time to bring their wives and sisters. She contributed articles, satire, and poetry to the society magazine, and from 1918–1919 served as editor-in-chief. Disagreement over the use of peyote, which Zitkala-Ša violently opposed, and internal dissension contributed to the society's demise in 1920.

Gertrude's career as a writer was boosted in 1921, when Hayworth Publishing House of Washington gathered her autobiographical stories, which had been previously published in *The Atlantic Monthly, Harper's Monthly,* and *Everybody's Magazine* and printed the collection as *American Indian Stories*.

She was one of the first Native American writers to say what she wanted, unfiltered by white mentors. She did not shrink from controversy or hesitate to express harsh opinions of America's treatment of its native people. She questioned Christian values, declaring boldly in one essay, "Why I Am a Pagan." Another story, "The Soft-Hearted Sioux," described the tragic consequences when a boy, trained in Christian boarding school that killing is wrong, has to feed his starving father.

Tireless and determined, she reached out to groups she thought might help the Indians' cause. That June she traveled to Salt Lake City, where she appealed to the General Federation of Women's Clubs annual convention, describing the deplorable state of Indian existence in the United States. She had a commanding stage presence, an assured yet modest manner, and delivered her dramatic facts in a pleasing, musical voice. When she had finished, the influential club women established an Indian Welfare Committee and hired her to head an investigation into the federal government's treatment of several tribes.

Gertrude traveled through the eastern Oklahoma back country with Charles H. Fabens of the American Indian Defense Association and Matthew K. Sniffen of the Indian Rights Association, documenting case after case in which local courts declared Indians who owned oil-rich land incompetent. Judges then appointed guardians who enriched themselves while the Indians starved. Trustees often took from twenty to seventy percent of an estate's income as administrative expenses. When lies and intimidation failed, those coveting the land resorted to kidnaping, rape, and murder. When their thirty-nine page report, *Oklahoma's Poor Rich Indians: an Orgy of Graft and Exploitation of the Five Civilized Tribes—Legalized Robbery,* was published in 1924, it was a sensation.

Tending at times to overblown prose, Gertrude had no need to embellish stories such as that of a Choctaw grandmother and her seven-year-old granddaughter, whose inheritance of oil-rich land brought harassment, starvation, and death to the child within two years. She documented another case of a woman who died in 1918, yet "appeared" in person—as a man—according to sworn statements, to lease her land to a white man in 1922. In Oklahoma, Bonnin noted caustically, "the grafters can bring the dead to life, and even change the sex!" For these and other victims, she appealed "for action, immediate action, by the honest and fairminded Americans of this 20th century."

The horrifying case histories shocked the public and led to further investigation and attempts at reform. That year Indians were granted U.S. citizenship, a cause for which Zitkala-Ša had long fought. Eventually, the Institute of Governmental Research established a commission headed by Lewis Meriam to survey education, health, hospital, and cultural resources available to Native Americans.

Citizenship was only a first step. In 1926, hoping to revive the cooperative effort of Indians working together to improve their lives, the Bonnins organized the National Council of American Indians, (NCAI). Zitkala-Ša served as president, traveling western reservations, lobbying Congress, and lecturing. "I am what I am. I owe no apologies to God or men," she had written in 1901. The statement was as much bravado as conviction at the time, but as the years passed, she became more certain that her methods and goals were the only correct ones. She found it difficult to accept criticism, and did not willingly share control. The NCAI failed to grow, but she remained its president as long as she lived.

Zitkala-Ša's championing of the Indian culture had several times put her in conflict with other Indian activists who wanted all focus on the future. To many of them, assimilation was not anathema, but a desirable outcome. They did not want to be reminded, or have a white audience reminded, of their tribal past. The voice Gertrude Bonnin raised, insisting native beliefs and practices were equal to—even preferable to—white culture, often sounded alone.

Impoverished and increasingly ill during the Depression years, she was thrilled to learn the New York City Light Opera Guild was to present *The Sun Dance* for its annual opera in April 1938. But the year had just begun when she died on January 26, in Washington, D.C., at the age of sixty-one.

Zitkala-Ša died a disillusioned and bitter woman. She had never made peace with her mother and always felt guilty that she could not be content on the reservation. Her struggle to effect meaningful, lasting reforms in laws concerning Indian's rights must have felt as if she again "trudged in the day's harness heavy-footed, like a dumb sick brute." She wondered if her lifelong struggle had achieved anything at all.

Her colleagues had no such doubts. Her aggressive use of the white man's tools of pen and book increased understanding, exposed wrongs, and substantially improved Indian lives. She was instrumental in securing citizenship for American Indians. Her contemporaries, including Commissioner of Indian Affairs John Collier, described her as "the most sincere and persuasive advocate," and the best defender and fighter for Indian rights.

She had spent her lifetime fighting for appreciation of Native American culture. Seeing *The Sun Dance* on a Broadway stage would have been a triumph. Knowing that two hundred soloists auditioned for leading roles and that the cast's singers and dancers represented the Cherokee, Chippewa, Hopi, Mohawk, and Yakima nations, would have gratified her soul. Watching her friend Will Hanson, by then a professor at Brigham Young University, and Guild director/conductor John Hand deal with dual crises might have provoked a rueful shake of her head. The day before the opening, theater management demanded an extra $300 for dress rehearsal time. The night of the opening the musicians' union demanded $600 to pay a standby orchestra. Contracts, written in white man's words, had confused, deceived, proved untrustworthy. Zitkala-Ša had battled them all her life.

The audience was gathered and growing restless by the time the final crisis was resolved. Then the curtain opened to tipis pitched by a mountain stream, the scent of sage, authentic Indian love chants, stirring choruses, whirling dancers, piping eagle-bone whistles, and drums that pounded until the beats reverberated in listeners' chests. Characters loved, longed, gossiped, intrigued, laughed, feared, prayed, and sacrificed in turn. Tension mounted toward the exhausting ordeal of dancers straining to fulfill their sacred vows to the Great Spirit in the Sun Dance finale.

The production sold out 3,100 seats for both performances, and applause stopped the show numerous times. It was, as opera historian Edward Ellsworth Hipsher noted, far removed from the familiar "dime-novel" Indian. Rather, he said, the opera "is a sympathetic portrayal of the real Indian"—the manners, customs, dress, religious ideals, superstitions, songs, games, ceremonials—"in short, the life of a noble romantic people too little understood."

In her preface to *Old Indian Legends,* Zitkala-Ša had expressed the hope her readers would feel a kinship, would realize Indians were "at heart much like other peoples." Having once left her people for education in the white man's way, she found, try as she might, she could never truly go home again. Yet she wrote from her tragic position with a passion that forced readers to recognize that pain, sorrow, joy, and love are felt by all people—even American Indians. The New Yorkers who exited the Broadway Theater that April in 1938 left with new understanding that the remote land of simple savages they had expected to experience was neither simple nor savage, and not so very far away.

"It is not what we give for nothing but what we inspire others to try or to do—that is the best, most valuable gift we can offer," Zitkala-Ša had written in 1901. Decades after her death, contemporary Native American authors evoke echoes of her trenchant voice. Zitkala-Ša's books, *American Indian Stories* and *Old Indians Legends,* were reprinted by the University of Nebraska Press in 1985.

RANALD MACKENZIE: THE FORGOTTEN HERO

Troy D. Smith

THE DASHING CAVALRY COMMANDER, defending settlers from Native American warriors, has become an ingrained image on not only our perception of the West but of American culture as a whole. One name jumps immediately into the minds of almost everyone in conjunction with this image: George Armstrong Custer, falling valiantly (some would say foolishly, or deservedly) at the Little Bighorn.

But there is another. One regimental commander in the Indian Wars compiled a record of success and efficiency—and of daring—which surpasses that of his more famous contemporary. This man was Ranald Slidell Mackenzie. His name is unknown now except to historians and enthusiasts of the Old West. This may be due, at least in part, to the circumstances in which his career ended: a descent into madness which was far less glorious than Custer's demise, but no less tragic. Nevertheless, an examination of Mackenzie's record shows that the public's infatuation, then and now, with Custer as the great hero of the Indian Wars has been sadly misplaced. A hero has been forgotten.

Another factor has contributed to Mackenzie's lapse into anonymity. Whereas Custer supplemented his martial activities with a penchant for self-promotion—often bringing reporters along to document his exploits for the reading public—Mackenzie shunned the spotlight. Custer's career blazed out in a violent, and disastrous, failure. Mackenzie, on the other hand, was always interested primarily in results. Mackenzie's aim was the destruction of the enemy's base and support rather than a "theatrical" victory. He planned and executed his campaigns meticulously, with no interest in publicity, and considered undue casualties as unacceptable. He lost fewer men in his entire career than Custer did on that one fateful day in 1876. Ironically, it was Mackenzie's Fourth Cavalry that was sent to the northern plains to engage the Cheyennes who had participated in the Battle of the Little Bighorn.

General Ranald Mackenzie came from a military family. He won a reputation as a courageous officer during the Civil War. As commander of the Fourth Cavalry during the Indian Wars he gained the confidence of his superiors. He defeated Quanah Parker's Comanches, won the respect of Cheyenne leader Dull Knife, convinced Sioux leader Red Cloud to return to the reservation, headed off an Apache crisis, and—in his proudest moment—prevented a war with the Utes. It was at the height of his career, when he had no enemies left to defeat and was about to finally marry the woman he had loved for years, that everything fell apart.

Mackenzie was not exactly the Hollywood prototype of a cavalry hero. He had a shrill voice and a nervous, temperamental disposition. He did fit the popularized mold in some ways, however. He was a man of few words. His old college classmates would complain that "he does not stop in one place long enough to write a letter." Even his reports were brief. This may have been due not only to his generally reserved nature but to the fact that his mangled hand made it difficult for him to write. He had lost part of the hand to a shell in the Civil War, and when in deep thought could be seen snapping the stubs of his two missing fingers together. Some of his men called him "Three-Finger Jack" (although almost certainly not to his face) and the Kiowas called him "Mangomhente"—Bad Hand.

When Mackenzie did speak, his words were effective. During his climactic battle with the Comanches at Palo Duro Canyon, he overheard a frightened trooper say, "How will we ever get out of here?" "I brought you in," Mackenzie said, "I will take you out." Mostly, however, he communicated through action—which helps explain the seven wounds he received in his career. His former subordinate James Parker put it best: "He was a *soldier*."

His accomplishments have been sufficient to inspire a good deal of entertainment. In September 1947, a short story based on his raid at Remolino appeared in *The Saturday Evening Post*. The James Warner Bellah story, "Mission With No Record," became the basis for the John Ford film *Rio Grande* (although Mackenzie's name and demeanor were changed for the role, played by John Wayne). This was followed by a 1955 novel published by Ballantine

Books—*The Mackenzie Raid,* by Colonel Red Reeder—and the television program *Mackenzie's Raiders* in the late 1950s and early 1960s. The television show, in turn, spawned a Dell comic book. In all these media, Mackenzie was portrayed as the typical steel-jawed Western hero.

The real Ranald Mackenzie was born in New York City on July 27, 1840. He took great pride in his Scots ancestry, bristling at anyone who thought his last name was Irish. His paternal aunt Jane was married to the famous Commodore Matthew C. Perry; his uncle John Slidell was a Senator and a senior advisor to President James Buchanan. Slidell would later be a diplomat for the Confederate government.

Mackenzie's father, Alexander Slidell Mackenzie, was a captain in the navy. The elder Mackenzie had been born Alexander Mackenzie Slidell, but switched the names as a favor to a bachelor uncle named Mackenzie who was afraid the name would die out. Captain Mackenzie was also an acclaimed naval historian, and a friend of Washington Irving. Irving described young Ranald as a "bright looking child."

Captain Mackenzie developed a reputation as a "sundowner," or a stern martinet. He was a harsh—and "sometimes psychotic"—disciplinarian whose men "feared, at times perhaps hated" him. He was very stingy with his praise—his men were only doing what was expected of them, after all—a feature which would be repeated decades later in his own son's command method.

The elder Mackenzie's approach to military discipline would embroil him in controversy. In December 1842, while in command of the Navy brig *Somers,* Mackenzie had three of his men hanged for mutiny. Unfortunately for Mackenzie, one of those men—Acting Midshipman Philip Spencer—was the son of the Secretary of War. This twist was sufficient to get the attention of both his superiors and the newspapers, who would have otherwise probably taken little note. Mackenzie was court-martialed and pilloried in the press.

It was in the midst of this troubled time that young Ranald, age three, suffered a sunstroke. It was years before he recovered, and in fact he was sickly for most of his childhood. It is possible that this early sickness may have contributed to his later mental problems.

The controversy surrounding the hangings did not prevent the elder Mackenzie from serving in the Mexican War. It was not long after returning home from this conflict, shortly after he had leaned down from his horse and kissed his little son Ranald and ridden away, that Alexander Mackenzie died of a heart attack at the age of forty-five. After his death the family moved to Morristown, New Jersey.

Ranald entered Williams College at Williamstown, Massachusetts, in 1858. In his junior year, having decided to pursue a military career, he transferred to West Point. He did well; in his senior year he was appointed assistant professor of mathematics, and graduated first in his class in 1862 (one year behind Custer.) He did have a considerable number of demerits on his record, however, as a result of the many pranks he had pulled—evidence that he was not always so reserved after all. He was commissioned second lieutenant in the Corps of Engineers. For the first time, Ranald Mackenzie was going to war.

His Civil War service was both exemplary and physically punishing. He was wounded at Second Manassas (known to Confederates as the Second Battle of Bull Run) on August 29, 1862. A sniper's bullet entered his right shoulder, skitted across his back, and exited the left shoulder. Lieutenant Mackenzie lay where he fell until discovered the next day. In the meantime, Rebels had robbed him and refused to give him a drink of water to ease his suffering. He later told his mother, "I am wounded in the back, but I was not running away." He was breveted to first lieutenant for "gallant and meritorious service." He received another brevet commission the following May, to captain, for his service at Chancellorsville. He was breveted to major on July 4 for service during the Battle of Gettysburg, where he received a minor wound. Less than a year later, on June 18, 1864, Mackenzie was breveted to lieutenant-colonel to replace Colonel Elisha Kellogg as commander of the Second Connecticut Volunteer Artillery. It was four days after this promotion that he lost the first two fingers of his right hand to a shell fragment.

On September 19, Mackenzie performed his most daring personal feat of all, at the Battle of Winchester. He held his hat up on the point of his saber and galloped back and forth over the battlefield, with Confederate bullets and shells whizzing all about him to no effect. One shell cut his horse in half, skinning the colonel's legs—he bound his wound and kept going. In yet another example of Hollywood borrowing from the life of Mackenzie without acknowledging him, Kevin Costner (as Lieutenant John Dunbar) portrayed this event in the opening minutes of the film *Dances With Wolves*.

A member of Mackenzie's command during these years would later say that "the men hated him with the hate of hell" for his strict discipline, but that they greatly respected him and "would follow him anywhere." There were still rumors that some of the disgruntled men under his command considered murdering him—he was already manifesting his father's harshness, but his unquestionable bravery seemed to offset it. The young officer was also beginning to show jealousy of other officers and a deep-seated distrust of Washington, both of which would stick with him throughout his career.

On October 19, at Cedar Creek, Mackenzie was injured yet again. This time he was wounded twice in the leg and received shrapnel in his chest, but he refused to leave the field. This time he was breveted two ranks, up to brigadier general. He was transferred to a cavalry command for the first time, the cavalry division of the Army of the James.

By the end of the war Mackenzie was breveted brigadier general in the regular army and major general of volunteers, making him the highest ranking officer of his West Point class. On January 15, 1866, he was mustered out a brigadier of volunteers but his regular army rank was reduced to captain, which was not unusual for Civil War officers who remained in the service after the war ended and there was no longer a pressing need for officers. Ulysses S. Grant wrote of Mackenzie in his memoirs:

> *I regarded Mackenzie as the most promising young officer in the army. Graduating at West Point, as he did, during the second year of the war, he had won his way up to the command of a corps before its close. This he did upon his own merit and without influence.*

Mackenzie was the last—and one of the few overall—of Grant's Civil War subordinates to be mentioned by name in his memoir.

In March of 1867 Mackenzie accepted command of a "colored regiment," the Forty-first Regular Infantry. He jumped three grades in rank, becoming the youngest full colonel in the army. He was assigned to Fort Brown, Texas—his new regiment quickly established a reputation as being first-rate, with the lowest desertion rate in the army despite being the object of much prejudice from the local Texans.

During his service in the West, Mackenzie further developed the reputation which would follow him as a commander. He was friendly enough when off-duty, and seemed to handle himself well in social circles—although he was much more dignified than most cavalry officers the public had seen—but his behavior toward subordinates was a different story. He saw no need to befriend them or even to be a popular commander, regarding this as a waste of time. One subordinate would report that no one ever saw the colonel smile except in the heat of battle, and that being in his company was an uncomfortable experience, another said that he was "irritable, irascible, exacting, sometimes erratic, and frequently explosive." That same officer, Mackenzie's Fourth Cavalry adjutant, went on to explain that the colonel was never unfair and was quick to apologize if he believed he had been.

In early 1868 the border was quiet, so Mackenzie was temporarily transferred to San Antonio to serve on a courts-martial panel. He was there from March until November. During this time the twenty-eight-year-old colonel lived in a boarding house owned by a man named Warrick Tunstall. Mackenzie developed a close friendship with Tunstall's eighteen-year-old daughter Florida. He soon learned that Florida was engaged to be married to a thirty-two-year-old army surgeon named Redford Sharpe, posted at the time at Fort Sam Houston; this fact did not prevent the two from spending time together, and before long their friendship had blossomed into a passion.

Colonel Mackenzie returned to his field duties, perhaps believing that he could win Florida away from her fiance. He was transferred in March of 1869 to Fort McKavett, in Menard County; the Forty-first and Thirty-eighth infantries had been consolidated into the Twenty-fourth Infantry, one of the four new black regiments which would come to be known as Buffalo Soldiers. As post commander, Mackenzie was also in charge of the Ninth Cavalry (also Buffalo Soldiers).

Mackenzie had a nasty surprise in store. The new post surgeon at Fort McKavett was none other than Doctor Redford Sharpe. Worse, Sharpe informed the colonel that he was to be married to Florida Tunstall on October 19. Not only was the woman whom Mackenzie loved going to marry someone else, he would be forced to see them together every day; in fact, the honeymooners' quarters were only a few yards from his own. It is easy to imagine what torture this must have inflicted on the young commander, but he gave no outward sign of it. Instead he threw himself into his work—and there was plenty of it, with the Kiowas and Comanches seeming to always be causing trouble.

In fact, Mackenzie had trouble enough with the Texans he was there to defend. One local hothead, John "Humpy" Jackson, grew incensed when a black soldier wrote a love letter to his daughter. Jackson grabbed his gun and shot a black trooper at random. Mackenzie was furious, and determined to bring the man to justice, but Jackson's friends hid him. When he finally was apprehended, a group of sympathetic neighbors mounted a rescue—killing two more of Mackenzie's buffalo soldiers. The colonel had several locals arrested, and one was killed while resisting, but Jackson evaded capture for two years. He surrendered himself after Mackenzie had been reassigned, and was promptly acquitted by a jury of his peers.

On December 29, 1870, at age thirty, Mackenzie was given command of the Fourth Cavalry. He relocated to Fort Concho on February 15. Comanches and Kiowas were coming and going at will from the reservation near Fort Sill, and it would be Mackenzie's job to put a stop to it. About 120 deaths had been attributed to the two tribes in Jackson County alone since 1859, and in the area as a whole hundreds had died and hundreds of women and children had been abducted. In addition to the Comanche/Kiowa problem, the settlers also needed to be protected from cattle thieves and *comancheros*—a loose-knit group of criminals (of all races) who trafficked with the marauding warriors.

In one early skirmish with Kwahadi (sometimes spelled Quahadi) Comanches led by the infamous Quanah Parker, on October 12, 1871, Mackenzie received an arrow wound in his thigh. He did not mention himself by name in the official report of the action. Instead, his laconic description was "one soldier wounded." The colonel was especially irritable after his injury—his adjutant noted that "nobody seemed to want to go near him even for sociability." The camp surgeon, mainly as a joke but perhaps also in hopes of smoothing the injured commander's ruffled feathers, told Mackenzie that unless he could behave more calmly the doctor would have no choice but to amputate the injured limb. The doctor barely escaped a blow aimed at his head from Mackenzie's crutch.

Mackenzie learned quickly from his initial encounters with the Indians. He adapted. He would not continue to make the same mistakes other commanders had made, that of fighting Native Americans using Civil War tactics. Colonel Mackenzie would meet the enemy on their terms, fighting as they fought. He would make lightning-fast strikes where they were the most vulnerable—in their home bases, on their food supplies and their horse herds. He determined to follow the Comanches into their formidable home territory, the *Llano Estacado,* the Staked Plains, an area that was "flat, featureless, and devoid of any natural landmarks." Newspapers often circulated rumors that Mackenzie had been killed, but he continued to prove them wrong. He also continued to show his opponents that the Staked Plains were no longer a sanctuary for them, because now they faced someone who was willing to chase them even in the most hellish environment and under any hardship.

And a hardship it was for the colonel. His many old injuries made camping in the extremes of the open desert especially hard on him. R. G. Carter described a hailstorm on the *Llano*: "Mackenzie had no overcoat, and somebody wrapped his shivering form in a buffalo robe. Several wounds received during the Civil War had disabled and rendered him incapable of enduring such dreadful exposure."

On September 29, 1872, Mackenzie's forces attacked a Comanche village at McClellan Creek. They destroyed the village and captured dozens of Indians and rescued several abducted Mexicans. They also captured a large horse herd, but some of the escaping Comanches managed to re-steal it. Nine Medals of

Honor were awarded to officers and men of the Fourth Cavalry for this daring action, but despite the acclaim for his victory Mackenzie was still severely irked by his own lapse in losing the horses. Henceforth he would immediately kill any mounts he took from the Comanches rather than risk letting them fall back into enemy hands.

Texas citizens were also being terrorized by Kickapoos and Lipans, who launched their attacks from below the border. The Mexican government seemed unable—or, as some Texans suggested, unwilling—to end these depredations. President Grant and General Sheridan gave Mackenzie special permission to attack the tribes in their Mexican homes. Since this would possibly lead to an international incident, Mackenzie asked for specific written orders. He later recounted Sheridan's reply to his adjutant, R. G. Carter:

> *Damn the orders! Damn the authority. You are to go ahead on your own plan of action, and your authority and backing shall be Gen. Grant and myself. With us behind you in whatever you do to clean up this situation, you can rest assured of the fullest support. You must assume the risk. We will assume the final responsibility should any result.*

Colonel Mackenzie crossed the border into the Mexican state of Coahuila with six companies from the Fourth Cavalry and a detachment of Twenty-Fourth Infantry buffalo soldiers. On the morning of May 18, 1873, the soldiers swept through several Indian villages near the town of Remolino, killing nineteen warriors and capturing dozens of women and children. He was back across the border at Fort Clark before the Mexican government knew what was happening. The main force of marauding Kickapoo and Lipan warriors, meanwhile, returned to their homes to find a nasty surprise: their villages were destroyed, as were their supplies, their reserve horses were taken, and their families were held captive. The Indians were dispirited, and ten years of raiding into Texas with impunity came to an end.

On the way back from the Remolino raid several of Mackenzie's officers were dismayed to learn that they had been operating without written orders, thereby placing themselves in legal jeopardy. One captain said that he "might not have crossed the Rio Grande if he'd known there were no written orders." Mackenzie calmly informed the officer that he would have shot any man who refused to follow him into Mexico.

After the Remolino raid Mackenzie was forced to take a four-month medical leave. The hard ride into Mexico had aggravated his many injuries, and he was suffering from rheumatism in his joints. The colonel was "never completely well after that time," his adjutant claimed, and "there was hardly a day that he did not suffer."

On September 28, 1874, Mackenzie struck the decisive blow against the Comanches, Kiowas, and Southern Cheyennes. He found their hidden base on the floor of the Palo Duro Canyon and launched a surprise attack. The Indians were routed, all their supplies and over 1,450 horses were destroyed, and they returned to the reservation. Ranald Mackenzie had achieved in only a few years what others had been trying to do for generations: the final defeat of the fierce Comanches.

Ironically, but not uncharacteristically, this significant achievement brought on an emotional malaise for the colonel. Biographer Charles M. Robinson noted, "it sometimes seemed he functioned best only when under severe stress, becoming increasingly nervous and irritable—and perhaps even irrational— once the situation stabilized." With the Comanches defeated and the border safe, the colonel was left with little to occupy his time except for the mundane bureaucratic functions which tended to strain his nerves.

Shortly after the death of Custer, Mackenzie got the new challenge which he had craved. In August, 1876 he was transferred to Fort Robinson, Nebraska, to assume command of the District of the Black Hills soon after his arrival he defused his first explosive situation. Cool and decisive under pressure as always, Mackenzie convinced Lakota leader Red Cloud to return peacefully to the reservation.

Mackenzie and his Fourth Cavalry were assigned to the Powder River Expedition, under the command of General George Crook, to campaign during the winter against Dull Knife's Northern Cheyennes. The Fourth engaged the Cheyennes in the freezing waters of the Red Fork. It was a vicious close-quarters fight. The cavalrymen won the day, but at the cost of seven dead and twenty-six wounded—extraordinarily high casualties where Mackenzie was concerned. To make matters worse, the Cheyennes managed to escape. While still in the field, the colonel was engulfed in a deep depression over what he considered a "failure" even though it had been a victory. He told one of his subordinates that he would "blow his brains out if only he had the nerve." General Sherman, meanwhile, was extolling Mackenzie's victory before the war board, saying, "I can't commend too highly his brilliant achievements and the gallantry of the troops of his command." When the colonel received word of that accolade his mood once more took an upswing and he was "quite jolly" again.

One thing that did not make Ranald Mackenzie "quite jolly" was his rivalry with Nelson Miles. Since his Civil War days Mackenzie had shown a tendency toward petty but intense jealousies, and often complained about fellow officers. Sheridan, one of his strongest supporters, acknowledged that Mackenzie was certainly "not bashful" about his wants—and one thing he wanted desperately was to win promotion to general before Miles did. Sherman was also a supporter and close friend of Mackenzie, but he was often annoyed and frustrated by the colonel's strange fits of temper. Sherman used it to his advantage, though, often playing Mackenzie and Miles off each other. He compared them to a "pair of 'vultures' hovering overhead until age or death left an opening in the higher ranks."

In December 1880, Mackenzie received the bitter news that Miles had been promoted to brigadier-general first. It is possible that Miles was chosen as a political concession, to appease the Democrats. A popular joke making the rounds at the time had Mackenzie staring longingly into the night sky, when another officer comments, "I'm afraid, General, there's Miles between you and the star."

Meanwhile, Mackenzie had become involved in a situation that would lead to what he considered the greatest accomplishment of his life. It was an accomplishment which only a handful of historians are aware of today, and this is *because* Mackenzie succeeded.

Like many other tribes before them, the Utes had the great misfortune of silver being discovered on the land which the government had promised would always be theirs. Now the Utes were told that they must all leave the White River Agency in Colorado and prepare to be removed to the Indian Territory. The Utes did not intend to surrender their homes without a fight. Instead, they began to "entrench themselves" in the mountains.

Colonel Mackenzie had his orders. The Utes must go. He met with a delegation of their leaders, taking with him only a handful of unarmed officers. The Utes stalled, and those among them who were the most intensely opposed to removal grew angrier by the minute. It was a volatile situation. If Mackenzie handled it wrong he and his men would most likely lose their lives, and a major war would be ignited. Finally he stood before them and spoke, his words carefully chosen and delivered in a calm and deliberate manner.

It is not necessary for me to stay here any longer. You can settle this matter by discussion among yourselves. All I want to know is whether you will go or not. If you will not go of your own accord, I will make you go. When you have sufficiently discussed this matter and have arrived at a conclusion, send for me. Remember, you are to go, at once.

The Utes, shocked by his seriousness, agreed to go. Mackenzie was "tinged by sorrow" when he watched the Indians abandon their homes and all they owned, but he was also satisfied. He had carried out his orders, and without the loss of a single life on either side. One wonders how Custer would have handled such a situation, had he still been alive. There is little doubt that more people would be familiar with the circumstances in that case, since there would likely have been a large number of dead Indians, troopers, and miners before it was all over.

Mackenzie was assigned command of the District of New Mexico on October 30, 1881. He was still officially in command of the Fourth Cavalry, but he was now an administrator rather than a field officer. His limited involvement in the Apache wars took place from behind a desk.

He got another chance for promotion when General Irvin McDowell retired. Benjamin Grierson, another Civil War hero and commander of the Tenth Cavalry, was also up for the position. Former President Grant intervened on behalf of his old subordinate Mackenzie, though, doing so "as a matter of simple justice." On October 26, 1882, Ranald Mackenzie received his promotion to the rank of brigadier general—a rank he had held two decades earlier as a brevet. The Fourth Cavalry passed completely into other hands.

General Mackenzie was given command of the Department of Texas— where many citizens now regarded him as their hero and savior from the Comanches—and took up his duties in San Antonio, the site of his great romance fifteen years earlier. It is possible that a return to San Antonio had been on his agenda, as he had been quietly buying land there for some years. He had suffered a brief mental breakdown in the spring of 1883, which friends attributed to the death of his mother, and by the time he arrived in Texas he was showing signs of mental instability. Nevertheless, he had finally secured his general's rank and was on his way to securing something else he had waited on for years.

Forty-eight days after his arrival at his new post, the *San Antonio Light* announced the marriage engagement of Brigadier General Ranald Slidell Mackenzie and Mrs. Florida Sharpe, *nee* Tunstall, who had been a widow since 1873. The impending union, according to the paper, "even had the approval of Mrs. Sharpe's twelve-year-old son, Red." The wedding was set for December 19, 1883. It seemed that Mackenzie finally had everything he had ever wanted.

In the first week of December Mackenzie began to act strangely. He lost weight, and started drinking heavily—he had never been a drinker before this. His orderlies noted that he was usually either "drunk or crazy." The doctor believed the behavior was only temporary, and convinced the orderlies to keep it quiet.

On December 18—the night before his wedding—the general slipped away from his aides and disappeared into a rainstorm. He turned up soon enough, attacking a storeowner with a broken chair leg. A crowd came to the man's rescue and beat the general into submission, holding him for the police. He was arrested. When the police realized that the madman in their possession was the famous and beloved General Mackenzie, they released him into the custody of the orderlies. The officers took him home. Mackenzie rambled incoherently all the way. He was in a paranoid rage for days, and the officers "became exhausted from the constant attention he required."

Mackenzie was sent to an insane asylum in New York. His aides convinced him to board the train by telling him that he was going to Washington to meet with General Sheridan so that the two of them could solve all the problems plaguing the army.

His doctors reported to the army's retirement board on Mackenzie's condition:

[The General] . . . is suffering from "General Paresis of the Insane." And that he is in our opinion unfit for any duty and it is also our opinion that the prospect of his ultimate recovery from the disease is entirely unfavorable. It is also our opinion that the disease originated in the line of duty and we would therefore respectfully recommend that he be placed upon the retirement list of the Army.

General Mackenzie also made a statement to the board:

I think that I am not insane. I think that I have served as faithfully as anybody in the Army. I would rather die than go in the retired list. The Army is all I have got to care for. I don't wish to stay here.

The board ruled that the general was incapacitated, and that his illness "was incurred from wounds received and exposure in the line of duty as an officer of the Army." Mackenzie was honorably—but forcibly—retired. Judged to be harmless, he was released from the hospital in June. He said in a letter that he planned to return to Texas to "look after my interests there"—perhaps meaning Florida—but he never did. He went to live with a cousin on Staten Island. Mackenzie gradually reverted to a childlike state, eventually unable to even speak and apparently unaware of the world around him. Florida would never speak publicly of him again. She would live to be ninety years old, but would never remarry.

Ranald Mackenzie died five years after his retirement, on January 19, 1889. He was forty-eight years old. His brief obituary was buried deep in the *New York Times*. The country seemed to have quickly forgotten him. There is no romance in a gibbering madman, no matter what his previous accomplishments. Also, unlike Custer, he had no devoted wife to continually praise his name and keep his memory alive to the public.

There have been many theories regarding Mackenzie's insanity. Some have suggested that it was a result of syphilis—it was by no means uncommon for frontier officers to resort to prostitutes, and Mackenzie was after all a very shy man. With all his war injuries, however, it is unlikely that such an illness would have escaped the notice of his doctors. Further, as unpopular as Mackenzie was with some of his men, any sexual improprieties would have been quickly made public by someone.

It has been proposed that the insanity resulted from a head injury—perhaps the childhood sunstroke which so ravaged his health when he was young, and which would have been aggravated by long campaigns in the desert. It may also have been sped up by the fact that he finally achieved all his goals and had nothing further to strive for. It has also been theorized by some that his romance with Florida Tunstall was actually little more than an obsession on *her* part. This theory holds that she had married Sharpe in order to be near Mackenzie, and had finally taken advantage of his waning sanity to pressure him into an engagement which finally pushed him over the edge because he did not really want it. There is little real evidence for this scenario.

The most likely explanation is that the doctors were right, although they did not have the modern terminology to express it. Mackenzie probably suffered from post-traumatic stress disorder. This phenomenon was especially common among Civil War veterans. He had all the classic symptoms—difficulty expressing emotions other than anger, a detachment from others, volatile aggression—and they did not begin until Mackenzie had experienced the horrors of war and physical disfigurement. The symptoms gradually worsened as he suffered more injury and privation and shouldered more and more responsibility. It is hard to imagine a man in that position not experiencing emotional and mental difficulties.

Ranald Mackenzie was an intense man. He gave his all, and more, until he burned himself out. His struggles and achievements are at least as heroic as other, more famous generals. Custer only gave his life, after all—Mackenzie gave his soul.

MURDER MOST FOUL:
A NEW MEXICO CAUSE CÉLÈBRE

Karen Holliday Tanner and John D. Tanner, Jr.

A RENAISSANCE PHYSICIAN WOULD have reasonably suspected the use of "inheritance powder" amid the court of the Borgia's, but in Sierra County, New Mexico, arsenic poisoning was not the customary method of ridding oneself of an undesirable spouse. It was certainly the last thing on Dr. Frank Given's mind as he rushed to the bedside of thirty-six-year-old Manuel Madrid on Friday evening, March 29, 1907.

Madrid had suffered gastrointestinal distress—intense abdominal pain, nausea, protracted vomiting, and diarrhea—for nine days. Yet, arsenic poisoning, with symptoms resembling some common illnesses, has always been difficult to diagnose. Although Dr. Given had encountered but three or four cases during his career, he concluded that Madrid suffered from symptoms associated with poison of some sort. The next morning, he returned to find that his gravely ill patient displayed "signs so evident that the merest novice in medicine would have recognized them." Before the pitiable man died, he experienced seizures, followed by shock, and probable kidney failure. The suspicious physician summoned the district attorney, Howard A. Wolford, who hurriedly gathered evidence sufficient to convene a coroner's jury that evening. The inquest's finding stunned the small mountain community. Madrid's seventeen-year-old wife, Valentina, had allegedly conspired with her lover, Francisco Baca, to prematurely end her husband's life. And, Valentina's sixteen-year-old black cook and confidante, Wyoming "Alma" Lyons, had helped them. Sheriff Eduardo Tafoya wasted no time in arresting the three suspects.

The day following Madrid's death, Dr. Given removed Manuel's stomach and sent it to the Agricultural College at Mesilla Park (now New Mexico State University at Las Cruces) for testing. The funeral was held later that afternoon; Valentina, confined to the Hillsboro jail, was not permitted to attend her husband's service.

The next day, she and her two coconspirators were escorted from the Hillsboro jail to their preliminary hearing. It had been eight years since the Sierra County courthouse had played host to the celebrated trial of Oliver Lee and James Gilliland for the murders of Albert Fountain and his son. Fascinated onlookers quickly filled the seats and confidently anticipated a similar spectacle.

Justice Ribera's courtroom stilled as Alma Lyons was summoned to the witness box. Uneducated and uncouth, the native of nearby Kingston was only nine months old when she had lost her mother, and the local newspaper concluded that, like Harriet Beecher Stowe's Topsy, she had "just growed up." Absent from the hearing was sixty-year-old Henry Lyons, who later explained that he had raised his daughter to the best of his ability, but she had received no schooling and little care. W. S. Hopewell, vice president of the Santa Fe Central Railway and Henry's past employer, described the former buffalo soldier and longtime New Mexico resident as an "illiterate and immoral man" and rationalized that Alma, brought up under such adverse circumstances, could only have "developed into a woman of weak-mind and very deficient morals."

On the stand, Lyons' tale of conspiracy and murder titillated the crowd. Some months before the murder, Valentina had invited her into the Madrid household as cook and companion. Manuel soon objected to her presence, but Valentina stood by Lyons and thereby earned the cook's devotion. When Francisco Baca plotted Madrid's murder, Lyons was drawn into the scheme to aid Valentina and her lover to marry, to come into possession of Madrid's property, to sell it, and to move away to live happily ever after. For her part in the conspiracy, Alma confessed that threatened by Baca, she had purchased two boxes of Ballard's Rat Poison. At the conclusion of her testimony, it remained unclear to many in the courtroom whether her acknowledged dislike for Madrid or her asserted fear of Baca better explained her involvement in the conspiracy.

The teenaged widow followed Lyons to the stand. Born in Mimbres, a small mining and ranching community in Grant County, Valentina Barela was barely fifteen when she married Manuel Madrid, well known in the area as a member of a good family, a hard worker, and a good citizen. The couple settled in Hillsboro, a town spawned by the 1877 discovery of gold, but now a casualty of mine closures and a dwindling population. The young bride soon caught the eye of Francisco Baca. Valentina also testified that Baca proposed the scheme to poison Madrid, and that he threatened to kill her, her husband, and Lyons, should she refuse. She confessed to lacing her husband's coffee with poison, starting nine days before his death.

Baca then took the stand. A twenty-five-year-old bachelor, and a recent arrival from Arrey, a small farming community twenty miles south of Hot Springs (now Truth or Consequences), he vehemently denied all charges, but Justice Ribera had heard enough. He ordered the three held without bail and set an arraignment date for May 8.

In contrast to the scandalous revelations at the preliminary hearing, the arraignment of the three prisoners proved anticlimactic. Judge Frank W. Parker read the three indictments charging murder in the first degree, accepted the defendants' pleas of not guilty, and set the trial of Lyons and Madrid to begin the following morning. He postponed Baca's trial until the next term of the court.

An associate justice of the New Mexico Supreme Court, Parker had no aversion to sitting in judgment of a capital offense case. Six years previously, he had upheld outlaw Tom "Black Jack" Ketchum's hanging and wrote, "The punishment of death is not cruel, within the meaning of the word, as used in the Constitution." Nevertheless, before the Lyons and Madrid trial, he gave consideration to the advisability of accepting a plea of guilty of murder in the second degree—a plea that mandated life imprisonment rather than execution. Ultimately, Parker decided that the community's interest would be best served "by putting them on trial and let the law take its course."

At ten o'clock, Thursday morning, May 9, Parker gaveled the courtroom to order, and District Attorney Wolford, assisted by the prominent, though frequently controversial, Albuquerque criminal attorney Elfego Baca, opened the case for the prosecution. Professor R. F. Hare of the Agricultural College presented the forensic evidence and established that Madrid's liver contained 2.75 grains of white arsenic—the cause of death. As both defendants had previously confessed, there remained little more for the prosecution to do.

Major James Waddell, the court-appointed defense attorney, faced a next to impossible task. Madrid took the stand first and told that court that she gave Manuel the poison, but insisted, "If no one had been advising me nothing would have happened." When asked who had advised her to do it, she replied that Francisco Baca "injected [it] into my mind." She claimed that Baca had threatened Alma by stating that if she did not buy poison that he would kill her, "and that if I did not give it to him that he would kill us both, wherever we were he would kill us three, myself, my husband and [Lyons] wherever we might be."

Lyons followed Madrid to the stand and again testified to her role in the crime and revealed little that was new. Baca had demanded that she and Valentina poison Madrid and had threatened to kill them if they refused. The two of them had "talked it over and agreed that we better do it than be killed ourselves." Baca gave her fifty cents to buy rat poison. She bought it, and Valentina put it in Madrid's coffee. He got sick the next day, lived for nine more days, and finally died.

Attorney Waddell attempted to portray his clients as young, ignorant, and the unwilling pawns of the villainous Francisco Baca. However, in the opinion of the reporter from *The Santa Fe New Mexican,* Waddell's effort was "smashed into smithereens" by Elfego Baca's closing argument. After all, attorney Baca told the jury, Lyons had purchased the poison, in two lots, at two different times, and she and Madrid had willingly fed it to Valentina's husband. Then, ignoring his suffering, for nine days they continued to administer the arsenic in Manuel's coffee. Rather than young and ignorant, the jury should recognize them as "old in dissolute and unchaste habits." That night the jury returned two verdicts of guilty.

Try as he might, Judge Parker could find no mitigating circumstances and labeled the crime "atrocious beyond description." "The fact that some man told you to do this, excuses not one particle of your guilt," he scolded Madrid. "You have committed the highest crime known to the law." With that, he sentenced her to be taken from jail on June 7, and then to be "hanged by the neck until you are dead." Turning to Lyons, Parker solemnly spoke, "You have been a party to the most outrageous crime that has ever been known in this part of the country. It strikes horror into the hearts of all men. It is simply terrible beyond description. You have forfeited your right to live." She, too, was sentenced to hang on June 7. Even as Sheriff Eduardo Tafoya returned the two convicted murderesses to the Hillsboro jail to await their date with the hangman, a furor arose over the sentences. Should the Territory of New Mexico, then actively seeking statehood, hang two naive teenaged girls?

On the day following the conviction, a number of Sierra County residents signed the first of many petitions that called upon the interim governor, James Raynolds, to commute the girls' sentences. The petition argued that hanging two young women would have a "demoralizing effect" and sought justice in the form of life sentences. Other petitions hurriedly followed from Lake Valley, Kingston, and Monticello residents. Within a week, even a Chicago dweller sought Raynolds's attention, "God gave life, let him take it in his own time and way." The timing of the appeals proved opportune for the girls.

Appointed the previous year, Governor Herbert James Hagerman proved idealistic but politically unskilled and was soon at odds with the Republican "Old Guard." To mend the rift in the party, President Theodore Roosevelt forced Hagerman's resignation only weeks before the Madrid-Lyons trial and appointed his old friend, former New Mexico lawman and Rough Rider George Curry to the post. Serving then as governor of Samar province in the Philippines, Curry could not reach New Mexico for some months. In the meantime, James Wallace Raynolds, secretary of the territory, assumed the interim governorship on May 3rd.

Amid the political upheaval, the prospect of New Mexico's statehood remained foremost in the mind of most of the territory's residents. The issue had assumed a new dimension during Hagerman's tenure with a controversial proposal of joint statehood for Arizona and New Mexico—the combined state to bear the name Arizona, but with the capital at Santa Fe. New Mexico, anxious for self-determination, had voted in favor of the measure, but Arizona's negative ballots defeated the plan. Nevertheless, a considerable majority of New Mexicans still held out hopes for statehood and feared that hanging two teenaged girls would be a serious setback. *The Daily Optic* (Las Vegas) expressed that concern when it editorialized, "It would be a blot on the fair name of the territory to have the news go out to the world that these two ignorant children have been executed within her borders." Mindful of the growing tempest, Raynolds expressed his own concern that "the eastern press is making preparations to give this hanging very liberal advertisement by way of special articles with illustrations, etc."

Several Sierra County officials took up the call for commutation. Julian Chavez, the under sheriff, wrote Raynolds that the girls acted like eight-to ten-year-old children, and failed to grasp the enormity of their crime. John Plemmens, the county treasurer, agreed that it would be "too much like hanging children."

As the condemned girls' youth and ignorance provided cause for many of the appeals, so, too, did their sex. One attorney expressed the opinion of many, "Death inflicted upon a man is always appalling; but, when death is to be visited upon a woman, our nature revolts. The very fact that they are women suggests that clemency is to be generously exercised." A resolution passed by the Albuquerque Woman's Club concurred.

As letters arrived at the governor's office seeking the commutation of the girls' sentences, in mid-May Sheriff Ed Tafoya and Deputy Adolfo Chavez reached Santa Fe with Francisco Baca in tow. Confined for safekeeping in the New Mexico Territorial Penitentiary while he awaited his forthcoming trial,

Baca joined his uncle, convicted murderer Jose Molino, serving a twenty-five-year sentence. Baca's confinement proved temporary—the territory afterward failed to convict him of any felony.

Still later in the month, Henry Lyons arrived in Santa Fe intent upon making a personal plea for his daughter's life. Employed as a cook in a Burro Mountain mining camp, the old man had been unaware of his daughter's arrest and conviction until well after the trial's conclusion. In seeking clemency from the governor, he begged "that for the good of humanity, in that these women are ignorant and young," life imprisonment would teach them "the way of righteousness, and the fear of God, and the laws of mankind." He then "broke down and cried bitterly."

As the commutation pressure on Governor Raynolds mounted, he also discovered that some defended the sentence. Dr. Given, the attending physician, reminded the governor that though sympathy might compel a commutation, knowledge that their life would be forfeit might deter other wives and husbands from committing similar crimes. Hillsboro banker W. H. Bucher wrote Raynolds of his belief that were honest opinions expressed, the majority of people would favor the extreme penalty, and that laws, in criminal cases, should apply as well to women.

As the date of the scheduled execution drew near, Raynolds sought additional advice from the district attorney and the presiding judge. Attorney Wolford stressed that both had been "leading a life of ill-fame since they were about twelve years of age." Moreover, he believed that they did, in fact, realize the import of their crime. However, he, too, defended a commutation; like many, he did so based upon the killers' sex and the certainty that "the Eastern papers are ready to do us all the injury they can do and this would be their opportunity." Judge Parker offered the viewpoint that although "the crime was without the slightest of mitigating circumstances," the hanging of any two women would "be brutalizing in the extreme" for the community. He counseled that a commutation "shortly before the day of execution" would serve the ends of justice.

These two judicious opinions provided Governor Raynolds with sufficient support for clemency, but he heeded Parker's advice and remained silent. On June 3, four days before the scheduled execution, Sheriff Tafoya read the death warrant to Madrid and Lyons. It failed to "disturb the peace of mind of the two women." The same day, V. F. Trujillo, the chairman of the Sierra County Commission, and responsible for the construction of the scaffold and the enclosure, telegraphed the governor requesting guidance. The next morning, with no word from Raynolds, construction of a scaffold for a double hanging began, only to cease in the midafternoon when Sheriff Tafoya finally received a telegram from the governor indicating that he had commuted the sentences of Valentina Madrid and Alma Lyons to life imprisonment. Interestingly, although the commutation order cited the volume of petitions, letters, and editorials supporting clemency, Raynolds's specific defense of the action was that the two girls were the only witnesses that could testify against Baca at his forthcoming trial.

On Friday, June 7, rather then leading Lyons and Madrid into an enclosure for a date with the noose, Sheriff Tafoya left Hillsboro with his two prisoners, bound for Santa Fe and the New Mexico Territorial Penitentiary. The threesome arrived the next day; Lyons (no. 2157) and Madrid (no. 2158) were swiftly inducted into the home that the law decreed to be theirs for the remainder of their natural lives.

New Mexico underwent a number of changes during the next seven years, including the coming of statehood in 1912. Alma Lyons and Valentine Madrid, long since forgotten by her citizens, remained confined behind the walls of the penitentiary. Events then thrust Alma back into the limelight—she was pregnant. Henry Lyons directed a number of serious charges against the prison matron, Mrs. James B. McManus, the wife of the warden.

Lyons claimed in his complaint to Governor William C. McDonald that Alma had been allowed to come in contact with a male prisoner, that upon the discovery of her condition she had been placed on bread and water for three weeks, and that no one could see or take a statement from her. He also alleged that Valentina Madrid had delivered a stillborn child during the previous few months.

McDonald acted promptly. The next day he convened the Board of Penitentiary Commissioners, chaired by former governor Miguel Otero, to investigate Henry Lyons's assertions. Later that afternoon, Warden McManus, also a member of the Board, responded to questions. He denied that female prisoners encountered male prisoners and explained that he had employed Lyons within the superintendent's dining room from about June 1, to July 21, 1913. She was then diagnosed with appendicitis, and Dr. J.A. Massie, the prison physician, had ordered her transferred to St. Vincent's sanatorium. She returned to the penitentiary on August 14, following an appendectomy. In mid-November, Massie diagnosed her pregnancy. McManus also denied the remainder of the charges and declared that although he "deeply deplored the occurrence," Henry Lyons's charges "were based on false statements concocted in the diseased mind of his poor, unfortunate daughter." McManus's protestations notwithstanding, one fact remained self-evident—Alma's pregnancy.

Mrs. McManus, the matron, filed a written statement with the Board. She, too, denied that she permitted Lyons to wander at large through the building, and she reiterated the chronology to which her husband had testified. After the discovery of her pregnancy, Lyons had been isolated, not as punishment, but "that for moral reasons her condition might not become known to the other prisoners." McManus also denied that Madrid had miscarried "as far as I am able to ascertain," and noted that her job required "constant vigilance." Again, rationalizations notwithstanding—Dr. J. A. Massie had confirmed Lyons's pregnancy.

On the afternoon of January 22, Chairman Otero, the McManuses, and board member C. F. Easley gathered to hear the principal witness, Alma Lyons. Lyons testified that she could not eat "cell-house" food, and she had received better food after complaining. She agreed that Mrs. McManus did not allow her to meet with male prisoners, and when asked if she had ever been placed on a diet of bread and water, she responded, "No, Sir, they just kept me in a room by myself." Otero then read a November 18, statement of Lyons's into the record. It revealed that she had first had sexual relations with prisoner Juan Trujillo, a hall porter, in early June 1913. On three or four occasions, he had somehow sneaked past the hall guard and up the stairs.

At five feet tall and one hundred and fourteen pounds, the diminutive Juan Trujillo, an alcoholic with three drunk and disorderly arrests immediately preceding his arrest for robbery, had testified at his trial that, due to drink, he had no recollection of having robbed anyone. As prisoner no. 3028 he had entered the penitentiary from Lincoln County on March 30, 1912, sentenced to a two- to three-year-term for robbery. Within six months, he had earned the job of porter. Trujillo had been paroled on January 5, 1914, and was no longer under the direct control of the Penitentiary Board. Lyons, however, remained under their administration; the investigation continued.

Warden McManus asked Lyons if she positively knew that Madrid had miscarried. She answered, "Yes, she showed it to me." From her response, and from her description of "a big piece of flesh," McManus next constructed a question designed to mislead.

"If you did not know positively what it was, why did you state it to your father, brother and sister as absolute fact?"

Lyons's response must have pleased. "I just stated it to them because I was just worked up."

The Board next examined Valentina Madrid, who denied having had a miscarriage. When Otero asked her if she had been a good girl, she replied, "Sometimes I have been doing wrong, writing notes and talking to the boys."

However, when he questioned whether she had been allowed to go around with the men convicts, she answered no. No one questioned how she might have talked to the boys without having been around the male inmates.

At the conclusion of the inquiry, Otero urged Henry Lyons to make amends by withdrawing his complaint and correcting the record. Otero then reported to the governor that no foundation for the complaint existed. Still, there remained one incontrovertible fact—Lyons's pregnancy—"it was due to the connivance, negligence or gross carelessness of the hall guard who is not now employed in the Penitentiary."

The Board's report effectively diffused a potential scandal. In retrospect, certainly Lyons designed some of her claims to secure better treatment. However, her father's complaint had a legitimate foundation—Alma Lyons had become pregnant while a prisoner at the New Mexico State Penitentiary during the administration of James B. McManus.

Lyons entered St. Vincent Sanatorium on February 7, 1914, and she delivered a son on April 1. A concerned family took the infant into their home; Alma returned to the penitentiary on April 10, and again stepped out of the public spotlight.

New Mexico's governors, possessed of the powers of pardon and parole, routinely exercised those powers, even in those instances where the sentence was for the remainder of the inmate's natural life. Indeed, between the opening of the New Mexico Territorial Penitentiary in 1884 and statehood in 1912, the average time served under a sentence of life was only seven years and nine months. On June 9, 1918, eleven years after her admission, Alma Lyons made application for parole to Governor Octaviano A. Larrazolo. Valentina Madrid made application the following November 27.

On their applications, their story remained consistent with their testimony at the trial. Francisco Baca had threatened to kill them if they did not poison Madrid; Lyons purchased the poison with money given to her by Baca; Valentina had put the poison in Madrid's coffee. Both also cited their youth at the time. Madrid, now twenty-nine years old, noted that she had an offer of employment in Parkview (Rio Arriba County); she accompanied her application with an appeal from her mother, Mrs. Tomasa Barela, and a petition signed by over 125 Hillsboro residents, including prosecutor Wolford. Twenty-six-year-old Alma Lyons reported that she had received an offer of employment in Santa Fe.

The governor commuted the sentences of the two young women from life to twenty-three years on May 12, 1919. As the records reported no bad conduct for either prisoner, their twenty-three-year prison time sentence, with credit for good behavior, would expire on March 3, 1920. Considering their age at the time of their sentencing, the period of time they had served, and their record of good conduct, the following day Governor Larrazolo granted them a conditional pardon. The two parolees were forbidden to leave the state of New Mexico or to enter Sierra County. They were also required to secure employment and to obey the laws. After almost twelve years, Valentina Madrid and Alma Lyons walked out of the New Mexico State Prison on May 13, 1919.

Since the advent of New Mexico's territorial status in 1850, her citizens had enthusiastically and repeatedly sought statehood. They had no sympathy for two girls who could have played the Brewster sisters of a later era (*Arsenic and Old Lace*), yet the need to properly punish these murderers had been at cross-purposes with that objective. On one hand, law and order dictated that a first-degree murder conviction justified, indeed demanded, the extreme penalty—death by hanging. On the other hand, to hang two women, and two teenagers at that, could fatally jeopardize the long-term goal of statehood. Having submitted close to fifty applications, and having experienced a like number of rejections, public sentiment in 1907 awakened to the realization that the dignity of the law and the fair name of New Mexico could be maintained by life imprisonment of the killers. For nearly twelve years, almost five years longer than time served by the average killer, Lyons and Madrid remained behind the walls of the New Mexico's penitentiary. It was during their incarceration that New Mexico, on January 6, 1912, at last secured her place on America's flag—the forty-seventh star.

IMAGES OF THE TEXAS RANGERS

Robert M. Utley

OF CONSTABULARIES AROUND THE world, only the Royal Canadian Mounted Police compete with the Texas Rangers in nearly universal name recognition. The Mounties began in 1873 as a frontier force designated the Northwest Mounted Police and evolved into a national institution admired for their scarlet tunics, precision drill, and efficient policing.

By contrast, the Texas Rangers began in the 1830s as a tradition rather than an institution. Officially they bore the Ranger designation only sporadically for decades. Not until after half a century fighting Indians did they evolve from sometime-citizen soldiers into full-time lawmen. In both incarnations, they disdained uniforms and all other military attributes.

Aside from these differences, the two institutions display another significant contrast. The Mounties have projected a consistently favorable image, prompting widespread admiration. The Rangers have displayed varied images, but most conspicuous have been polar images almost from the beginnings in the 1830s to the present day. At the one pole the image is firmly positive, at the otherfirmly negative. Thus, unlike the Canadian Mounted Police, the Texas Rangers are either idolized or deplored.

The positive Ranger image is rooted in the decade of the Republic from 1836 to 1945, the Mexican War, and the decade preceding the Civil War. Outstanding leaders captained some of the companies called out to fight Indians or contend with Mexicans—Jack Hays, Matt Caldwell, Ben McCulloch, and Rip Ford, to name four. The model for all subsequent captains, John Coffee (Jack) Hays, pioneered mounted combat by adopting the first revolving pistol, the five-shot Paterson Colt. At the Battle of Walker Creek in 1844, he and fourteen Rangers took on seventy Comanche warriors and employed the revolver so effectively that only twenty Indians escaped the battlefield unhurt.

In the Mexican War of 1846–48 Hays commanded the federalized First Texas Mounted Volunteers, all former Rangers. General Zachary Taylor kept one of Hays's companies, Ben McCulloch's Gonzales Rangers, attached to his headquarters because of their unsurpassed reconnaissance skills. At the Battle of Monterey (the contemporary spelling), Hays's regiment proved themselves first-rate combat soldiers and arguably the critical factor in Taylor's victory. Later, under General Winfield Scott, Hays's men proved their excellence in antiguerrilla operations. Armed with the new Walker Colt, the first six-shooter, they repeatedly defeated overwhelming numbers of Mexican lancers.

The Mexican War transformed the Texas Rangers from men celebrated by Texas to men celebrated by the entire nation. They emerged as national heroes not only because of their battlefield success but because of media appeal. Their unorthodox ways attracted journalists. They wore no uniforms, carried no flags, enjoyed an easy camaraderie between officers and enlisted men, and scorned military regulations. They also indulged in unmilitary ruffianly high jinks that correspondents delighted in describing.

The opposite polar image also gained prominence in the Mexican War. For both Generals Taylor and Scott, the undisciplined Rangers constantly made trouble. But their worst misdeeds sprang from vivid memories of the Alamo and Goliad massacres perpetrated by Mexicans during the Texas Revolution and incidents of Mexican cruelty during the decade of the Texas Republic. The Rangers came to Mexico to exact revenge, and they gained it not only on the battlefield but in atrocities against noncombatants. In February 1847, for example, reacting to the destruction of a military supply train, Captain Mabry B. ("Mustang") Gray's Ranger company put to death the entire male population—twenty-four men—of the nearby village of Ramos. And in Mexico City in December 1847, after one of Hays's Rangers was slashed to death in a district called Cutthroat, Rangers rode the streets throughout an entire night, systematically shooting down anyone who appeared in the sights of their heavy Walker Colts. The next morning, wagons hauled eighty corpses to the morgue.

Little wonder that Mexicans called the Rangers *Los Diablos Tejanos*. And little wonder that General Taylor asked superiors "that no more troops may be sent to this column from the State of Texas."

The 1850s brought Ranger units into repeated collisions with Comanches, both along the frontier of settlement and in their homeland north of Red River, the Indian Territory. The widely applauded captain of this period was John Salmon Ford, "Rip" Ford, who had served as Hays's adjutant in the Mexican War. In fact, the Rangers proved no more successful than the Regular Army at keeping raiding parties out of the frontier settlements; and Ford's celebrated victory over Iron Jacket's Comanches at the Battle of Antelope Hills in 1858 merely intensified the raids, both in revenge and to restock the horse herds Ford had seized. But because Ranger fights could be easily glorified, the Ranger image flowered.

Although a Confederate Ranger regiment faced Comanches on the northwestern frontier during the Civil War, the contrasting images faded in the turmoil of war and Reconstruction. Not until 1874 did the state legislature bring the Rangers back to life, now as a permanent institution. Created to fight Indians, they discovered that the Regular Army had finally conquered the Comanches, leaving few Indians to fight. But Texas was a violent place, overridden by stock thieves, feudists, and other varieties of criminals. The Rangers transformed themselves into lawmen, and such they have been ever since.

The last of the citizen soldier outfits, however, revived the negative image. From 1874 to 1877, Leander McNelly's Ranger company contended with Mexican stock thieves. McNelly not only crossed the Rio Grande to violate Mexican sovereignty but also used intimidation, torture, and even execution to carry out his mission. Mexicans did not forget McNelly.

As Old West lawmen, the Rangers of the last quarter of the nineteenth century regained their fame and revived the fading legend among Anglo Texans. The state's adjutant general commanded the Rangers, and during this period he constantly extolled the deeds of the lawmen in expansive rhetoric. Newspapers and pulp fiction portrayed them in even more glowing terms. The image vastly inflated the reality; but for the most part the Rangers of this period, even though constantly thwarted by a criminal justice system that made convictions almost impossible to obtain, performed their duties efficiently and effectively.

Most of the good Ranger captains were quiet and modest, but one reinforced the grandiose facade. Captain Bill McDonald was a showman, a colorful character, a self-promoter who reveled in notoriety and played to the media and the politicians. Often quoted for years afterward was Captain Bill's motto: "No man in the wrong can stand up against a fellow whose in the right and keeps on a-comin'." The fallacy of course lies in who defines right and wrong. With Captain Bill, he was always the man in the right.

McDonald is also behind another persistent Ranger myth. A town mayor frantically wires the governor to send Rangers because a riot is about to break out. A single Ranger arrives. When asked where the others are, he replies, "Ain't but one riot." The story appears in many variations, but several of Captain Bill's exploits provided the inspiration. "One Riot, One Ranger," is still a vibrant element of Ranger legend.

The negative image endured throughout the era of the Old West lawmen principally among border Mexicans. The excesses of the Mexican War and of Leander McNelly's company remained deeply buried in their memory. Moreover, they regarded almost any violent encounter between an Anglo lawman and a Mexican as ethnic stereotyping, as many were. *Rinches* was their word for Rangers, but they applied it equally to any white man on horseback with a gun-federal, state, or county lawmen and even cowboys. They all looked alike. During the final decades of the Old West period, roughly 1885 to 1910, the Ranger Force rarely numbered as many as twenty for the entire state. Rangers along the border were few indeed, but they bore the blame for many a local lawman's mistreatment of Mexicans.

The prime example of false image-making remains the saga of Gregorio Cortez, a young Mexican who in 1901 killed two sheriffs and led hundreds of possemen on an extraordinary ten-day chase across South Texas. It ended at the border when a Ranger captain quietly arrested him. Cortez was probably a horse thief, but the Mexican balladry that still celebrates his exploit presents him as a simple tenant farmer mistakenly victimized by the law and ruthlessly run down by the Texas Rangers. Aside from the officer who arrested him, only one Ranger participated in the chase. Yet the folk tale pits the lone hero against a horde of Rangers and enjoys currency not only among Mexicans and Mexican Americans but, thanks to the work of the revisionist scholars, among politically correct elements of the larger population.

As the Old West passed into history, many Texans thought the Rangers should slip into history also. Not only Mexican Americans but many Anglos also wanted the Rangers gone. Their impartiality in local crises, whether feuds or courtroom dramas that aroused partisan sentiment, gained politically powerful enemies and frequently brought the force to the edge of extinction by the legislature. But beyond the special interests, Anglo Texans still venerated the Rangers and Mexican Americans still hated them.

The Old West lawmen lived within what may be termed a "six-shooter culture." They not only set high value on mastery of the Winchester repeater and Colt six-shooter but admired men who had validated their skills against human targets. The culture embraced physical strength, courage, and fearlessness as well as a readiness to apply violence where deemed necessary. A frontier lawman needed all these qualities, but if not kept in check they could easily drift into excess.

With several exceptions, the captains of the 1880s and 1890s were superior leaders who, both in recruiting and in operations, kept the worst features of the culture under control. When misdeeds did occur, unless directed at Mexicans, the governor and state legislators usually heard of it, and each biennium the Rangers had to contend against still deeper cuts in their appropriations. Even as the force shrank to hardly a dozen, however, the Rangers basked in a bright image. How Mexicans regarded them, of course, did not count.

The last of the accomplished captains, John R. Hughes, retired in 1915, the very year in which the six-shooter culture spun altogether out of control. The Mexican Revolution had spilled over into Texas and created border troubles along the Rio Grande all the way from Brownsville to El Paso. In South Texas gangs of Mexicans from both sides of the border robbed, murdered, and destroyed symbols of Anglo domination such as railroads, irrigation works, and telephone and telegraph lines. Sincerely or cynically, they operated under the Plan de San Diego, a wild scheme to throw off Anglo oppression and regain all the territory lost in the Mexican War.

The politicization of the Ranger Force was well underway by 1915, when Governor James E. Ferguson turned to the troubles in South Texas. He commissioned as a Ranger captain Henry L. Ransom, a convicted murderer free on appeal, to recruit a company and end what had become known as the "Bandit War." Under Ransom's leadership, a reign of terror swept South Texas as Rangers, local lawmen, and vigilantes turned on any Mexican deemed "suspicious." Anointing themselves judge, jury, and executioner, they "evaporated" as many as three hundred Mexicans and brutalized and turned from their homes many more. County officers and vigilantes inflicted many of the barbarities, but Ransom and his men set the example and provided the validation.

That politically appointed captains of dubious qualifications failed to contain the six-shooter culture became dramatically apparent three years later, in 1918. Far to the west, in the rugged Big Bend country, Rangers of Captain Monroe Fox's company joined with local ranchers to launch a nighttime raid on the border village of Porvenir, suspected of harboring bandits. It did not, but the attackers hauled fifteen men from their rude homes and methodically executed them.

The atrocities committed by Ransom and Fox exemplified the worst of the six-shooter culture. But the force included enough toughs to uphold the tradition by treating citizens, mainly Mexicans, in thuggish, often unlawful, and sometimes homicidal ways. Captains ignored or excused such methods. Meantime, with the advent of Governor William P. Hobby, the Rangers sank ever deeper into a political quagmire. In 1919, prodded by Brownsville legislator José T. Canales, the state legislature undertook an investigation of the force. It revealed ample abuse but led to only token reforms.

The contrasting images endured as the Rangers moved into the 1920s and made headlines taming oil boomtowns, smashing whiskey stills, facing lynch mobs, and chasing bank robbers. It was former Ranger Frank Hamer who finally got Bonnie and Clyde. That he was no longer a Ranger reflected the nadir of politicization of the force. Governor Miram Ferguson was the ostensible culprit, but she merely fronted for her husband, Jim Ferguson, kept off the ballot by his impeachment in 1917. Ma and Pa Ferguson rode roughshod over the Rangers during her first term from 1925 to 1926, but at the beginning of a subsequent term in 1933 she fired the entire force, replacing them with political cronies. Reform came soon, however, with the advent of Governor James Allred in 1935. With his support, the legislature removed the Rangers from the Adjutant General's Department and combined them with the Highway Patrol in a new Department of Public Safety.

Reform and increasing professionalism marked the history of the Texas Rangers in the Department of Public Safety. The six-gun culture never entirely dissipated, however, as the late 1960s dramatically revealed. Efforts to unionize the predominantly Mexican laborers in the orchards and farms of the lower Rio Grande Valley revived some of the thuggery that had given the Rangers a bad name in the past. In effect, Governor John Connally used the Rangers as strike breakers, and his captain in South Texas, A. Y. Allee, reminded Mexicans of all the reasons for their hatred of Texas Rangers.

The "blunderbuss efforts" of the Rangers, as a federal judge characterized Allee's response to the strike of 1966–67, deprived the farm workers of their constitutional rights. In 1974, the U.S. Supreme Court agreed, holding the Rangers guilty of lawlessness. It was a severe blow, one that set them on a new course that gradually ate away at the six-shooter culture. By century's end, they functioned as the efficient and effective criminal investigative arm of the State of Texas.

They still bore the stigma of a black side and a white side, however, and they still had to fight off periodic attempts to abolish the force. The positive image gained professional support from two eminent Texas historians, Walter Prescott Webb and T. R. Fehrenbach. Neither discerned much of the black side in their portrayals of the fearless and peerless horsemen who tamed the Indians and Mexicans and brought law and order to a raucous frontier. The negative image gained similar professional respectability from the studies of the distinguished folklorist and historian Américo Paredes. He and his acolytes discerned nothing but black in the lawless, brutal, pistoleers who avoided the tedium of legal process by shooting prisoners "while attempting to escape."

Academic respectability seems to ensure immortality for the competing images of the Texas Rangers. The reality of course is not as simple as the images. History discloses instances reflective of both but validating neither. The Rangers have both a black side and a white side but mostly, like all institutions composed of people, a range of grays separating the two. Sound history records the range as well as the poles.

"MORE THAN A LOCOMOTIVE
TO SEPARATE US"

Lori Van Pelt

WRITING TO HER HUSBAND on March 4, 1866, Frances Casement put up a good front regarding his risky new railroading venture. "Jack," she wrote, "you know what you are *determined* to do you will do with all your might, & if you are so determined *I have no fears.*" The couple, who had been apart for a time during the Civil War, faced another separation. Now, Jack headed west to Omaha, Nebraska Territory, to guide tracklayers for the Union Pacific Railroad. Frances remained in Painesville, Ohio. Jack had written to her on the very same day. He expected to return within a month.

The building of the transcontinental railroad, however, became a prolonged and demanding duty. Casement's work stretched into years of labor instead of weeks. As his tracklayers broke the boundaries of the frontier, he held tight to his bond with his wife while forging opportunities for commerce and development for others throughout the country.

By the time the Casement brothers, John and Dan, received the 1866 contract to lay tracks for the Union Pacific west of Omaha, railroad construction in the United States had been proceeding for more than thirty years. In 1825, Congress instructed a committee on roads and canals to explore the usefulness of railroads. When the Erie Canal connected Albany to Buffalo, New York, in 1825, Baltimore's progressive citizens pushed for a railroad, hoping to increase their chances for profit. In 1827, the pioneer of American railroads, the Baltimore & Ohio (B&O), the first state-chartered railroad, was created. In 1830, the Charleston & Hamburg, the nation's second railroad, became the first railroad to regularly operate a steam engine. At that time, railroads had not yet surpassed canals as the favored mode of transportation. Railroad mileage totalled only seventy-three miles as compared to 1,277 for canals. The cost of building railroads was enormous. By 1838, the census reported $43 million of debt incurred by states supporting railroads. The costs were heavy, but the opportunities for profits remained enticing, and railroads continued to grow.

The Casements's 1866 contract represented an immense challenge in railroad work. Tracks laid for this job would eventually stretch from Omaha to Utah, meeting those of the Central Pacific coming from Sacramento, California, and connecting the nation from coast to coast. William Withuhn, curator of transportation at the Smithsonian Institution, likens this nationwide railroad link which speeded the arrival of goods at the marketplace to modern-day high technology. He calls the progress of railroads "the biggest national project of the nineteenth century on land," and explains the railroads themselves became "a hugely energizing factor in the economy, similar to the Internet today." As railroads grew, canals soon proved too slow a mode of transportation for the bulk of the nation's commerce.

Tracklaying duties for the westward moving railroad fell to a diminutive but capable man. John Stephen (Jack) Casement, who stood just five feet four inches tall, brought years of tracklaying experience with him to this mission. Railroading had already become an important part of his life. Born on January 19, 1829, in Geneva, New York, Casement began working on railroads as a teenager. The family moved to Ann Arbor, Michigan, to farm, but strenuous agricultural work led to the premature demise of Casement's father. Casement's mother faced supporting several children alone, so the older children found jobs as soon as they could. When he was eighteen, Casement began laying tracks for the Michigan Central Railroad, working near the family's farm. In 1850, when that railroad neared completion, Casement traveled to Ohio to work on the Cleveland, Columbus & Cincinnati Railroad. That same year, railroads inspired another new development for the country when the United States Congress allotted the first land grants to the Illinois Central and the Mobile & Ohio Railroads. The grants were given to assist the railroads in building a north-south route from the Great Lakes to the Gulf of Mexico.

Land grants became the basic financial foundation for railroad corporations. During the years 1850 to 1871, the government granted 131,350,534 acres of land to eighty railroads. At that time, settlement did not extend much beyond the Mississippi River. Lands west of the river were considered worthless because there wasn't suitable transportation to take people there. The federal government held public domain to about 1.4 million acres of the property. The land grant policy would, therefore, achieve two goals as railroads tracked through the region—settle the West and increase land values west of the river. Because the federal government at the time was small and had not levied an income tax, it relied upon excise taxes and custom duties for revenue. The government charged a set price for the land ($1.25 an acre) and granted railroads alternate sections. The sections not allotted to the railroad, the government sold to settlers. Railroad corporations could sell their land to raise cash. Other forms of financial aid became necessary to help build railroads and were received in various forms such as cash donations, land and securities, stock subscriptions, loans, and the guaranty of principal or interest or both of railroad bonds from state and local sources.

Railroad work appealed to Casement, and he held a variety of jobs on different railroads during the 1850s. Following his promotion to foreman for the Cleveland, Columbus & Cincinnati Railroad, he soon traveled to Cleveland, where he worked on the Lake Shore Line as track-gang foreman. When construction on that line ended in 1852, Casement worked as a freight-train conductor for the company. In 1853, he earned the contract to lay ballast—material used to stabilize the track placed between and under cross-ties—for the Lake Shore Line. As Casement accumulated more work experience, he found romance in his personal life. On October 14, 1857, he married Frances Marian Jennings, the only child of a Painesville, Ohio, nursery owner. He called his seventeen-year-old bride "Frank." His next job, in Pennsylvania, lasted longer. Working on the three-hundred-mile long Philadelphia and Erie Railroad kept him busy until 1861.

Jack and Frances's time together proved short, disrupted by the war which tore the nation in two. In April 1861, Casement volunteered for service in the Seventh Ohio Volunteer Infantry. Though he had no previous military experience or training, he handled men well and survived battle, earning honor through his conduct at the Battle of Franklin. He became colonel of the 103rd Ohio Volunteer Infantry and earned a brevet brigadier generalship by the war's end. From this service, he gained his nickname, "General Jack." Battle most likely toughened him, but so did sobering aspects of personal life. During the war, Frances and Jack's five-year-old son, Charles, died from a fever. Frances continued to visit the child's grave regularly after Jack headed west to work on the Union Pacific, perhaps hoping to assuage her loneliness.

During the war, a block of legislation referred to by some historians as "Lincoln's New Deal" was passed that directly impacted the development of the railroads and the settlement of the western frontier. Because the nation was divided, any southern opposition was effectively silenced. The 1862 Pacific Railway Act (PRA) coincided with the Homestead Act, the Federal Banking Act, and the Land Grant College Act. Under the terms of the PRA, the Union Pacific became the first federally chartered railroad. The government gave the Union Pacific alternate sections of land in a twenty-mile strip on both sides of the track for every mile of track built. Odd-numbered sections were granted to the railroad, and the federal government retained the even-numbered sections, resulting in the "checkerboard" pattern that remains part of maps today. Land patents (titles) were issued to the railroad company after each forty miles of road was completed and certified as such by government officials. The government retained all mineral rights. The railroad was granted timber rights. The PRA set the price for lands at $1.25 per acre and created bond subsidies for the railroad. For every forty miles certified completed, the Union Pacific Railroad received United States bonds in varying amounts related to the construction difficulties expected in each area of the route. The company received $16,000 in bonds for each mile constructed on the plains, $32,000 for each mile laid between the Rocky Mountains and the Sierra Mountains, and $48,000 per mile in mountainous areas.

The Union Pacific's first rail was placed on July 10, 1865, but Jack Casement was not yet in charge of tracklaying for the company. By the middle of November, just twenty-eight miles of track had been laid, although one hundred miles had been graded. The company struggled to improve its internal organization and developed its organizational style based on the military model used during the Civil War. Delays in tracklaying had been in part due to the company's slow pay policy and also to supply shortages. Because there was not yet a rail connection to Omaha, supplies had to be transported by river from St. Joseph, Missouri. Spring ice in the river led to aggravating delays, as did low water and fickle steamboat transportation, forces beyond the company's control. Most materials had to be shipped. Limestone, used in masonry, was readily available and cottonwood, used for lumber, was in abundant supply, but cottonwood was not as sturdy as some other woods. The Union Pacific used a chemical process, burnettizing, to treat and preserve the wood. Lumber was cut into ties at Omaha or at portable sawmills upriver. Progress was impeded but not completely stopped by these frustrations. By winter, the workers had laid forty miles of track.

Thomas C. Durant, the vice president of the Union Pacific, began to implement changes in the company in 1866 to increase efficiency. He named Samuel B. Reed, who had been working on surveying, as Superintendent of Construction of Operations. General Grenville M. Dodge was appointed chief engineer. Jack and Dan Casement received the tracklaying contract. Jack managed the men while Dan served as bookkeeper and supervised the supply flow. The military model of organization proved beneficial for the Union Pacific since many of the workers were Army veterans, both Union and Confederate. Skills the workers learned during the war would also become useful as the railroad passed through Indian country. Confrontations were expected. The men were trained to defend themselves and the lengthening railroad.

The Casements received their contract just a few months before Grenville M. Dodge joined the Union Pacific as chief engineer. Their pay was $750 per mile above the labor and material costs of laying track. The contract, dated February 8, 1866, signed by Sidney Dillon, gave the Casements, doing business as the firm of J. S. & D. T. Casement, three-fourths of the net profits from the work. Dillon was to receive one-fourth. None of the parties to the contract would receive a salary, and further, they had to pay into the capital stock "an amount sufficient to prosecute the work and in proportion to their relative interests." This was the Casements' first major business venture together. While they focused on tracklaying, other contractors completed additional necessary construction, including grading, building culverts, bridges, water tanks, and stations.

In March 1866, the Casements hired workers and built boarding cars for the men. Still, they faced a frustrating waiting game. The river level was too low for iron to be shipped. The closest railhead was St. Joseph, Missouri, about 135 miles distant, and that situation did not change until a year later when a railroad line reached Council Bluffs, across the river from Omaha. On March 29, 1866, Jack wrote to his wife about the low water on the river, explaining that the situation resulted because of cold weather. "We were four days coming from St. Jo. [sic] and we pushed boats that started out four days ahead of us." On April 1, his predicament had not yet improved. Jack told Frances people could travel from St. Joseph to Omaha "twice as quick by Stage and for the same price." He had no iron yet and the boarding cars were not completed. Jack shared his frustration, writing, "It is a slow country to drive business in." By April 6, their separation felt more wearing than ever, and Jack wrote, "I do believe that when I get you with me again it will take more than a locomotive to separate us." When that reunion would occur was unknown. The iron had not yet arrived although the river had begun to rise. He explained, "I have been working a few men grading and putting in a side track. We will commence tracklaying next Monday but our boarding cars will not be ready for more than a week."

The Casements' labor force consisted mostly of army veterans and included many Irish immigrants. The Casements treated their men well. The brothers organized an innovative construction train to help speed the work and provide some comforts for the workers. Dining and sleeping cars were included with a blacksmith's car, a carpentry shop, a washroom, harness shop and feed for horses, and separate dining and sleeping cars for managers. A baker's car was also included. Historian John White, Jr. termed this "a city on wheels providing a functional if not luxurious living environment for about five hundred construction workers." The sleeping cars for the workmen housed 144. Strong workers needed good food and plenty of it, and the Casements kept the men well fed, relying on staples of fresh beef, sugar-cured ham, bacon, beans, and fresh bread. Twelve hundred pounds of flour were used each day to make bread. According to White, the kitchen car also housed the telegraph office and paymaster's office. The bunk and dining cars were custom-made, while most of the others were box cars. Water cars followed, and fresh water was collected down line and brought forward to the end of the track. The typical workday began at 5:30 A.M. Tracklayers washed up and ate breakfast before reporting trackside by 6:30 A.M. They worked twelve hour days, six days per week. Basic pay was thirty-five dollars per month.

In mid-April 1866, only sixty-three miles of track had been laid, but the organizational changes in the Union Pacific and the abilities of the Casements began to show soon after. Casement first drove his men to complete a mile of track each day. He then increased the goal to three and then to five miles daily. White explains how the task was accomplished so efficiently, writing, "Supply trains were in constant motion from Omaha with all that was needed to push the job forward. At the same time, the single-track railroad was accommodating trains of empty cars headed back to the Omaha yards for a fresh load. Once a train was emptied, it backed down the line to a siding so that another loaded train could take its place. About five or six hundred tons of material were delivered each day." Each mile of track used 2,500 ties, 400 rails, and 10,000 to 12,000 spikes. A new rail was placed every thirty seconds. The thirty-foot long rails weighed 560 pounds each and had to be lifted from wagons by four men.

Tracklayers made quick progress across mostly flat Nebraska Territory. Casement's men worked so fast that he completed the terms of his contract in the summer of 1866. Money remained tight, however. Durant urged Casement to keep steady pace of three miles per day but didn't release funds to help him pay the extra expenses for additional workers needed for that task. When Casement complained, Sidney Dillon came to his assistance. In early October, the tracklayers reached the 100th meridian, 247 miles west of Omaha. Dodge created a public relations event to recognize this noteworthy achievement, probably hoping to garner further financial support.

The Great Railway Excursion took 140 people west to see the progress of the transcontinental railroad. The *Chicago Tribune* in late October contained regular reports of the adventures of the Union Pacific excursionists. Travelers left New York on October 15, arriving in Chicago two days later to pick up tourists from that city. The route then took the travelers to St. Joseph, Missouri via the Chicago, Burlington & Quincy and the Hannibal & St. Joseph railroads. A steamboat hauled passengers from St. Joseph to Omaha, but an alternate route by train was made available. Passengers could ride either the Chicago & Northwestern or the Rock Island & Pacific railroad if they wanted to travel through Iowa instead. On October 17, 1866, the *Tribune* correspondent explained the trip "is expected to be and should be, in proportion to the magnitude of the enterprise it inaugurates, the most magnificent ever gotten up in the country." Excursionists traveled in grand style. Subsequent reports explained the train was "one of the most magnificent ever sent out of Chicago." The train contained five coaches, three of which were luxurious Pullman sleeping cars, each of them costing twenty thousand dollars. A commissary car complete with a restaurateur, H. M. Kinsley, provided the tourists with remarkable repasts. Explaining on October 20 that "everything is unqualifiedly lovely," the unnamed newspaper correspondent told about the wealth represented by those on board the excursion train. "The capital represented by a limited number of individuals on board amounts to over fifty millions. As an instance, among the few of those at this time present with us, when in the East recently a call was made for a subscription to the completion of the Iowa Nebraska line . . . in fifteen minutes three millions were planked down. Such wealth affords power to build a road so rapidly as the Union Pacific road which has been constructed."

The correspondent's October 24 dispatch from Lone Tree, Nebraska, explained the tourists camped at Columbus and were treated to unusual entertainment. "Through the exertions of General Casement, an ample supply of bedding was provided for all those who chose to occupy the tents, and although the night was very cold and windy, by means of blankets and buffalo robes all were kept warm." All were kept fascinated by the legendary West as well, for Durant had arranged with a local group of Pawnees to perform a war dance for the visitors. The group of Indians consisted of 110 men and seven women, and the reporter explained, "When visited by our party, the braves were all found standing round a large fire, and the picturesque wildness of their appearance far exceeded anything we had expected." He commented on their scanty attire, writing, "Some of them were wrapped in huge blankets, adorned with paint, birds, animals, skins, beads, ornaments . . . and strange contrivances of feathers." A few "sported the airy costume of a breech cloth eight inches long, and a pair of bracelets on each arm." One wore only a blue swallowtail coat and nothing else. In addition to the war dance, the Indians also created a "sham fight on horseback." Tourists traded "greenbacks for tomahawks" and "stamps for arrows" to keep souvenirs of the event.

The Indians rated much more press coverage than did the tracklaying, which was also demonstrated for the benefit of the excursionists. The reporter noted that track was laid "as rapidly as a man would walk," and stated, "The work was all done with excessive rapidity, simply because each man had but a certain thing to do, was accustomed to doing it, and had not to wait on the action of anyone else." The excursion had gone so well Durant decided to send tourists when the Union Pacific reached other important goals along the route.

Under Casement's supervision, the railroad tracks expanded the West quickly, until freezing winter weather halted progress. By December 1866, tracklayers arrived at milepost 305, just past North Platte, Nebraska Territory. When winter weather stalled construction, Casement did not sit idle. He built a blacksmith shop, ice house, slaughterhouse, wash house and stock pens in preparation for the next season. Casement had been buoyed by news from Frances in November about the arrival of their second son, John Frank. On November 25, she wrote to her husband in Omaha, saying she was rested but "far from feeling very strong." In letters written on November 28 and 29, Frances admitted how lonesome she felt for him and how the Thanksgiving holiday amplified her melancholy feelings. In December she reminded Jack again to "beware of the *tempter* in the form of strong drink." On December 7, 1866, Jack wrote of having "started quite a store and a ranch. Generally we are boarding men for the Company while they get up their buildings. Next week the stages will commence running here and we will have to take them, men passengers, horses and all. We are just getting our fast freight line started which will make this quite a busy place for a while. I hope to finish track laying for this season next week." The next week, he explained to Frances that the work had stopped at milepost 305 for the winter and remarked that he hoped to be home for Christmas. On December 23, he was still in North Platte, feeling "positively homesick." He assured her that he and his brother Daniel had no wine or liquor, saying, "we have the only temperance house in this country."

Casement's store allowed him an additional profit opportunity because he could sell sundries to his workers without facing competition from other merchandisers, few and far between on the still lonesome frontier. Casement also bought cattle and earned profits by selling the beef. However, the Union Pacific soon put a damper on Casement's entrepreneurial spirit. He had been relying on the company to ship his merchandise to him free of charge as part of the railroad building effort, but the company considered Casement's enterprise a separate venture and began charged him shipping fees for his goods.

Although the Union Pacific squelched a portion of his independent earnings, Casement's wealth increased. In 1867, the brothers' new contract afforded them $850 per mile. Work began again in April, although this time floods hampered the efforts. During the winter, the group stored enough supplies to lay 150 miles. By May it took forty cars to haul all the material, equipment, fuel, and supplies needed to lay one mile of track. Dodge estimated that when construction reached its peak, Union Pacific employed ten thousand men and used as many animals.

In the summer of 1867, the tracks reached Julesburg, one of the worst hell-on-wheels communities on the route. The events occurring in that end-of-the-track town led to legends arising about Jack Casement. Historians disagree on the exact turn of events, and records are scarce but basically, the toughs of the town wreaked havoc with Casement's tracklaying crews. Julesburg was said to have murders occur in broad daylight, and with its numerous saloons and gambling houses, abundant opportunities existed for workmen to succumb to the temptations of liquor, dally with prostitutes, and lose their paychecks in card games and other pursuits. Angered by the loss of work due to illness and injuries his men suffered, Casement asked Dodge for permission to handle the situation as he saw fit.

Dodge agreed to Casement's request. Some sources explain Casement's ire was aroused because scoundrels in the town had purchased land from the railroad, but refused to pay for it. Whatever the cause, Casement issued an ultimatum to the ruffians. He instructed them to ride their horses out of the town or else be on the next train bound within the hour for Omaha. Many of them remained, gambling that Casement's elfin size ensured their safety. Here again, stories about the actual conflict differ. Some say the general responded by arming a hand-picked group of his labor force and shooting the toughs who had stayed to make more trouble. Others report that the rogues who elected to remain in Julesburg were treated to a necktie party and hanged on telegraph poles because of the dearth of available trees. The tales do agree that an impromptu and somewhat crowded cemetery sprang up in Julesburg following Casement's ultimatum and the conflict that followed.

On June 30, 1867, Frances took an excursion to the end of the tracks, mentioning Julesburg in a letter to her mother but leaving out any details as to whether or not the grisly vigilante incident occurred. Instead, she wrote of leaving Omaha on Monday, arriving in North Platte on Tuesday morning, and then heading for Julesburg, located "about two miles across the river and opposite the old town of Julesburg or what is now Fort Sedgwick." She continued, writing, "The city had been commenced about two days when we reached there, and they had erected several tents, one or two frame buildings, a hotel almost finished." She had watched a good-sized frame building being erected while she was there, and explained she rode to the end of the track five miles distant at Lodge Pole Creek. Frances had been more concerned about Indian attacks than about the villains of Julesburg. She wrote, "A journey of 385 miles and back in two days and three nights. 385 miles from Omaha, almost across the plains, and tell Aunt Lide we *didn't see an Indian, not one*." Conflicts with the Indians were minor. Some resulted in train wrecks or in men's deaths, but most of the difficulties arose from incidents of stolen horses and did not interfere much with the continuing westward movement of the tracks.

The railroad arrived in Cheyenne, Dakota Territory, in mid-November 1867. On April 8, 1868, the *Cheyenne Leader* reported the railroad tracks had reached the peak of Sherman Hill between Cheyenne and Laramie City, explaining, "the outside world was informed by telegraph that the highest eminence on the roadbed between the Missouri and the Pacific Ocean had been conquered. . . ." The elevation measured more than 8,200 feet. A few days later, Jack Casement informed Frances that he planned to begin laying three miles of track each day. He and Dan had taken on more grading jobs and were "starting work 150 miles ahead of the track." Later that month, he told her he expected Indian troubles, but not enough to delay the work. He admitted his optimism because of the good weather. Frances's experience of Jack's career and his absence felt much less bright. On April 19, 1868, she wrote to him saying, "I wonder if we will be settled again and go to church as we used too [sic] before the war—we seemed quite christianized in those days—since that every thing is in confusion & we have never been settled in any thing." In a letter he wrote to his wife a few days later, Jack confided, "The only real comfort I have here is in reading your letters." As he traveled further west, he advised her, "Keep the music box running and be as happy as possible."

The Casements continued their correspondence throughout the years Jack helped push the rails westward to Utah. They shared news of snowstorms delaying the tracklayers and the Union Pacific Railroad's financial difficulties, which thwarted Casement's ability to pay his workmen. In 1868, five hundred miles of track had been laid, and by December, the railroad reached Echo

Canyon, Utah Territory. The Union Pacific and the Central Pacific united at Promontory on May 10, 1869. The transcontinental railroad brought settlers west and expanded and energized the nation's economy. Jack and Frances Casement's necessary separation had helped unite the country via railroad tracks.

Railroads were his mainstay, but Casement also dabbled in politics. In 1868, Casement, a Republican, earned election to the U.S. Congress as a representative from Wyoming Territory, serving during the winter hiatus of the railroad construction. In the 1870s, he served in the Ohio Senate. Following their Union Pacific venture, Jack Casement returned home to a hero's welcome in Painseville along with his brother. Although Jack's father-in-law, Charles C. Jennings, built a large and elegant brick home for his daughter and son-in-law in 1870, Jack continued tracklaying, and as a result, traveled much. His employer, included the Canada Southern, the Union & Titusville, and the Nickel Plate among others. Although he had free rail passes which afforded him the comfort of Pullman cars, Casement preferred to ride in the smoking car, puffing on a cigar as he traveled.

In 1897, Casement, nearing seventy, took on yet another railroad job, this time in Costa Rica. His brother Dan, was dead by that time, so Casement relied on the help of his only surviving son, Dan Dillon Casement. John Frank, born when Casement worked on the Union Pacific, had died in 1885. The Casements' job was to build a narrow gauge line from San Jose (the capital) to Tivives, a distance of fifty-five miles. Due to yellow fever outbreaks, mudslides destroying work already completed, and poor sales of bonds to finance the railroad line, the Casements did not complete this job. They toiled until 1903 when they reached Santo Domingo de San Mateo, thirty-five miles from San Jose. The Costa Rican government hired another American contractor who completed the remaining twenty miles of the line in 1910.

Even in the early 1900s, Jack Casement continued to travel. When the San Francisco earthquake struck in 1906, he was staying in a San Jose, California, hotel. The hotel collapsed and a chunk of ceiling crushed Casement's chest but did not kill him. He recovered and was traveling two weeks before he succumbed to pneumonia at home in Ohio on December 13, 1909. Frances survived her husband by twenty-seven years. After his death, she became active in the women's suffrage movement. She died in 1928.

The transcontinental railroad opened the West and achieved the goals of promoting settlement and expanding the nation's economy. Broad changes swept the country as locomotives became a familiar sight. Farmers switched from self-sufficiency to commercialization, industry increased due to the de-

mand for engines and materials to operate railroads, and other businesses—
like the legal field—profited from the emergence of the railroads. The railroads
owed their existence to workers like Jack and Dan Casement who persevered
despite their own personal sacrifices. Jack and his wife, Frances, sustained their
love for each other through their letters while revealing the poignant and
immeasurable human cost exacted from building the railroads. Letter by letter,
rail by rail, they showed that "more than a locomotive" was needed to keep
them apart and to connect the nation.

R.I.P.
THE WHEREABOUTS OF FORTY
CELEBRATED WESTERNERS

Dale L. Walker

JESSE JAMES'S REMAINS WERE exhumed in 1995 and DNA tests were conducted to prove that it was Jesse in Jesse's grave at Mount Olivet Cemetery in Kearney, Missouri.

Billy the Kid's tombstone has been stolen several times, giving some doubt as to the precise location of his bones at the Fort Sumner, New Mexico, graveyard.

Meriwether Lewis's grave is said to be under the monument dedicated to him on the Natchez Trace near Hohenwald, Tennessee, but nobody really knows if he is under there, or nearby.

Insofar as anything in history can really be known, these forty whereabouts are known.

Just don't bet the farm.

CLYDE BARROW (1909–1934). This Teleco, Texas, boy, his shoes off, his necktie hanging on the rear-view mirror, was driving a stolen 1934 Ford V-8 "Fordor Deluxe" just after 9 A.M. on May 23, 1934, in the piney woods of Bienville Parish, northern Louisiana, when the car was hit by 107 bullets, 27 of which ventilated Clyde Barrow. His companion-mistress, Bonnie Parker (see below), was also killed in the ambush staged by Texas Ranger Frank Hamer and five other lawmen. Bonnie and Clyde were accused of murdering a dozen people in a two-year armed robbery rampage in the Southwest. *Western Heights Cemetery, Dallas, Texas.*

ROY BEAN (c. 1827–1903). He fined a lawyer for using profane language in court when the attorney announced he intended presenting a writ of *habeus corpus* in defending a client, and once, after inspecting the corpse of a railroad worker who had fallen from a bridge, he fined the victim the forty dollars found in his pocket "for carrying a concealed weapon." The self-proclaimed "Law West of the Pecos," Bean set up his court in the "Jersey Lilly" saloon in the south Texas railroad construction camp he named Langtry—after the British courtesan-actress Lily Langtry, who Bean admired but never met—and dispensed rough justice and whiskey with equal alacrity and humor. *Del Rio Cemetery, Del Rio (on the Texas-Mexico border above Ciudad Acuña, Mexico), Texas.*

BILLY THE KID (1859–1881). Born Henry McCarty in New York ("Billy" derives from the alias "William Bonney" he used after 1877), he was raised in Silver City, New Mexico, by his mother and stepfather. An outlaw by age seventeen, he was a central figure in the Lincoln County War. He escaped from the jail in Lincoln, New Mexico, on April 28, 1881, killed two of his jailers, and fled north. On the night of July 13, 1881, Lincoln County Sheriff Pat Garrett found the Kid at cattleman Pete Maxwell's ranch in Fort Sumner. The Kid, armed and cornered in a dark bedroom, was shot and killed by Garrett. *Old Fort Sumner Military Cemetery, Fort Sumner (150 mi. southeast of Albuquerque), New Mexico.*

MARTHA JANE CANARY ["CALAMITY JANE"] (c.1852–1903). A Missourian, Canary claimed in her autobiography to have been an Army scout between 1870 and 1876, but there is no record of this service or to her claim to have been with Gen. George Crook against the Sioux at the battle at Slim Buttes in 1876. She did work as a bullwhacker, mule-driver, camp-follower, volunteer nurse during diphtheria and mountain fever epidemics, and appears to have been in Deadwood, South Dakota, at the time her alleged paramour, James Butler Hickok, was killed. Her claim to have been married to Hickok is fiction but she died near Deadwood and was buried next to Wild Bill. *Mount Moriah Cemetery, Deadwood, South Dakota.*

CHRISTOPHER HOUSTON "KIT" CARSON (1809–1868). Among the most recognizable of all Westerners, Carson, born in Kentucky, came west in 1826 and became a Santa Fé Trail trader, mountain man, Indian fighter, exploration guide for John C. Frémont, a colonel of volunteers in the Civil War in the West and in subsequent campaigns against the Apache and Navaho. He died at Fort Lyon, Colorado, one month after his beloved wife Josefa died in childbirth, and is buried with her. *Kit Carson Cemetery, Taos, New Mexico.*

CHIEF JOSEPH of the Nez Perce (c. 1840–1904). Born Hiemot Tooyalatket in the Wallowa Valley of Oregon, Joseph became a peace-seeking chief of the Nez Perce and in 1877 led 350 of his people on a 1,200-mile retreat across Idaho and Montana to the Candian border, fighting four battles and fourteen skirmishes with the pursuing U.S. Army. In finally surrendering to Gen. Nelson A. Miles, Joseph gave his celebrated soliloquy which contained the words, "From where the sun now stands I will fight no more forever." *Colville Reservation, Colville, Washington.*

WILLIAM CLARK (1770–1838). Brother of George Rogers Clark, hero of the trans-Allegheny campaigns of the American Revolution, William Clark, a veteran of Indian fighting in the east in the 1790s and of the War of 1812, is best known as Meriwether Lewis's partner in the great transcontinental expedition from St. Louis to the Pacific from 1803 to 1806. The only surviving physical trace of the Lewis and Clark expedition is the

Wm. Clark

July 25 1806

chisled by Clark on a rock at Pompey's Pillar, a limestone outcropping that overlooks the Yellowstone River near Billings, Montana. *Belleffontaine Cemetery, St. Louis, Missouri.*

WILLIAM FREDERICK "BUFFALO BILL" CODY (1846–1917). No person more personified the Old American West than Cody. While much of his great fame rests on his role as showman-proprietor of "Buffalo Bill's Wild West," he had, in fact, a notable career as Pony Express rider, army scout, Indian fighter and buffalo hunter before he was "discovered" by dime novelist E. Z. C. Judson ("Ned Buntline") in 1869 and transformed into the internationally celebrated "Hero of the Plains." He died on January 10, 1917, and was buried, with a throng of 18,000 people attending his funeral, on *Lookout Mountain, five miles west of Golden, Colorado.*

COMANCHE (c. 1861–1891). This claybank gelding, only survivor of Custer's command at the Battle of the Little Bighorn on June 25, 1876, was owned by Capt. Myles W. Keogh of the Seventh Cavalry. Comanche was badly wounded in the battle but, nursed back to health, became a regimental mascot and favorite of the ladies at Fort Abraham Lincoln until retired from service. He died at Fort Riley, Kansas, on November 7, 1891, and was "mounted"—stuffed—and donated to the University of Kansas. *University of Kansas Museum of Natural History, Lawrence, Kansas.*

GARY COOPER (1901–1961). Born Frank James Cooper in Helena, Montana, son of a Montana supreme court justice, he was educated in England and Grinnell College, Iowa, and traveled to California in 1924 hoping to land a job as a political cartoonist. He began his movie career as an extra in westerns and won his first big role in 1926 in the film *The Winning of Barbara Worth* starring Ronald Colman and Vilma Banky. Always the shy, laconic hero, he twice won the Best Actor Academy Award (for *Sergeant York* in 1942, and for *High Noon* in 1952). *Sacred Heart Cemetery, Southampton, Long Island.*

GEORGE ARMSTRONG CUSTER (1839–1876). Born in New Rumley, Ohio, graduated last in his West Point class of 1861, and at age twenty-three he became a brigadier general, youngest in either army of the Civil War. He was a lieutenant colonel in command of the Seventh Cavalry Regiment during the Sioux War of 1876 that culminated in the June 25 battle on the Little Bighorn River of Montana. There, in about an hour, Custer and five companies of the seventh—about 215 men—were killed, engulfed by upwards of two thousand Sioux and Cheyenne warriors. Buried with his wife, Elizabeth "Libbie" Bacon Custer (1842–1933) at the *West Point Cemetery, U.S. Military Academy, West Point, New York.*

WYATT EARP (1848–1929). Most recognizable of all lawmen of the Old West, Wyatt Berry Stapp Earp was more saloonkeeper, gambler, and mining speculator, than "badge." He worked as a teamster, buffalo hunter and sometime policeman before arriving in Tombstone, Arizona Territory, in 1880, with his brothers Virgil, Morgan, and James. He was a saloonman in Tombstone before being deputized by his brother Virgil to assist in the feud with the Clanton family of rustlers. In the famous gunfight at the O.K. Corral (actually *near* the corral) on October 26, 1881, three members of the Clanton gang were killed. *Hills of Eternity Cemetery, Colma (south of San Francisco) California.*

PAT GARRETT (1850–1908). Best known as the Lincoln County lawman who tracked down and killed Henry McCarty, known as Billy the Kid (see above), Patrick Floyd Jarvis Garrett was a buffalo hunter, cowboy, rancher, and Texas

Ranger. He was killed, allegedly while standing alongside his buckboard and relieving his bladder, in the Organ Mountains of New Mexico on February 29, 1908. The man who confessed to killing him, a goat rancher named Wayne Brazel, was found not guilty in a jury trial in April, 1909, and freed. *Masonic Cemetery, Las Cruces, New Mexico.*

GERONIMO (1829–1909). Originally called Goyathlay ("Yawner"), he apparently adopted his Spanish name (Geronimo is "Jerome" in Spanish) in the 1850s after his wife and children were killed by Mexican raiders in Sonora. He was a member of the Deindai band of the Chiricahua Apaches. When the Chiricahua were forced on to the San Carlos Reservation in Arizona, Geronimo and his band fled into Mexico. He surrendered in September 1886, and in 1894, Geronimo and the Apaches who survived exile in Florida were removed to Fort Sill, Oklahoma. *Apache Cemetery, Fort Sill (near Lawton), Oklahoma.*

JOHN WESLEY HARDIN (1853–1895). Killer of, some say, forty men, Hardin was the product of Reconstruction Texas and his killings included numbers of blacks, former Union soldiers, at least one lawmen and others who stood in his way or whom he disliked. He was imprisoned at Huntsville, Texas, and between escape attempts, wrote his autobiography, learned theology and law. After his release from prison in 1894 he moved to El Paso to practice law. On August 19, 1895, as he stood at the bar of the Acme Saloon in El Paso he was shot in the back of the head by Constable John Selman. *Concordia Cemetery, El Paso, Texas.*

JAMES BUTLER "WILD BILL" HICKOK (1837–1876). Hickok came off a farm in Homer, Illinois, and as a youth worked as a teamster, stagecoach driver and occasional lawman. He was given the name "Wild Bill" in an article about him in *Harper's Weekly.* He was a civilian scout and wagonmaster during the Civil War and afterward a scout, hunting guide and city marshal in Abilene, Kansas. In 1876 he married and settled down in Deadwood, Dakota Territory. There, on the afternoon of August 2, 1876, he was playing poker when a drifter named Jack McCall came up from behind and fired a single shot from a .45 Colt into Hickok's head. *Mount Moriah Cemetery, Deadwood, South Dakota.* (*See* Martha Jane Canary.)

JOHN H. "DOC" HOLLIDAY (1852–1887). Wyatt Earp's deadly, tubercular friend was born in Griffin, Georgia, and trained in dentistry in Pennsylvania. He moved to Dallas, Texas, in the early 1870s and there pulled teeth, drank heavily and gambled. He was in various shooting incidents in Jacksboro and around Fort Griffin, and in other fracases as he drifted to Denver, Cheyenne, Las Vegas, New Mexico, and Deadwood, Dakota Territory. In Tombstone he was suspected of a stage robbery and was on bail when he participated in the O.K. Corral gunfight on October 26, 1881. In 1887, Holliday moved to Glenwood Springs, Colorado, seeking treatment for his disease. He died there on November 8, 1887. *Glenwood Cemetery, Glenwood Springs (100 miles west of Denver), Colorado.*

TOM HORN (1860–1903). Before he became a hired gun, Horn, a Missourian, had been a stagecoach driver, teamster, scout in Apache campaigns under the legendary Al Sieber, top rodeo roper, lawman, and Pinkerton detective. In 1894, he was employed by the Wyoming Cattle Growers' Association as a stock detective but his main enterprise was to locate and kill rustlers. After a break for service as a teamster in the Spanish-American War in Cuba, he returned to this work and on July 19, 1901, allegedly shot and killed a fourteen-year-old son of a prominent sheepman in the Iron Mountain area of Wyoming. Horn was hanged for this crime on November 20, 1903, in Laramie. *Columbia Cemetery, Boulder, Colorado.*

SAM HOUSTON (1793–1863). He came to Texas in 1832 after careers as Indian fighter under Gen. Andrew Jackson and as governor of Tennessee. With the outbreak of the Texas Revolution in 1835 he became commanding general of the Texas Army and after the fall of the Alamo led his ragtag Texas Army of under eight hundred men against Santa Anna's 1,500-man force and defeated the Mexicans at the San Jacinto River on April 21, 1836. Houston served as the first and third president of the Republic of Texas and after statehood was elected to the U.S. Senate. In 1859, he was elected governor of Texas but opposed secession at the outbreak of the Civil War and retired to his farm near Huntsville. He died there on July 25, 1863. *Oakwood Cemetery, Huntsville, Texas.*

FRANK JAMES (1843–1915). Alexander Franklin James was side-by-side with his younger brother Jesse riding with Quantrill and in all the James-Younger Gang robberies. After the Northfield, Minnesota, disaster, he and Jesse lay low in Tennessee for over three years before returning to Missouri. After Jesse's death, Frank surrendered and stood three trials for murder and armed robbery but the juries would not convict him. He went free and lived a quiet life on the family farm. He died on February 15, 1915, in the room in which he was born near Kearney, Missouri. *Hill Park Cemetery, Independence, Missouri.*

JESSE JAMES (1847–1882). When he was fifteen, Jesse Woodson James rode with Confederate guerillas under William C. Quantrill. At war's end he formed an outlaw gang with his brother Frank and the Younger boys, robbing banks, trains and stagecoaches as far south as Texas and Alabama. The gang's work effectively ended on September 7, 1876, in the attempt to rob a bank in Northfield, Minnesota, an ambush in which Jesse and Frank alone escaped wounds or death. On April 3, 1882, Jesse was straightening a picture on the wall of his home in St. Joseph, Missouri, when he was shot in the head by Robert Ford, a former James-Younger gang member who hoped to collect the $5,000 bounty offered for the outlaw. *Mount Olivet Cemetery, Kearney (outside Kansas City), Missouri.*

MERIWETHER LEWIS (1774–1809). A soldier and President Thomas Jefferson's private secretary, Lewis became co-commander, with William Clark (see above) on the first transcontinental exploration expedition of 1803–1806. Lewis became governor of Upper Louisiana Territory after his return from the Pacific and died under quite mysterious circumstances—perhaps murdered, probably a suicide—on October 11, 1809, en route to Washington, in the wilds of the Natchez Trace of Tennessee. *Meriwether Lewis Park, Natchez Trace Parkway, Hohenwald (35 mi. southwest of Columbia), Tennessee.*

JACK LONDON (1876–1916). The best known and bestselling writer in the West in the years between 1903 (the year his best-known novel, *The Call of the Wild*, appeared), and 1916, London grew up in poverty and was largely self-educated. In his brief, incandescent, writing career—1900 to 1916—he produced fifty books, twenty-two of them novels, and managed to find time to marry twice, sail his own yacht to the South Seas and build a huge baronial estate in the Valley of the Moon in northern California. He died of uremia and an accidental overdose of drugs on November 22, 1916, two months before his forty-first birthday. *Jack London State Park, Glen Ellen (a few miles southeast of Santa Rosa), California.*

WILLIAM BARCLAY "BAT" MASTERSON (1853–1921). Another Illinoisian (like Hickok and Earp), Masterson came West to Kansas in 1871 and worked as a scout, Indian fighter, buffalo hunter and railroad laborer before establishing a reputation as a fearless lawman in Dodge City and later in Deadwood, Dakota Territory, and in Tombstone, Arizona Territory. He moved to New York City in 1902 and worked as a sports writer for the New York *Morning Telegraph*. He died at his desk on October 25, 1921. *Woodlawn Cemetery, Bronx, New York.*

TOM MIX (1880–1940). Between 1910 and the mid-1930s, Mix starred in over 170 short and feature-length Western films, usually as a lawman with an adeptness at horsemanship. In 1935, he left the movie business and took his celebrated horse Tony into circus performances. Various stories about his early life generated by Hollywood publicists—that he was a real-life lawman, that he fought in the Boxer Rebellion in China in 1900 and as a mercenary in the Mexican Revolution—are unsubstantiated. He was killed in an auto accident in Arizona on October 12, 1940. *Forest Lawn Memorial Park, Glendale, California.*

ANNIE OAKLEY (1860–1926). Born Phoebe Ann Oakley Mozee in Patterson, Ohio, she may have been the greatest markswoman of all time. Proficient at shooting as a child, by the time she was sixteen she had challenged and beaten Frank Butler, a noted sharpshooter whom she later married. From 1885 until 1902 she and Butler toured with Buffalo Bill Cody's Wild West, a feature attraction of the show. Among her stunts: dividing a playing card by shooting through its edge, breaking as many as eleven glass balls tossed in the air at a time, and hitting targets with her back turned, using a shiny hunting knife as a mirror. *Brock Cemetery, Greenville (30 miles northwest of Dayton), Ohio.*

BONNIE PARKER (1910–1934). This Rowena, Texas, girl was eating a bacon-tomato sandwich when she was hit by 50 of the 107 bullets that struck the car driven by Clyde Barrow on May 23, 1934, in Louisiana. *Crown Hill Memorial Park, Dallas, Texas.* (*See* Clyde Barrow)

QUANAH PARKER (c. 1845–1911). Quanah ("fragrant" in the Comanche tongue) was the son of chief Peta Nocona and Cynthia Ann Parker, a white captive woman taken by Nocona's band in an east Texas raid in 1836. As a young man, Quanah led the Kwahadi band of Comanches in raids on white frontier forts and was among the last of his tribe to surrender to the whites (in 1875). He became a master of reservation politics, principal Comanche chief in 1890, and a wealthy man by the turn of the century. He was a devotee of the peyote religion, a polygamist, and owner of a fine twelve-room home near Cache, Oklahoma, in which he entertained visiting dignitaries. *Post Cemetery, Fort Sill (near Lawton), Oklahoma.*

BILL PICKETT (c. 1860–1932). One of the greatest rodeo performers of all time, Pickett was the son of black and Choctaw parents and was born on the San Gabriel River in Texas. He worked as a cowboy on the Miller 101 ranch in

Oklahoma and there "invented" what was to become the rodeo event of steer wrestling. Pickett called it "bulldogging" and his version of it, much modified later on, was to leap on a steer's back, bite into the animal's lip and throw his body off, taking the steer to the ground with him. He died on April 2, 1932, eleven days after being thrown from a horse on the 101. *White Eagle Monument, Marland (20 miles south of Ponca City), Oklahoma.*

ZEBULON MONTGOMERY PIKE (1779–1813). Pike was a soldier, born in New Jersey, when he was dispatched in 1805 to find the headwaters of the Mississippi (he fell short of finding it by twenty-five miles) and in 1806 to explore the headwaters of the Arkansas River. On November 15, 1806, he discovered the peak, east of present-day Las Animas, Colorado, that bears his name. He and his men were captured by Spanish authorities in February 1807, and taken to Mexico before being released. He served in the War of 1812 as a brigadier general and died on April 27, 1813, on the deck of an American warship on Lake Ontario. *Military Cemetery, Sackets Harbor (west of Watertown, on Lake Ontario), New York.*

FREDERIC REMINGTON (1861–1909). With a prolific legacy of some 2,700 paintings, illustrations and sculptures, most on his favorite subject of the Old West, Frederic Sackrider Remington is among the most revered of Western artists. He wandered the West beginning in 1881 and often returned. His Western works were a mainstay in *Harper's Weekly* and numerous other magazines and he worked as a war artist-correspondent in the Spanish-American War in Cuba. His sculptures, a medium he began using in about 1895, are even more prized than his paintings. *Evergreen Cemetery, Canton (southwest of Potsdam) in northern New York State.*

WILL ROGERS (1879–1935). The man who claimed he never met a man he didn't like and who said "I don't make jokes. I just watch the government and report the facts" was born William Penn Adair Rogers in Indian Territory (Oklahoma today). He made his first public performance as a trick roper in Johannesburg, South Africa, during the Boer War and subsequently performed in vaudeville, musical comedy with the Ziegfeld Follies, and in movies from 1918. His homespun philosophy and humor made him a sort of roving ambassador, a favorite of presidents and common folk everywhere. He was killed in an airplane crash near Point Barrow, Alaska, on August 15, 1935. *Forest Lawn Memorial Park, Glendale, California.*

PHILIP SHERIDAN (1831–1888). Among the toughest and most relentless of generals in the West's Indian campaigns, Sheridan fought against tribes from Washington and Oregon to the Rio Grande, commanding army units against Kiowas, Comanches, Cheyennes, Sioux, Nez Perces, Utes, and Bannocks. He was a Civil War divisional commander who fought at Stones River, Chickamauga, Missionary Ridge, the Wilderness, and the Shenandoah campaigns, among many battles. After the retirement of his old chief, William T. Sherman, in 1884, Sheridan became commanding general of the Army. *Arlington National Cemetery, Arlington, Virginia.*

SITTING BULL (c. 1831–1890). Tatanka Iyotanka, spiritual leader of the Hunkpapa tribe of the Lakota Sioux, he was born on the Grand River of South Dakota. He first warred with white interlopers in 1863 after prospectors discovered gold on Hunkpapa lands in Montana, and he became a staunch opponent of all government programs and treaties affecting his people. He is said to have had visions of the defeat of U.S. troops at the Rosebud and Little Bighorn battles in 1876. He and his fugitive band fled to Canada in 1877 but he finally surrendered in 1881 at Fort Buford, Dakota Territory. He was killed by Indian police on December 15, 1890, resisting efforts to remove him and his followers to a reservation. *Sitting Bull Monument, Mobridge (60 miles south of Bismarck), South Dakota.*

SMOKEY BEAR (1950–1976). In the aftermath of a fire, started by camper carelessness, that devastated 17,000 acres of forest in the Capitan Mountains of New Mexico, a badly burned two-month-old, four-pound black bear cub was found clinging to the trunk of a charred tree on May 19, 1950. Originally named "Hot Foot Teddy" by firefighters, he was adopted by the U.S. Forest Service, renamed Smokey and became—along with his successors—a powerful national symbol of forest fire prevention. The original Smokey died at the Washington, D.C., Zoo in November 1976, his body returned to New Mexico and buried at the *Smokey Bear Historical Park, Capitan (near Lincoln), New Mexico.*

BELLE STARR (1848–1889). Myra Belle Shirley of Carthage, Missouri, is said to have ridden with Confederate guerillas led by William C. Quantrill during the Civil War, and came to know the James, Younger, and Dalton boys before she was out of her teens. In 1880, she married Sam Starr, a Cherokee with Irish blood, and joined him and others in horse and cattle thievery in Indian Territory. She was a rough-edged, profane, unhandsome woman who wore velvet dresses and plumed hats, her sixguns hanging from a belt around her slim waist. She was killed by persons unknown on February 3, 1889, as she rode with her husband from Fort Smith, Arkansas, to their home at Younger's Bend, Indian Territory. *Belle Starr Cabin, Eufaula (20 miles south of Muskogee), Oklahoma.*

JOHN A. SUTTER (1803–1880). Born in Germany of Swiss parents, Sutter emigrated to the United States in 1834 and settled in San Francisco three years later. After he became a Mexican citizen he was awarded nearly 50,000 acres in a land grant in the Sacramento Valley and built a fort at the juncture of the American and Sacramento Rivers. Sutter's Fort became an important wagon train station and Sutter encouraged emigrants to the farmlands and vineyards he had named New Helvetia (New Switzerland). Gold was discovered on the American River in January 1848, and soon Sutter's land was overrun with "Forty-Miners." He spend much of the rest of his life shuttling between his home in Pennsylvania and Washington, seeking payment from Congress for his losses. He died on June 18, 1880. *Liditz Moravian Cemetery, Liditz (near Lancaster), Pennsylvania.*

TRIGGER (1932–1965). Roy Rogers's Palomino, who could stamp up to the number twenty-five, rear up on his hind legs and whinny, carried Roy (1912–1998—born Leonard Franklin Slye in Duck Run, Ohio), through most of his eighty-seven movies. Rogers once said, "When I die you can skin me and put me on top of Trigger and I'll be happy." Trigger is mounted in a rearing position in the *Roy Rogers-Dale Evans Museum, Victorville (60 miles northeast of Los Angeles), California.*

MARK TWAIN (1835–1910). Born Samuel Langhorne Clemens in Florida, Missouri, and raised in Hannibal, Twain adopted his famous penname in 1863 while writing humorous sketches for the *Virginia City Territorial Enterprise* in Nevada. He worked as a printer and newspaper correspondent and began his climb to fame in San Francisco in 1865 with publication of his story "The Celebrated Jumping Frog of Calaveras County." While his *Tom Sawyer* (1875) and *Huckleberry Finn* (1884) are his most familiar works, he wrote many American classics and is considered one of the principal influences in American, and world, literature. *Woodlawn Cemetery, Elmira, New York.*

JOHN WAYNE (1907–1970). Marion Michael Morrison, born in Winterset, Iowa, played football for USC and played in bit roles in films before winning the role as Ringo Kid in John Ford's *Stagecoach* (1939), considered the turning point in his career. In the war decade of the 1940s he made some of his most celebrated western films—*Red River, Fort Apache,* and *She Wore a Yellow Ribbon*—as well as a number of war movies. In 1956 he made what many consider his finest film, *The Searchers.* He won the Best Actor Oscar in 1969 for his role as Marshal Rooster Cogburn in *True Grit* and gave a bravura final performance, and one touchingly true to life, as the gunfighter-dying-of-cancer in *The Shootist* (1976). *Pacific View Memorial Park, Newport Beach, California.*

THOU SHALT NOT,
OR "HOW TO TAME A TEXI-KAN"

Sandy Whiting

GOD DID IT WITH ten. Abilene thought seven sufficient; Wichita threw in a few extras, and Dodge City reduced it to three. From the first steps westward, settlers have sought to legislate behavior in public as well as dictate morality on both sides of the bedroom door.

The Great Cattle Drives in the years following the Civil War brought with them a vexing factor to the End Of Cattle Trail Towns—EOCTT. Besides bringing Texas "beef on the hoof" north, the drives brought a new breed of man, the cowboy. Within hours of his arrival to an EOCTT, "soiled doves" descended from their roosts to coo over the visitor and his friends. After months in the saddle on a "dry" trail, this fellow had an unquenchable thirst for "bitters." Also in desperate need of a view other than the southend of a northbound longhorn, he searched for entertainment on either side of the rail-road tracks and occasionally between the rails.

Of a certainty, this "fresh off the trail" hand had sixty to one hundred dollars coming to him. First and foremost though, he needed a bath, shave, and fresh clothes. No reason to put "new cotton" onto "old flesh." Spiffed up with coins jangling in his purse, it was time to let loose of his own drive. After all, God had created both man and his needs and surely He would understand a "personal drive." And what better way to have fun than with marked Aces, Kings, and a few purchaseable Queens? Or a little stampeding, pistols blazing, down mainstreet? On busy days, residents needed iron umbrellas to protect heads from the lead rain drops.

Enter civilization, or the "not in my back yard citizens" composed of families and businessmen. With the urge to own homes, a new generation of founding fathers picked up and moved west. The dice hadn't stopped rolling before these genteel folk arrived to cultivate homes, raise children, and invest in the new land.

Promenade back to the cowboy. Mama, if she still breathed, was no longer within skirt's reach to make her son conduct himself as a proper gentleman. With older, but not necessarily better men for company, the "boy" soon discovered the pleasures available at trail's end: spirits, gambling, and soft warm women—most certainly missing around hearth and home.

These "pass through" cowboys met their match with the "here to stay" citizens. The tender eyes of youngsters, the Godly wife, even salvation itself was at stake. Folks felt they needed these trespassing ruffians and their ilk as much as a cottonwood needed a Texas twister. In terms clear enough for the blind to read, the locals said to these "bloody demons of disaster", "Take your gambling, drinking, and whoring somewhere else."

While promoting the civilized north lane of the street, the mercantiles waltzed on both sides of this EOCTT conflict of "us" versus "them". On the left hand, shop proprietors welcomed these denizens in disguise because new people meant more sales, which meant more profit at every swing of the door. On the right hand, the owners dreaded the messes and utter chaos the cowboys left in their wake.

A walk on the south side of this proverbial street found the dancehalls and saloons thriving on the cowboy and his soon-to-be-spent wages. Many of these hands were young and greener than new sprouted grass and of a mindset that they could beat the quick draw of the card. They never considered the professional gambler who could snake a game under a rattler's fangs. Other greenhands only cared to hear the owl hoot at the bottom of a glass or find a willing woman.

Occasionally, settlers would agitate an issue, refusing to leave a hand until the cards played in their favor, preferring to take up arms until all out war threatened. One such event befell Abilene, Kansas.

The Bull's Head Saloon, built in 1871 and owned by Texans Phil Coe and Ben Thompson, sported a painted bull in all its male glory on the building's second-story facade. The bull's portrait had been modeled after one in a livestock journal.

Stuart Henry recounted what happened.

Though as far from any knowledge of art or desire for it as any people could well be, the picture made them instinctively revolt. Once again a baffling question almost as old as humanity! Bulls were frequently driven or led through the town without causing anybody a moment's thought, much less an objection, yet the image on that saloon stunned. It met with denunciation as immoral, degrading, hateful. And this in a cattle country whose present and future depended on stock breeding! . . . Bulls did breed before the public in that open "God's country," yet man with a brush was ignoble if he reproduced in paint the all-desired virility. The natural human cry: Nature is good, Art-indecent! So influential citizens, suddenly possessed of the thin-skinned susceptibilities of their mid-Victorian epoch, could not overlook the defiant animal on the Bull's Head. It must be considered an insult to the good women of the town, a shame in plain sight of children. To let the bull stand unobjected to or forbidden was held to be an outright "knuckling under" to the Texans and to open the full road to unsupportable transgression. . . .

When violence appeared on the horizon, Coe and Thompson relented and had the offending feature painted out—more, but mostly, less. The paint lacked sufficient pigment leaving the outline of said "male organ" clearly defined.

Satisfied they had won the battle, Abileneians went their way. On the sidelines, Coe and Thompson chuckled at the Bible thumpers. Perhaps they should have only painted the head of the bull, but then, that wouldn't have been one-tenth of the "oyster on the half-brush."

Still, the farmers and town businessmen were there to stay, long after the cowboys disappeared. If the county and state wouldn't compel "virtuous behavior" for those ruffians, then by jingo, residents would incorporate into a city and hire their own law to enforce moral codes, uphold their own "Thou Shalt Nots," and give God a hand.

In May 1870, Abilene passed seven ordinances seeking to tame the unruly segment of town. As residents would have described them, these "anti" laws sought to control:

Gambling. The "bad luck" of the draw or toss of the dice. Persons who make their fortune through the lost shirts or grocery money of others, are wrong. Their actions are contrary to God's moral laws. Cards and the playing thereof bring with it the "cold game" in which the "cold player" has as much of a chance of winning a nickel as a turkey has of surviving to the day after Thanksgiving. Had not God said "Thou Shalt Not Steal?" And what is gambling but theft in sheep's wool?

Guilt by association. Vagrancy. To be destitute, without *legitimate* means of support *and* to loiter around establishments where gambling occurs makes either man or woman guilty of being a vagrant—but only if in proximity of these houses of ill-fame. Hide your activities under that bushel basket, and we will not bother you. One tiny candle peeks out, you are in the calaboose.

Sale of "bitters." Persons who wish to sell intoxicating spirits within Abilene's city limits must first obtain a petition signed by a majority of the town's residents, both male and female over age twenty-one, attesting to the suitability of said persons to properly run the establishment. In other words, those already living there must approve before a new license is issued. Woe be unto those who cross the local citizens. Provoke them, and you will not see so much as an inkblot on paper.

Public drunkenness. If you imbibe liquid spirits, do not allow yourself to drink until sloshed. Such activity will lead to conduct unbecoming a proper resident.

Use of the lariat on a person or animal, running horses through town, riotous conduct, threats of any kind likewise are prohibited. It is also forbidden to carry firearms or other deadly weapons within the city limits. (Ladies, take care with your pots and rolling pins less they too be banned!)

This town absolutely will not tolerate the oldest profession within its boundaries—that is they buying and selling of "female wares." Jesus pardoned Mary Magdalene, but we will not excuse. To those who rent rooms to such women, patronize their services, reside with or otherwise act in a lewd manner or use language that would be offensive to God and country, please board the next train east, west, north or south.

Sundry, that is to say, minor, offenses. Neither disturb the peace and tranquility of even a pond, nor throw stones or sticks. And to promote a serene milieu for our families, fire crackers are prohibited—except on New Years and Independence Days.

And so dictated the residents of that time.

Abilene passed these ordinances, but the question remains. Did the Board of Trustees believe they could simply jot a few "Thou Shalt Nots" of their own and the cowboys would acquiesce? Perhaps they were of the mindset of "If you write it, they will mind it."

Several lawmen, including "Wild Bill" Hickok, were hired to enforce the ordinances. However, residents turned a dim eye toward Hickok when his *modus operandi* of "shoot first and ask later" became evident. An early citizen said, "Such a policy of taking justice into his own hands exemplified—of course—

but a form of lawlessness." Only after the locals made the city an uncomfortable EOCTT did the Texas drovers find reason to seek another soft and comfortable bosom.

Now that Abilene had turned conservative and had withdrawn its open invitation to cattlemen, cowboys, and the herds, along with the immorality that accompanied them, the town at the confluence of the Big and Little Arkansas Rivers wove its own welcome mat promising, EVERYTHING GOES IN WICHITA.

Having been kicked out of cities along the Kansas Pacific Railroad (roughly now Interstate 70), the gaming houses descended from the north into Wichita. Cowboys came up the trail from the south. Poised to flame the city, the primer cord and match stood head to head.

Ben Thompson, of Abilene's Bull's Head fame, set up shop at the Keno House in this burg so named after a local Indian tribe. Soon he and the cowboys had shaped their own version of the law—whatever they wanted to do, they did. Settlers, again miffed, decided to dispose of this volatile box of matches before the flames ignited and burned the streets.

Incorporated in 1871, Wichita had a fledgling lawforce, which included Wyatt Earp for a short time. Contrary to many movies and popular myth, Wyatt settled many disputes by convincing the rascals that acceding to the demands of law and order was in their best health.

And as long as the "wilted flowers," gambling and intoxicating liquors stayed on the westside of the Arkansas River in Delano Town, all was well. However, several ladies, in keeping with the letter of the law, though certainly not its spirit, enjoyed frolicking—sans clothes—on the western shores in full view of the civilized folks on the east side.

When the gambling and saloons eventually spilled across the river, residents petitioned to have the establishments declared a nuisance. If labeled as such, then the houses of pleasure could be eradicated, but only if the police were of a mindset to do so. It seems that ordinances were enforced only when a representative of the law desired to punish the miscreants, leaving personal friends to "abscond with the gold."

Instead of enforcing ordinances, Wichita's police focused on disarming revelers, that is to say cowboys, of lethal weapons. They could not physically enforce moral standards and therefore didn't try to do so.

During one instance in 1874, Officer Sam Botts faced twelve armed Texans. Any attempts to shoot his way out would have resulted in his death. Although outnumbered, Botts wasn't alone. Out of the doors and alleys came shotguns toted by locals—many being owners whose livelihood depended on keeping order—to assist the lone officer. Wichita might be the moral dreg of the state, but it *could* do something about keeping the peace when it came to breaking written laws.

By the book, immorality and lawlessness were not considered the same. Moral laws were dictated by God. Failure to adhere to those laws result in immorality. All other laws (man's laws) were rules or actions written and recognized by a controlling authority, for instance a city council. Those in office, such as police and city marshals, could enforce man's laws and therefore the city could avoid lawlessness. Often a city passed an ordinance identical to one of God's laws, an example being sex for hire. However, just because prostitution was both an act of lawlessness and one of immorality, it didn't make the violation any easier to prosecute or control.

The trains that met the cowboys at trail's end didn't pull in with empty cars. Westbound travel brought groceries, household goods and other sundries. Settlers also heeded this westward call with its promise of free land, arriving in their own "herds" on the rail stop's platform.

By 1873, Wichitans had become so annoyed with the immorality, outright theft, and violence associated with the cattle trade and cowboys that they jumped on the pulpit of reform. At an anti-vice rally, attendees agreed that "the general moral climate of the city was tied to its long-range economic health." Only those cities that were morally upright and virtuous would endure. Hadn't Rome fallen when its debauchery caught up with it?

That in mind, Reverend Hason preached a sermon from Jeremiah 29:7. "Seek the peace of the city . . . pray the Lord for it; for in the peace thereof shall ye have peace." He and public opinion believed that the cowboy and cattle would eventually stop coming to Wichita. Local citizens would be left to deal with the skeletal remains of bawdy houses, saloons, and dancehalls. What family man wished to bring his wife and children into such wickedness even if he hoped for a little clandestine entertainment of his own?

By 1877, violent crime in Wichita had diminished almost to the point of total disappearance. Local police carried clubs instead of guns. As said by Marshall "Marsh" Murdock, "There has been no call for an armed patrol in this town for two years."

The first Texas cattle reached Dodge City in 1875. On Christmas Eve of that year, a temporary town council passed Dodge's first "Thou Shalt Nots" relating to licensing of dramshops, crime, and punishment.

These and future ordinances mirrored those passed in Abilene in 1870; disturbing the peace, carrying or use of deadly weapons, and the commission of nuisances upon any street, sidewalk, or other public place. Especially important was the one forbidding horses to be ridden in buildings. After all, another century would have to turn before the nation would embrace the "drive thru."

These ordinances put some of the wealthier merchants at odds with the civilizing force. Businessmen wanted the Texans' money, and by instituting harsh laws, these owners believed it would cause the Texans to go elsewhere. God might have His laws, but He would have to take a back saddle to the needs of Dodge's Front Street.

With a mere one thousand residents, in 1877, Dodge City's saloons numbered sixteen. In another year, ordinances to collect fines from bawdy houses and those who dwelled there, prostitutes, and gamblers were passed. Although written on the books, the laws were enforced only when those currently in office were of a mind to, which seldom happened. If the lawmen called you friend, vice was in. If he called you foe, vice brought woe.

This careless attitude changed with the election of Alonzo B. Webster in 1881. Webster gave fair warning with this notice: "To all whom it may concern: All thieves, thugs, confidence men, and persons without visible means of support, will take notice that the ordinance enacted for their special benefit will be rigorously enforced on and after tomorrow. April 7th, 1881. A.B. Webster, Mayor, Dodge City, Kansas."

Pistol-packing Mayor Webster was not cut from the fat but from lean muscle. He took no lip from those who thought the sun rose in the west, a place where a man wrote his own laws. Being mayor, Webster's duties included appointing city marshals and assistant marshals. After firing Jim Masterson from the office of city marshal, Webster appointed Fred Singer to the post. Fred also tended bar at the Old House Saloon, which was owned by Webster.

The mayor showed his "cut of cloth" at one particular scrape between Bat Masterson and Misters Peacock and Updegraph. Peacock and Bat's brother Jim co-owned the Lady Gay Dancehall and Updegraph kept bar for them. The shooting ended when Mayor Webster and Marshal Singer, both toting shotguns, "compelled Masterson to give up his pistols. . . ." Four months later, Assistant Marshal Tom Nixon purchased the Lady Gay from Peacock and Masterson.

Now Mayor Webster controlled the Lady Gay Dancehall and the Old House Saloon, both managed or owned by men who were also in his employ as law enforcement officers. Webster also owned the newly opened Stock Exchange Saloon. With this arrangement, a few of his hidden colors slipped through.

Webster collected fees from the saloons he did not own. Owners, gamblers, and prostitutes all paid money in the form of licenses and fines. These funds, in turn, paid the salaries of law enforcement, i.e. himself and the managers of his saloons.

Asked why he could morally fine his competition, Webster said it bluntly. He wanted control of Dodge and its seedier side and to share in its profits. If he enforced the law equally, he would soon have no way to cover his salary as mayor and the salaries of the marshal and assistant marshal, his friends. In addition, his saloon's income would be wiped out from fines—and why shoot your own foot?

Dodge City passed more rules over the next years. Ordinances 70, 71, and 83 all worked together to suppress vice and immorality and to punish vagrancy. Number 83 also banned music, vocal or instrumental, where immoral acts took place. Or so the city hoped. These ordinances served merely to push the vice it sought to eliminate behind closed—though certainly not locked—doors.

Only when the city's livelihood ceased being linked to the cattle trade and the associated cowboys did it begin to exhibit any vestige of civilization. Samual S. Prouty, editor of the Dodge City *Cowboy* stated: "The experience of all cattle towns is that their growth had been held in check during the period when they depended upon the cattle trade for support. The country surrounding could not be developed while it was being held for stock ranges. . . . The cattle traffic made money for its citizens but did not make a town."

With the disappearance of the cattle and cowboy, the gamblers and prostitutes no longer had a steady market and drifted away. With their disappearance, prohibition gained a foothold and ordained the end of the saloons. With vice kicked out of these towns and the institution of Sunday closing laws, families sprouted, seemingly overnight, to cultivate the earth.

Many more ordinances and "Thou Shalt Nots" have been passed in the hundred-plus years since the cattle drive days. All were intended to aid in civilizing the new land and new people—hopefully with more success than the "white wash" was on a single bull's portrait.

NOTES ON THE CONTRIBUTORS

DARRELL ARNOLD

Darrell Arnold is the founder and longtime publisher of *Cowboy Magazine,* a quarterly journal expressly designed "for and about the working ranch cowboy." A wildlife biologist by training, Arnold has written extensively for the magazine market and concentrates on issues that affect today's ranching industry. His contribution to the present anthology, "Survival of the Cowboy," is, in his own words, the "result of all I have learned as a writer, editor, and publisher of nonfiction articles about ranchers and cowboys." The piece is especially relevant in today's world that, all too often, witnesses environmentalists and ranchers on opposite sides of an increasingly difficult historical problem.

ALLEN P. BRISTOW

Allen Bristow is a Spur Award winner for "Secrets of the Lost Cannon." A former sergeant with the Los Angeles County Sheriff's Department, he has also taught public administration on the college level. Bristow has written more than a dozen textbooks on law enforcement, and he is currently pursuing his interest in Western and Military history publishing. His present article, "A Medical Necessity," regarding a late-nineteenth-century manhunt for a Hawaiian cowboy, reminds us that the last state to enter the Union is a Western one.

LARRY K. BROWN

Larry Brown's writing credits include many articles for such national magazines as *Wild West, American Cowboy, True West, Persimmon Hill,* and *Old West.* For his book *Hog Ranches of Wyoming: Liquor, Lust, and Lies Under Sagebrush Skies,* Brown was presented the "Western Horizon Award" by Wyoming Writers, Inc. His other book titles include *Petticoat Prisoners of the Wyoming Frontier Prison* and *You Are Respectfully Invited to Attend My Execution."* He is the current membership chairman for WWA. The present article deals with murder and mayhem in early twentieth-century Wyoming.

ROBERT F. CASEMORE

Robert F. Casemore is a retired officer from the U.S. Army. He is the author of four scripts that were made into films by the Department of Defense. He has also written several "self-help" books, including *How to Sell Yourself* and *Mastering Your Way to the Top*. Casemore has written for national magazines and has published articles in Western fiction and nonfiction. His current offering deals with the little-known story of the man who first reported "Custer's Last Stand" to the world.

JAMES A. CRUTCHFIELD

James A. Crutchfield is the secretary-treasurer of Western Writers of America. He has authored almost forty nonfiction titles that cover all aspects of American history, including *Tragedy at Taos, The Santa Fe Trail, Mountain Men of the American West,* and *Eyewitness to American History*. Crutchfield is a regular contributor to several national magazines and has written for television as well. He has received the Spur Award for his short nonfiction article "Marching with the Army of the West." He has also received two writing awards from the American Association for State and Local History. Crutchfield's current selection deals with Zebulon Pike's mysterious southwestern expedition of 1806–07.

DAVID DARY

David Dary is a former president of WWA and the Owen Wister Award winner for 2002. He is the author of such groundbreaking books as *Cowboy Culture,* winner of the Spur Award, *The Buffalo Book, Entrepreneurs of the Old West, The Santa Fe Trail,* and *Seeking Pleasure in the West,* which also garnered a Spur. Dary has been a TV news director, a journalism professor, and the director of the H. H. Herbert School of Journalism at the University of Oklahoma. In addition to his titles of national interest, Dary has authored three regional books about his native Kansas. His present article, "Western Trails," provides a comprehensive overview of the early trail system of the American West.

RILEY FROH

After teaching Texas and United States history and British literature at San Jacinto College for twenty-eight years, Riley Froh has recently retired to devote his full time to writing. He has contributed articles to three Western

Writers of America anthologies and has written several nonfiction articles and book reviews for scholarly journals. His two published nonfiction books are *Wildcatter Extraordinary* and *Edgar B. Davis and Sequences in Business Capitalism.* His current offering details the history of Luling, "the toughest town in Texas."

CARMEN GOLDTHWAITE

Carmen Goldthwaite writes for a number of western heritage magazines, including *Wild West* and *American Cowboy.* She also reports on Texas business for *The New York Times*—Financial Desk. Her story on "The Yellow Rose of Texas" appeared in *Wild Women of the Old West,* an anthology from Fulcrum Publishing. A Texas journalist of long standing, she was syndicated with *Scripps-Howard News International* and has won the Society of Professional Journalists' "Headliner" award for state and national investigative reporting. Goldthwaite's selection for the present anthology explores the colorful life of a legendary Texas female whose political and social graces were legends in their own times.

JANET E. GRAEBNER

Janet E. Graebner's works have appeared in *The Bloomsbury Review* and *Roundup Magazine,* as well as in the anthologies *Woven on the Wind, American West,* and *Westward.* A former freelance corporate communications consultant, she has also penned two nonfiction books. Her article herein chronicles an almost-forgotten battle on the Tongue River between forces led by the famed Sioux warrior Crazy Horse, and U.S. army Colonel Nelson Miles.

WILLIAM GRONEMAN III

Bill Groneman is a retired New York City Fire Department captain who recently pulled up stakes and moved to Texas. An authority on such diverse subjects as the Texas Revolution and John Steinbeck, he has authored several books, including *Roll Call at the Alamo, Defense of a Legend: Crockett and the De La Pena Diary,* and *Battlefields of Texas.* He has also contributed articles to many national magazines, including *True West, Wild West, Alamo Journal,* and *Military History of the West.* His present offering vividly describes the horrors of the last days at the Alamo.

BILL GULICK

Bill Gulick's name is synonymous with the history, legends, and lore of the Pacific Northwest. Beginning his writing career with the early pulp magazines, he later became one of *The Saturday Evening Post*'s most popular and prolific contributors. Two articles appearing in that magazine, "Thief in Camp" and "The Shaming of Broken Horn," won Spur Awards. Three of his works, *The Man from Texas, Bend of the Snake,* and *The Hallelujah Trail,* were made into movies. Gulick, a former president of WWA, was awarded the Saddleman Award (the forerunner to the Owen Wister Award) in 1983. His contribution here, "Pacific Northwest Steamboat Days," traces the history of early steam transportation on the Columbia River and its tributaries.

ABRAHAM HOFFMAN

Abraham Hoffman has contributed articles to such noted journals as the *Western Historical Quarterly, California History, Southern California Quarterly,* and *Journal of the West.* A college history instructor by profession, Hoffman has also penned numerous books, including *Unwanted Mexican Americans in the Great Depression, California Then and Now,* and *Vision or Villainy: Origins of the Owens Valley–Los Angeles Water Controversy.* His current article deals with the national dissemination of the news following the discovery of gold in California in January 1848.

PAUL ANDREW HUTTON

Paul Andrew Hutton is the executive director of the Western History Association and a past president of Western Writers of America. He has been seen in numerous on-camera interviews on the History Channel and has written several of the programs as well. He has been awarded multiple Wrangler and Spur Awards from the National Cowboy Hall of Fame and Western Writers of America. He regularly contributes articles to national magazines and is the author of *Phil Sheridan and His Army* and *Ten Days on the Plains.* He is also the editor of *Soldiers West: Biographies from the Military Frontier.* He wrote the Introduction to the present anthology.

ELMER KELTON

Former WWA president Elmer Kelton is one of the nation's most honored writers of the American West. The recipient of seven Spur Awards, the Levi Strauss Saddleman Award from WWA, and several Western Heritage Awards, Kelton has authored fifty novels and several nonfiction books. He has been voted by his WWA associates as the Best Western Writer of All Time, surpassing such names as Louis L'Amour, Zane Grey, and A. B. Guthrie. Kelton's current selection deals with the later lives of the fifty-nine signers of the Texas Declaration of Independence.

JOANN LEVY

JoAnn Levy has performed extensive research on the California gold rush. Her first book on the subject, *They Saw the Elephant: Women in the California Gold Rush,* has been acclaimed "one of the best and most comprehensive accounts of gold rush life to date." Levy is a two-time winner of the coveted Willa Award for *Daughter of Joy, A Novel of Gold Rush San Francisco* and *For California's Gold.* Levy has also been published in numerous magazines and journals. Her present contribution, "The Intrepid Females of Forty-Nine," traces the oftentimes harrowing journeys of several women from their civilized homes, through the wilds of either the American West or Central America, to their final destinies in California.

JUDY MAGNUSON LILLY

Judy Lilly has contributed short stories to several anthologies, including WWA's *American West: Twenty Stories from the Western Writers of America,* as well as *White Hats, The Enchanted Rocking Horse,* and *Maybe It's the Moon.* Her fiction has also appeared in *Louis L'Amour Magazine.* In her role as professional librarian, Lilly has researched extensively in Kansas history. Her present contribution, "The Jayhawking of Salina," documents the day during the Civil War when guerillas struck her hometown as a prelude to William Quantrill's later, bloody attack on Lawrence, Kansas.

DOUGLAS V. MEED

Douglas Meed is the author of nine books dealing with some phase of Texas, Southwestern, or Mexican border history, among them *Soldier of Fortune: Adventuring in Latin America and Mexico with Emil Lewis Holmdahl* and *The Texas Navy: 1832–1843.* During his years in journalism as both reporter and editor, he was awarded a Hearst newspapers writing award while on the staff of the *San Antonio Light.* Meed currently pursues a full-time writing career. His present offering details Pancho Villa's daring attack on the town of Columbus, New Mexico, in 1916.

LEON CLAIRE METZ

Leon Metz is one of America's foremost authorities on Western outlaws and lawmen. Metz, a past president of WWA, was the recipient of the Saddleman Award (the forerunner of the Owen Wister Award) in 1985, and his book *John Wesley Hardin: Dark Angel of Texas* has received the Spur Award. Other Metz titles of interest are: *John Selman, Texas Gunfighter; Pat Garrett, the Story of a Western Lawman; The Shooters; An Encyclopedia of Gunfighters, Outlaws, and*

Lawmen; Fort Bliss; and *Border.* In addition to his prolific book writing, Metz is a frequent contributor to national magazines and scholarly journals as well. In his current article, Metz gives his readers a real treat with an authoritative look at one of his favorite characters.

ROD MILLER

Rod Miller's short stories and poetry have appeared in numerous national magazines, including *Western Horseman* and *American Cowboy.* He also has been published in several anthologies, among them WWA's own *Westward: A Fictional History of the American West,* edited by Dale L. Walker, and Robert Randisi's *White Hats* and *Black Hats.* Miller's present selection describes the events surrounding a hair-raising adventure in the life of a youthful William Cody, who later, of course, became famous as "Buffalo Bill."

CANDY MOULTON

Roundup Magazine's editor and a former WWA board member, Candy Moulton has written eleven Western history books, including the immensely popular *Everyday Life Among American Indians* and *Everyday Life in the Wild West from 1840 to 1900.* Moulton was a finalist in the Spur competition in the documentary film category for her "Footsteps to the West." Her contribution to this anthology, "The Fourth Company," documents the grueling passage of her husband's great-great grandmother from her departure in England to her arrival in Salt Lake City in 1856. In presenting the hardships of this journey, Moulton provides an excellent overview of the trials and tribulations of the Mormon migrations across America during the 1850s.

PAT DECKER NIPPER

Pat Nipper is the author of *A Life Within a Life,* which chronicles the life and adventures of Libbie Custer. She has also written for such national magazines as *Ranger Rick's, Teen, Roundup,* and *Landscape.* Her short story "Who Really Killed President Lincoln?" appeared in the western anthology *Black Hats.* Her present offering details an elusive murder case that occurred in Idaho during the gold rush there.

NANCY M. PETERSON

Nancy M. Peterson has authored *People of the Moonshell,* a history of the Platte River, and *People of the Troubled Water* and *People of the Old Missury,* which both focus on the Missouri River. She has received a Spur award for her article "Captain Marsh: Master of the Missouri." Peterson has published historical articles in *American History, Persimmon Hill, Wild West, True West,* and other national magazines. Her present contribution is a fascinating account of a half-blood Yankton Sioux woman who devoted her entire life to the advancement of her people.

TROY D. SMITH

Troy Smith has received the Spur Award for his book *Bound for the Promise-Land.* He contributes to several national magazines as well. Smith belongs to a newer, younger breed of Western chronicler, whose credo is absolute accuracy and a fast-paced, yet engaging, writing style. His contribution to the present anthology documents the little-known story of a career army officer whose troubled and complex life was overshadowed by other, more flamboyant, members of his brotherhood who possessed much less talent, ambition, and experience.

KAREN HOLLIDAY TANNER AND JOHN D. TANNER, JR.

The prize-winning husband-and-wife writing team of John and Karen Tanner has contributed articles to a host of historical magazines and journals, including the California Historical Society *Quarterly, The Journal* of the Western Outlaw-Lawman History Association, *True West, Wild West,* and the *Tombstone Epitaph.* The pair's joint effort has also resulted in a book, *Last of the Old-time Outlaws: The George West Musgrave Story.* The Tanners' current offering graphically depicts the greed, lust, and politics involved in a forgotten early-twentieth-century murder case in New Mexico.

ROBERT M. UTLEY

To the serious student of Western history, Robert M. Utley needs no introduction. The former chief historian for the U.S. National Park service and a past president of the Western History Association, he is the author of more than a dozen authoritative books on subjects ranging from the American military presence in the West to the Rocky Mountain fur trade, and from Plains Indian warfare to the Texas Rangers. Recipient of WWA's coveted Owen Wister Award in 1994, Utley also won the Spur Award for his biography of Sitting Bull, *The Lance and the Shield.* His current offering provides an interesting and valuable insight into the multifaceted history of the Texas Rangers.

LORI VAN PELT

Lori Van Pelt's works have appeared in many national magazines, including *Persimmon Hill, Old West True West,* and *Western Horseman.* Her articles have also appeared in several anthologies, among them *American West: Twenty New*

Stories from the Western Writers of America. Van Pelt's book *Dreamers and Schemers: Profiles from Carbon County, Wyoming's Past* has established her as a leading voice in popularizing regional history. She is the recipient of the Wyoming State Historical Society's Publication Award. Her contribution here details the poignant correspondence exchanged between John Stephen Casement and his wife, Frances, during the building of the Union Pacific Railroad.

DALE L. WALKER

Former WWA president Dale L. Walker is no stranger to anthologies, either as editor or contributor. His latest compilation is *Westward: A Fictional History of the American West,* with contributions by twenty-eight members of WWA. Walker, the former director of Texas Western Press in El Paso, has also written a number of popular books, including *Pacific Destiny,* which won a Spur Award. He has also been awarded Spurs for his short nonfiction articles "Killers of Pain's Transcontinental Journey" and "The Boys of '98." Walker was bestowed the Owen Wister Award in 2000. In the current selection, he has revealed the final resting places of such noted Western figures as Roy Bean, Billy the Kid, Belle Star, and even Roy Rogers's legendary horse, Trigger.

SANDY WHITING

Sandy Whiting was awarded a Spur for "Charity," the first short story she ever wrote. She has written for such magazines as *Louis L'Amour Western Magazine, True West, American Cowboy,* and *Country Woman.* One of her short stories also appears in the anthology *White Hats.* A rock, mineral, and gem aficionado, she has written extensively for *Quarry Quips.* Her present article reveals what a young Texas cowboy had to look forward to when his outfit rode into town at the end of the trail.